sg · june · 03

The Rise of Mass Literacy

Themes in History

Published

M. L. Bush, *Servitude in Modern Times*
Peter Coates, *Nature: Western Attitudes since Ancient Times*
J. K. J. Thomson, *Decline in History: The European Experience*
David Vincent, *The Rise of Mass Literacy: Reading and Writing in Modern Europe*

The Rise of Mass Literacy

Reading and Writing in Modern Europe

DAVID VINCENT

Polity

First published in 2000 by Polity Press in association with Blackwell Publishers Ltd.

Editorial office:
Polity Press
65 Bridge Street
Cambridge CB2 1UR, UK

Marketing and production:
Blackwell Publishers Ltd
108 Cowley Road
Oxford OX4 1JF, UK

Published in the USA by
Blackwell Publishers Inc.
Commerce Place
350 Main Street
Malden, MA 02148, USA

A catalogue record for this book is available from the British Library.

Library of Congress Cataloging-in-Publication Data

Vincent, David, 1949–
    The rise of mass literacy : reading and writing in modern Europe / David Vincent.
        p. cm.—(Themes in history)
    Includes bibliographical references (p.) and index.
    ISBN 0-7456-1444-2 (B)—ISBN 0-7456-1445-0 (P)
    1. Literacy—Europe—History. 2. Literacy—Social aspects—Europe—History.
    I. Title. II. Themes in history (Polity Press)
LC156.A2 V55 2000
302.2'244'094—dc21   00-027871

Typeset in 10 on 12 pt Times
by Best-set Typesetter Ltd., Hong Kong
Printed in Great Britain by T.J. International, Padstow, Cornwall

This book is printed on acid-free paper.

Contents

Figures

For
Caroline Millington and Michael Robinson

Acknowledgements

In the preparation of this survey I am grateful variously for advice, encouragement, information, and technical assistance to Onno Boonstra, Jack Corrigall, Steven Hicks, Lindsey Howsam, Mark Jacob, Egil Johansson, Martin Lawn and the Silences and Images group, Jane Mace, Anders Nilsson and his comrades from Lund, Fabrizio Pischedda, Frank Simon, Margaret Spufford, Graham Tattersall, Istvan Tóth, Liz Zsargo, and the staff of the Post Office Archives and Record Centre, London and the International Bureau of the Universal Postal Union, Berne. My particular thanks to David Mitch, who found the time to read more than I asked him to. And, as ever, to Charlotte Vincent.

1

The Rise of Mass Literacy

The European project

Literacy in modern Europe came of age on 9 October 1874. The era of mass communication was formally inaugurated by the Treaty of Berne which led to the creation the following year of the Universal Postal Union.[1] Every inhabitant of every country from Sweden to Greece, from Russia to Ireland, was to be linked together in a common system of flat-rate postage.[2] Businessman would be connected to businessman, worker to worker, parent to child, lover to lover, through their common ability to read and write. For the local equivalent of a fifteen-centime stamp, their thoughts and feelings would be conveyed rapidly and securely along the roads and railway lines of the Continent and across the sea to Britain and to the only non-European signatories of the Convention, Egypt and the United States. It was a practice without social or economic barriers. As the UPU's journal observed, 'there is a scarcely a single individual, however wretched, in any civilized country who has not, at least once in his life, been put in communication with his fellow creatures by means of the post.'[3] Such an achievement was widely celebrated. *The Times* was in no doubt of its significance:

It is a literal truth that the Postal Union not only corresponds with the most advanced humanitarian spirit of the times, but is itself the most practical realization which human ingenuity has yet achieved of those floating aspirations towards universal brotherhood, regarded generally as of the nature of dreams, however decorative of the pages of poetic literature.[4]

The success of the Berne Convention reflected the growing sense of a single European project in the field of written communication. Since at least the middle of the eighteenth century, states had learned from each other's progress in the struggle to disseminate the skills of reading and writing. Educational pioneers such as Pestalozzi and Lancaster were visited and consulted by reformers from all over the Continent in search of solutions for what were coming to be seen as common problems. As the nineteenth century progressed, successful innovations were copied with increasing rapidity. Most European states embraced the ambition of instructing the poor in their letters in the years following the defeat of Napoleon, and most moved to the imposition of compulsory education at around the time of the founding of the Universal Postal Union. Within the schools, methods of instruction became less and less distinctive as writers and administrators travelled from country to country to study the most cost-efficient ways of instilling literacy. The UPU itself was the consequence of a concerted set of domestic reforms. Rowland Hill's dramatic transformation of the British postal system in 1840 was closely scrutinized by other national post offices. As soon as the twin devices of pre-payment and flat-rate postage were seen to be working, plans were laid for similar schemes.[5] By 1850, most of Britain's rivals had freed their postal services of the constraints on mass correspondence, and it was the resulting increase in international flows of mail which created need for a single co-ordinating institution. In turn, the success of what was one of the first modern international bureaucracies was convincing proof of the potential for co-operation between states. The prime mover of the Berne Convention, Heinrich von Stephan of the German post office, claimed in the first edition of the *Union Postale* that 'such a complete unanimity of the governments of the great majority of the civilized nations of the globe constitutes a fact, up to the present, unequalled in history.'[6]

The UPU's only forerunner as a modern international agency was the International Telegraph Union, founded ten years earlier in the same Swiss city, which could now claim to be the capital of world communications. At the moment when the victory over illiteracy was in sight, the written word lost its monopoly in the transmission of information over distance. The telecommunications era began just three years after the introduction of the Penny Post with the installation of a telegraph along the Great Western Railway's line from Paddington to Slough, and the telephone was patented in the first year of the UPU's operation. However, a mode of communication which was as old as civilization itself was still far from obsolete. In 1876, more than three decades after the first messages were sent down the first wires, forty-two letters were being sent within, into and out of the countries of Europe for every one telegram. During the years up to the first world war, the written word almost kept pace with the electronic, the proportion of telegrams rising marginally to one in forty. By this time, the telephone was introducing many of the populations of Europe to the pleasures of making connections over distance without the need either to read or write. The spread of Bell's invention was much more rapid than the telegraph. In 1913, twenty-one phone calls were being made for every hundred items of mail. The average concealed wide variations between countries. Some, such as Russia and Spain, had yet to install a system, but in Scandinavia, where mass reading had been the earliest to take root, there were instances of the telephone overtaking the letter. Sweden was the first country to record a lead for the spoken voice in 1899, followed by Denmark in 1909.[7]

The phones were ringing as Europe went to war, but inscribing and deciphering written messages had remained the dominant mode of communication during the century since the defeat of Napoleon. The continued expansion of the telephone systems once peace was restored took place largely at the expense not of reading and writing letters, but of the much younger telegraph. By 1928, for every hundred mail items, there were twenty-five telephone calls and just one telegram. As late as 1950, there was two and half times as much work for the postman as for the telephone operator. Not until 1972, almost a century after its invention, did the telephone finally gain pre-eminence over a still expanding postal service.

The practice of counting

From the outset, the Universal Postal Union assumed a responsibility not merely for co-ordinating a particular use of literacy, but for counting it. The very first edition of the organization's journal, *Union Postale*, addressed the system by which statistics were to be collected, setting out the standard form to be followed by every member state. Year after year, broken only by an unusually disruptive revolution or invasion, each national post office calculated the flows of different categories of mail, and of all the attendant costs and labour involved in their carriage. These were summarized by the bureaucrats in Berne, who published annual

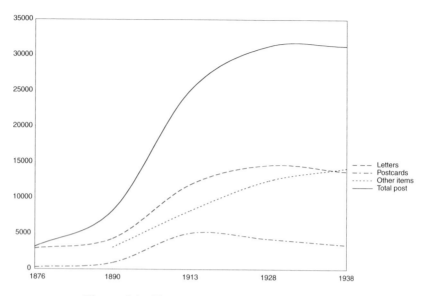

Figure 1.1 European postal flows, 1876–1938

tables of the advance of civilization. The sheer scale of the achievement matched the hyperbole of the most ardent reformer. In the first full year of operation, three billion letters and postcards a year were circulating within and between the countries of Europe, and between Europe and the rest of the world. By 1913, continued expansion in the basic forms of correspondence, allied to a growth in ancillary mail services such as the parcel and sample posts, and in the range of overseas countries which had joined the organization, had driven the total flow up to twenty-five billion, or fifty thousand items a minute (see figure 1.1).[8] Growth was maintained at a slower rate after 1918, reaching thirty-one billion in 1928 and levelling out during the remainder of the inter-war period.

If the post disconnected distance from time, it wedded time to progress. The ambitions of the Universal Postal Union could be expressed in figures, and the annual returns displayed a constant upward movement. In this respect, the civilization of the letter reflected the outlook of all those engaged in the struggle to promote literacy. It is no accident that Sweden was at once the first country to envisage universal literacy, at least at the level of reading, and also the first to generate reliable statistics by which to measure the achievement of the goal.[9] The annual examination registers in which the seventeenth- and eighteenth-century Lutheran pastors recorded the progress of children in learning their letters and the catechism were the forerunners of what by the middle decades of the nineteenth century had become a Europe-wide industry of cultural counting. The outwards signs of competence, especially signatures on marriage registers but also the educational attainments of army recruits, the answers to census enumerators, and the examination performance of schoolchildren were added up and then compared to other measures of social advance or regression. The practice was by no means confined to those societies which had the most to celebrate. Russia, for instance, was at or near the bottom of virtually every European index of progress except that of the quality of the means by which it measured its backwardness. Those seeking to modernize its culture mounted a series of increasingly sophisticated investigations into the need for and consequences of educational reform.[10] Contemporary reformers and administrators bequeathed to historians a wealth of figures about what was held to be literacy, although ironically with very few about prevailing standards of numeracy.

The counting of reading and writing was founded on an act of discrimination. A social practice was abstracted from the pattern of living in which it was embedded, and then further simplified in order that it might be given a cardinal value. Literacy was disentangled from the bundle of devices by which individuals communicated with each other, and through the tables and graphs presented as a discrete moral, social and political problem. In the same way, 'education' was separated out from the complex means by which the growing child discovered about its world and equipped itself for adulthood, and was given an identity which was divorced from and in many respects hostile to the sequence of learning which took place in the home, the neighbourhood and the workplace. The process was comparable to the contemporary emergence of 'crime' as a social issue and indeed extensive efforts were made from the early nineteenth century onwards to establish a convincing statistical relationship between law-breaking and educational deprivation.

The act of decoding texts had of course been distinguished from speech since the invention of writing. The schoolroom and the schoolteacher were scarcely the inventions of the modern era. The first specialized text for assisting a child to learn its letters in post-Roman Europe dates back to Bede in the early eighth century.[11] What translated a discourse into tables of figures and a distinction into a fixed category was the emergence of the state as the dominant force in the provision of literacy. Prior to the nineteenth century, the major burden of specialized instruction had been borne by the church, assisted in some countries by largely superficial statutory regulation. Sweden was unusual in that its Church Law of 1686 was widely observed, and that the ministers tried to count both the technical proficiency and the religious knowledge of those whose education they were responsible for supervising. In general, the churches, whether Protestant or Catholic, found it difficult to distinguish between the interdependent forms of spiritual training in which they were engaged, and impossible to calibrate the progress of souls towards God. The most that could be achieved was the compilation of parish registers, whose information about literacy remained dormant until they were visited by nineteenth-century researchers. Once, however, the state entered the field in its own right, the statistical data began to appear. In France, for instance, calculations of the literacy of conscripts started in 1827, just five years before the first effective government intervention in schooling. Analyses of marriage register signatures were published in 1854, and in 1866 and 1872 the census machinery was appropriated for a study of the educational level of the population. In 1877 a retired schoolmaster named Louis Maggiolo secured a government grant to undertake the first large-scale historical study of literacy based on the registers kept by past generations of parish priests.[12]

The association of the state with statistics is partly explained by the interdependence of literacy and bureaucracy in the nineteenth century and beyond. Alongside or in place of the multi-functional church organizations, specialized public officials were employed in ever-increasing numbers to maintain the systems without which the inculcation of mass literacy now seemed impossible. They developed a regime of annual returns on standard forms and encouraged teachers to accept a culture of report and inspection. The success of Maggiolo's enterprise was founded on the presence of 16,000 state-employed schoolteachers willing to participate in a co-ordinated programme of statistical research. As the levels of public investment grew, so literacy rates and examination results could be entered on the other side of the balance sheet to demonstrate value for taxpayers' money. The evidence of reading and writing became the means by which the officials could read and communicate the success of their endeavours. Beyond the school systems, the state post offices rapidly became the largest civilian organizations of their time, with almost a million employees across Europe on the eve of the First World War.[13] Literacy provided a living for a new species of literate worker, whose labours were most readily recognized in a numerical form.

The figures reflected a new concentration of authority in society. They were calculated and published as part of a complex power struggle which accompanied the creation of mass literacy. What mattered was not just a particular outcome, but also the capacity to measure it. Indeed a poor or unacceptably variable performance could be of more use to the proponents of state action than a display of consistent achievement. In France, for instance, a study of the educational level of recruits undertaken by General Morin in 1864 was translated into a series of grey-shaded maps by the Minister of Education, Victor Duruy, who used them to further his campaign for free and compulsory public elementary education.[14] The energetic Russian investigators identified the immense variations between their country and those of the west, and within the vast territories of the Empire, in order to strengthen their case for a radical extension of government action. Homogeneity of basic literacy levels within societies and, as the international data became available, across the whole of Europe, was gradually established as a necessary goal. The capacity of other structures of power, the family, private philanthropy, the market place and the church, to realize this objective was called into question both by the statistics and by their own inability to count. The absence of the kind of systems which could supply a measure of progress across a state became itself a statement of failure. This applied not only to the extensive structures of informal education which existed in most parts of Europe, but also to the churches, which alone of the providers of literacy in the nineteenth century had the capacity to develop their own large-scale provision. For all the increasing significance given to them, the skills of reading and writing remained subordinate elements in the religious curricula, and thus second-order indices of progress.

The tables reflected a downgrading of the moral objectives of education in favour of the mechanical, and of the consumers of education in favour of the suppliers. As they gained increasing corporate self-awareness, the teachers themselves often resisted the cruder devices for measuring their performance. Payment by results, pioneered in England and Wales through the Revised Code of 1862, was the first round in an unfinished struggle between educational professionals and bureaucrats. But at least the teachers participated in the debate. The parents who were encouraged and then required to cede control over their children's education were at no point consulted about the appropriate indicators of success. They now had to begin to learn how to use a new currency for measuring the worth of their sons and daughters.

The final victims of the nineteenth-century bureaucrats' conception of achievement are historians themselves. Any engagement with the literacy statistics forces upon the modern observer the language of progress. In terms of marriage register signatures or data on recruits or census populations, every country in this survey starts low and ends higher. There are occasional plateaux and troughs in the returns, although many fewer than in other contemporary indicators of change such as mortality rates or gross national product. There are variations in the gradient of improvement, but no doubt about its direction. A common destination is apparent, with the arrival merely a matter of timing. Countries lag behind their rivals and then catch up, and within them groups defined by occupation, gender, age, religion or spatial location display gaps in performance which close as the years pass. What gives the history of literacy in modern Europe its outward identity is the sense of imminent victory. A journey with distant origins is everywhere reaching its conclusion. Sooner or later the figure at the foot of each column of figures approaches 100 per cent. Illiteracy seems as doomed as the handloom or the stagecoach. The more effort that is invested in establishing the causes of the sharply rising levels of reading and writing, and the greater the sophistication of the statistical analysis, the more endorsement is given to the association of a particular way of measuring communication skills with a specific conception of cultural progress.

The language cannot be divorced from the figures, and the figures themselves cannot be excluded from an account of change in the skills of reading and writing in modern European history. This is partly because they are so central to how the promoters of mass literacy conceived and communicated their purpose and their achievement. And it is partly because the act of counting constitutes a necessary point of entry for a general survey of the period. As will become apparent, the central questions of how literacy was used and given meaning take us deep into the economic, social and political structures of individual countries, and it is important at the outset to gain some sense of the general framework of change. If notions of progress and victory need constantly to be interrogated, there is no doubt that in these basic forms of communication, a European-wide event was taking place with enough common features to permit systematic comparison. Although there remain gaps and inconsistencies in the data, there now exists a sufficient volume of roughly similar long-run returns to permit the outlines of a picture to be drawn. The extent to which the figures remain abstractions will become more evident as their implications are pursued through later chapters.

The framework of change

At the most general level, it is possible to identify three phases of change, and three groups of countries within Europe. Prior to 1800, a handful of countries in the north and north-west had achieved something like mass literacy in terms of reading skills. Sweden, Denmark, Finland, Iceland, Scotland and Geneva had disseminated the capacity to decode a text across most of their population, and parts of France, Germany and England were nearing that level of competence. Behind them, in terms of statistical scores, were an adjacent group of countries where there were rarely to be found communities without at least a scattering of households in which books were owned and could be read, and in which there were high levels of literacy amongst the middling and upper

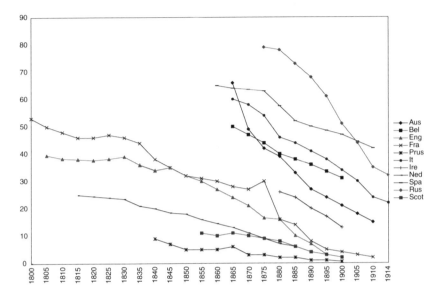

Figure 1.2 Male illiteracy in Europe, 1800–1914

reaches of society. Beyond them, in the further reaches of eastern and southern Europe, were countries in which the capacity to read and write could not be taken for granted at any level, and in which there were wide tracts of society and the countryside into which the written word rarely penetrated. The gentry in the comparatively advanced Hungarian province of Vas, for instance, could only manage to improve their ability to write from 22 to 39 per cent during the course of the eighteenth century, and their wives remained almost wholly illiterate.[15] In Russia, the eastern side of the Austro-Hungarian Empire, southern Italy, the Iberian peninsula and the Balkans, aggregate literacy, on the rare occasions when it could be counted, was below 25 per cent and often in single figures, with little sign of movement.[16]

As figures 1.2 and 1.3 indicate, the period after 1800 can be divided into two phases.[17] Before the 1860s, there was in the two more advanced sectors a general but relatively modest decline in illiteracy, which in this context may be taken as an inability to sign the marriage register, and equivalent tests for army recruits and census respondents. Most of the countries in the inner and middle bands showed falls of between 10 and 20 points for men, and similar if less consistent movements for women. The relative positions of these countries remained largely constant, although very rapid progress was made in Sweden, which until the beginning of the nineteenth century had neglected writing at the expense of

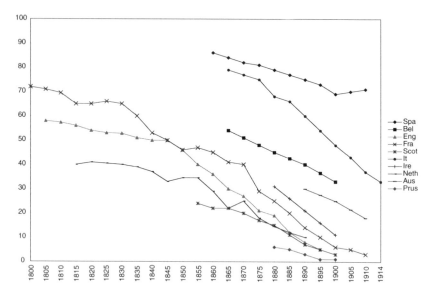

Figure 1.3   Female illiteracy in Europe, 1800–1914

reading, and now began to catch up with other northern and western countries, where some form of calligraphy had been more broadly taught before 1800. By the 1860s these countries could regard illiteracy as a problem for a minority of their populations, and might begin to plan its total eradication. At this point only Prussia was within sight of achieving this goal. It was otherwise in the outer band, where such changes as had taken place since the previous century were both small and fragile. In Spain for instance, male illiteracy was still above 80 per cent and female above 90. The only discernible movement was in the level of awareness amongst the more progressive forces in these countries of the scale of their backwardness.

During the final third of the nineteenth century, the pace of change picked up throughout the whole of Europe. The countries in the inner and middle bands set about the task of eliminating nominal illiteracy from their societies. In much of northern and western Europe, the figures were driven down to 10 per cent and below. Those parts of the region which ended the century with as much as a quarter of their men still unable to sign their names, such as Belgium and Ireland, were clearly heading in the same direction. As Europe prepared for war, most of the potential combatants had ensured that their recruits would be able to read the instructions on their weapons and write back to their families. The exceptions remained the countries on the eastern and southern fringes of the continent. In terms of their overall returns, Russia, Italy, Hungary and Spain had yet to achieve the levels of literacy in 1900 that had been recorded in much of the west 100 years earlier. At this time the countries of the Balkan peninsula displayed overall percentages of between 12 and 39.[18] It would take most of the first half of the following century for the last pockets of illiteracy to be eradicated from these areas. But even here, the period from around 1860 onwards saw a decisive shift in the distribution of communication skills. The ability to engage with the written word became a commonplace amongst the middling and upper ranks of society and spread out into the ranks of the superior urban workers and rural craftsmen. These countries were neither as isolated from the rest of the Continent as once they had been, nor were sections of their population as divorced from each other. Everywhere universal literacy was now seen as an inevitable destination, a common railway line with a single terminus. Church and state all over Europe had embraced the objective, even if many still lacked the institutional and material resources necessary to achieve it.

From the Urals to the Atlantic coasts, from the Mediterranean to the Baltic, there was a sense of a converging history. By the end of the nineteenth century, there was a broad diffusion of aspiration, and in the north and west, a growing homogeneity of performance. Whereas France and Prussia had been separated by 30 points in their male illiteracy at the end of the Napoleonic Wars, they were almost as one as they approached military conflict once more. Together with most of their neighbours to the east and north, the differences between them were now of little size or significance. And as the young men in these countries came to resemble each other in their capacity to sign their names, so the young women came more to resemble those they married. In the inner and middle bands at the beginning of the nineteenth century, female literacy generally lagged between 10 and 25 points behind male, and in the outer band the shortfall could be much higher. In the Spanish province of Northern Meseta, for instance, the gender gap was 53 points in 1860.[19] Girls had always suffered relative neglect in the education systems, especially in respect of learning to write in the formal classroom. As in poor developing countries of the late twentieth century, scarce cultural resources always went first to sons rather than daughters.[20] However a little after the boys in their community had commenced their journey towards universal literacy, they joined in the pursuit. Although the gap in achievement could initially widen, over the nineteenth century as a whole their illiteracy rates fell faster than those of men, with the differentials reduced to a few decimal points by 1913. Not only was the scale of change greater, but amidst the transformation, there were incidences of brides reversing their centuries-long tradition of subordination and actually outperforming their grooms. In later nineteenth-century Estonia for instance, women who had grown up in rural areas displayed consistently higher literacy than men, probably because they had been permitted to spend longer in the classroom before being sent out to work.[21] In England at the beginning of the final third of the century, female illiteracy was lower than male in a stretch of rural counties in the south and east. In some areas the differentials were very marked, with twice as many illiterate grooms as brides marrying in Oxfordshire, Suffolk and Sussex by 1884.[22] Again the reasons had to do with the nature of the local demand for child labour, and may also have exposed a wider tradition of reading ability hitherto concealed by the marriage registers.[23] Behind the rising graphs were the labours of the official schoolteachers, who in England as in most of Europe were now formally committed to achieving the same levels of literacy amongst girls as boys.

The spread of national education systems was also associated with the erosion of the equally traditional differentiation between the town and what its inhabitants frequently regarded as the mute countryside.[24] Since the invention of printing, books had belonged to the urban world, as had the institutional means of disseminating the skills for using them. In the towns and cities of early modern Europe were to be found not only the seats of advanced learning, but the concentrations of adults and children which made possible a thriving consumer culture in print and a diverse provision of charitable and commercial elementary schooling.[25] Here were the expanding professions whose authority and prosperity were founded on their display of codified knowledge, and here also were those manual occupations which developed their own traditions of literacy. In late eighteenth-century Paris, most artisans spent several years in the classroom, and there were few domestic servants who could not sign their wills.[26] Both print and schooling found their way into the rural areas, but always the flow was outward from the towns, and usually the levels of possession and use were lower. Only where industrial centres were undergoing periods of exponential growth did urban rates temporarily lag behind.[27] In general the rural hinterland tended to take its cue from the urban centre, with levels in the town determining the threshold of the surrounding countryside and the point of take-off.[28] Reading, which might be taught informally and practised on a basic devotional litera-ture, could spread widely in the countryside if the church was organized for the purpose. Towns were few and far between in the Scandinavian countries which led the way in the seventeenth and eighteenth centuries. But with writing skills, the gap between urban and rural literacy could be measured by the century right across Europe.

In those countries which remained predominantly agricultural in the nineteenth century, the slow process of change did little to alter the disparities. In Russia, for instance, rural literacy stood at 6 per cent in the 1860s, against a national average of 21 per cent; a doubling of the national figure over the next half-century still left rural literacy 15 points in arrears.[29] In late nineteenth-century Estonia, the countryside was in some areas marginally more literate than the towns in terms of reading skills, but everywhere lagged behind when it came to writing.[30] In the states of northern and western Europe where illiteracy was defined as a problem to be solved in the early nineteenth century, the main focus of attention was the countryside, together with the communities of unskilled labourers in the expanding towns, many of whom were themselves recent migrants from the surrounding villages. Where large areas of the countryside were bypassed by the twin forces of industrialization and urbanization, progress in achieving homogeneity of literacy rates was slow. Even in Prussia, the educational flagship of Europe, the male rates at unification ranged from 98.8 per cent in Berlin to 66.8 in West Prussia.[31] The eventual success of these campaigns dissolved the recorded inequalities between the urban and rural worlds. As was the case with female attainment, the common destination of virtually universal literacy by the early twentieth century demanded dramatic trajectories of improvement. Grooms and, even more so, brides from families of unskilled labourers began at below 30 per cent at the end of the second third of the nineteenth century, and were returning scores of over 90 within little more than two generations. Amongst these groups of the population a revolution was taking place. By contrast, the nominal literacy of urban artisans barely has a history in this period. The skilled male workers in the towns and cities of England, France and Prussia started in 1800 as they ended in 1914, altered only by their diminishing contempt for the idiocy of rural life.

The struggle against patterns of differential possession in terms of gender, space and occupation was not won easily. If the clock is stopped in any of the advancing countries, the outlines of ancient topographies of illiteracy are still visible. In France, the Saint-Malo–Geneva line which divided the more literate north and north-west from rest of the country remained apparent as church and state fought to establish an effective system of national education, with the area of backwardness shrinking to a triangle in the south west.[32] In England, the counties in the far north, around London and along the Channel coast retained their lead as the national illiteracy levels fell during the middle and later decades of the nineteenth century.[33] The differentials were narrowing, but as the ambition of homogeneity took hold, their significance increased. Amongst those countries with the greatest gap between aspiration and achievement, the scale of variation called into question the very existence of the state as a single cultural entity. Illiteracy in the newly united Italy in 1911 ranged from 11 per cent in Piedmont in the industrialized north to 70 in Calabria, far away to the south.[34] As the Austrian Empire struggled to hold itself together, the census of 1900 revealed disparities extending from 1 per cent in Vorarlberg to 73 in Dalmatia. Categorized by linguistic group, the returns were spread between 3 per cent amongst the Bohemians, Moravians and Slovaks to 75 amongst the Serbo-Croats and Romanians and 77 amongst the Ruthenians.[35] Within Hungary, a national average of 72 per cent male literacy in 1910 dissolves on closer examination into a complex map of local performance, with rates varying from 90 per cent in some western provinces to 40 per cent or less in parts of the north-east. Amongst women a rate of 61 per cent concealed a variation of between 90 and less than 20.[36] The new Bolshevik state inherited a polyglot society in which, according to official figures, literacy rates ranged from more than 70 per cent in the major cities to less than 1 per cent amongst the remote Chechens and Ingush.[37]

The act of setting and eventually achieving a target of universal possession of the skills of reading and writing separated the modern history of literacy from all the preceding centuries. But as we go forward to examine the implications of this final period of transition in later chapters, it is important to retain a sense of the complexities which were concealed by the smoothly descending national graphs. What was increasingly coming to be seen as residual illiteracy was visible not just in terms of geography and linguistic group, but also in relation to age. Given that most of the acquisition of nominal literacy took place in childhood, it followed that in periods of rapidly improving performance, gaps opened up between cohorts in the population. This phenomenon was visible in the first mass literacy campaign in late seventeenth-century Sweden, and in Spain during the first half of the twentieth century.[38] Where improvement was still sluggish, the generations remained close to each other. In Napoleonic France there was no discernible relationship between literacy and age, and in Italy in 1881, fifteen- to nineteen-year-old boys were only 6 points in advance of sixty-five- to sixty-nine-year-old men.[39] In England on the other hand, children educated in the 1830s and 1840s were on average 20 points more literate than their parents' generation when they came to be married in early adulthood, and in turn lagged behind their own children by a similar amount a quarter of a century later.[40] By 1900 in Belgium, the young were entering the realm of universal literacy, with rates of 90 per cent or more amongst teenagers, whereas their grandparents were locked into the semi-literate world of the mid-nineteenth century, with more than a third of men of sixty or more and almost half of women still unable to write.[41] In France at the turn of the century, virtually all the young brides and grooms could sign their names, but 30 per cent of women over fifty and of men over sixty-five had never learned to do so. Translated into absolute figures, the population still contained nearly 2,000,000 illiterate men and around 3,000,000 illiterate women.[42] With the possible exception of Prussia, whose levels fell into single figures in the middle of the nineteenth century, those countries claiming victory by 1914 would not in reality gain nominally literate populations until around the time of the next world war. By the same measure, the fact that much of southern and eastern Europe based their figures on census returns rather than marriage registers or conscript tests may have caused the extent of their backwardness to be overstated. The residual illiteracy between the wars in countries such as Italy, Spain, Austria and Russia had some parallel in the incidence of the undereducated elderly in the societies of their apparently more advanced neighbours to the north and west.

The descending graphs of illiteracy were further complicated by the factor of the family as a cultural unit. Reading and writing were promoted by the public authorities in the nineteenth century as an antidote to the oral and communal forms of recreation and protest which increasingly were seen as inimical to an ordered society. The means by which the consequences of investment in education were measured tended constantly to exaggerate the shift towards privacy. Both the marriage registers and the census returns recorded the attainments of individuals as discrete units. The aggregate tables displayed an atomized population, each member of society capable or incapable of communicating through the printed word. But the census enumerators called upon households, and the marriage registers recorded the making of new families. Their raw evidence, which has generally been neglected by historians, displayed the combined skills of couples or larger domestic groups.[43] It was widely assumed by contemporary observers that illiteracy was so shameful a condition that marriages would be founded on an educational endogamy, with the occasional incidence of an uneducated groom and an educated bride concealed by the latter modestly declining to sign her name. Embarrassment would cleanse the registers of undue complexity.

However detailed studies of the actual patterns of signatures and marks in English and Belgian marriages suggests that the new family units were far from consistent in their combinations of skills.[44] Only amongst the middling and upper ranks of society were the traditions of education for both sexes sufficiently well established to guarantee equality of attainment amongst the partners. Lower down the social scale, the brides of artisans were at the beginning of the nineteenth century less literate than their new husbands, and amongst the farm labourers and unskilled urban workers, all kinds of patterns of signatures and marks were possible, and remained so for much of the century. Contrary to the received view, there was little evidence of brides failing to sign out of consideration for their unlettered grooms, an impression strengthened by an examination of the literacy of the witnesses whom the couple chose to participate in the ceremony.[45] In Belgium, the proportion of marriages involving literate brides and illiterate grooms ranged from a seventh to almost a third across a sample of urban populations.[46] The immediate consequence of the variegated patterns was both to accelerate and to retard the graph of progress. At the beginning of the state campaign against illiteracy, only one in three unskilled labourers in England could sign his name, but there was a literate partner in almost half the marriages formed at this level of society. Across the marrying population as a whole, the proportion of new households in which at least one partner could sign passed 90 per cent a generation before the figure for grooms alone. Conversely, illiteracy lingered longer in families than the separate returns for brides and grooms implied.[47] At the end of the nineteenth century, one marriage in eight involved at least one partner failing to sign their name, and if the witnesses are included, one in six of the participants in the ceremony found it necessary to make a mark.

This reworking of the official returns introduces two of the themes of this survey. The first is that in their basic social groups, literate and illiterate were rarely strangers to each other. They married each other or mingled in the streets and other public places.[48] They lived with parents who had been raised with fewer opportunities to learn their letters or with children brought up with more. Some male occupational groups amongst the labouring population, especially the skilled urban artisans, had achieved a consistency of attainment by the early nineteenth century, and other sectors joined them as the decades passed. But outside the workplace, the divisions were rarely absolute. The kind of cultural cleansing which reformers hoped to achieve through the promotion of mass education was slow in coming. Most schoolchildren throughout most of this period will have encountered adults who never knew or had long since forgotten how to read or write.

A second theme is the social possession of the skills of communication. The element of privacy which is necessarily associated with the practice of reading a book or writing a letter must always be tempered with the sense of shared resources which characterized all aspects of the material culture of the labouring poor. Communities survived on the basis of the self-sufficiency not of each individual but of larger collectivities such as the family, the kinship network, the village or the urban neighbourhood. Consumables and services were begged, borrowed or purchased as necessity or availability dictated. Reading and writing were transferable skills. They could be hired out from specialist scribes who flourished for as long as the demand exceeded supply. In Italian towns at the beginning of the nineteenth century for instance, the uneducated victims of crime turned to professional assistance for the necessary task of writing their complaint to the police.[49] At the end of the century, the gap between peasant literacy and the need to correspond, especially with emigrated relatives, enhanced the role of paid and powerful intermediaries in the rural communities.[50] On a more casual basis, the service was rendered by a neighbour to those who had a document to be written or deciphered, or wanted to gain access to the contents of a broadside or a newspaper. Only between the wars in the countries of northern and western Europe could every citizen be expected, for instance, to conduct correspondence without the help of another, and even then, the escalation in the demands of bureaucratic procedures renewed the need to seek the help of others. In their influential study of the psycho-linguistics of literacy, Scribner and Cole compared the practice to basket-weaving.[51] Both were everyday skills, of general use to the community, taking their place amongst a wide range of tools for living. Neither was new to the modern period, and each had a long history in traditional cultures. They were relatively complex activities, which took some time to learn, but they could be taught in a variety of informal settings, and their mastery was not a matter of especial achievement. Indeed a basic literacy could be acquired at an age when a child was incapable of learning much else of value to itself or anyone else.[52] It might be an advantage if individuals were able to undertake the activities without assistance, but access to the skills of others would frequently suffice.

Literacy, however, raises more problems of definition than basket-weaving. It is at the very least two skills, with immense variation across Europe before the middle of the nineteenth century in the association between reading and writing. Since the state began to compile its own records of possession, questions have been asked about what was signified by the inscribing of a couple of words in a register once or sometimes twice in a lifetime, or by the self-ascription of capacity in response to a census enumerator or an army recruiter. In 1873, for instance, the Ministry of War in Denmark decided to classify the abilities of recruits with particular rigour, distinguishing six categories above total illiteracy: ability to compose a text; to sign a name and to read print and handwriting; to sign and read only print; to read print and handwriting but not sign; to read print only and not sign; and to sign but not read at all.[53] A mere 2 per cent of the 9,000 soldiers were wholly illiterate, with a further 1 per cent able to perform the task of writing their names but otherwise defeated by the written word. Just over one in five could read but either not write at all, or just manage their own names. This left three in four whose command of writing was sufficient to attempt some form of prose. In 1886 an examination was made of what was nominally the most literate society in Europe. Of 50,000,000 Germans, 20,000,000 could manage the Bible, hymn books or almanacs, 30,000,000 could cope with a newspaper, 10,000,000 could tackle 'demanding literary subjects', 2,000,000 regularly read the German classics, and 1,000,000 'followed literary developments'.[54] These studies emphasized the range of conditions which might be covered by the term 'literate'. They look forward to the late twentieth-century preoccupation with the persistence or growth of functional illiteracy, with measures of practical incapacity in contemporary Britain rising as high as a fifth of the adult population.[55]

The studies also offered comfort to those who argue that the names on marriage registers are evidence of more than a mere party trick. By the time these exercises were undertaken, a number of European countries were generating information from a variety of different sources, which could be related to each other. Furet and Ozouf have contrasted returns from marriage registers, the census and military recruits in France of the early 1870s, and found a striking consonance between them.[56] By and large, the capacity to sign the register constituted a crude index of communication skills, standing somewhere between an ability to make some sense the printed word, which it understated, and a full fluency with the pen, which it may have overstated.[57] The measure was not far removed from what most parents and children expected of schooling during the nineteenth century. The question of the marriage register signatures thus shifts from one of possible deception to one of potential application. The meaning of the statistical evidence resides in how the skills of reading and writing could be used, and for what purpose.[58] This involves a study of what actually was being taught in what were soon to become compulsory education systems, which will be the concern of the next chapter, and how the struggles of the schoolchildren were applied throughout their lives, which will be the topic of the succeeding chapters. In the meantime, however, some light can be cast on the relation between the passive and active possession of the skills if we return to the use of the postal systems in later nineteenth-century Europe.

Marriage register signatures should not be excluded altogether from the realm of functional literacy. By signing their names, bride and groom entered into what might well be the only enforceable legal contract of their lives. Even their marks were seen as a kind of immanent literacy, to be converted into *de facto* writing by the educated officials present at the ceremony. Correspondence, however, represented an altogether more sustained and sophisticated application of the written word. There is evidence of letters being written for or read to illiterate neighbours or family members in communities in which the skills of reading and writing were only partially distributed. Pierre-Jakez Hélias recalled his

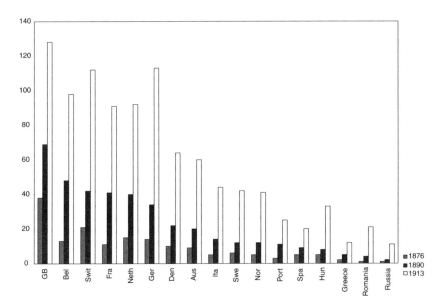

Figure 1.4 European per capita postal flows, 1876–1913

Breton grandfather, who could read but chose not to: 'It was my mother who deciphered all the letters from uncles and aunts out loud, and it was she who answered them, but he knew how.'[59] Conversely, with the appearance of the typewriter and the typist in the last two decades of the nineteenth century, the days when captains of industry or heads of government departments would conduct every scrap of business in their own hands were numbered. We can begin to glimpse a sight of the modern executive, whose power and status may be measured by his functional illiteracy, his refusal even to open an envelope let alone write a reply, and his proud inability to inscribe a legible signature. Nonetheless as most of Europe moved towards universal nominal literacy, it is likely that the majority of letters were written and read by the individuals who signed them and were named on the envelopes.

Between 1876 and 1928, the bureaucrats at the Universal Postal Union calculated the total national and international flows of the member countries on a per capita basis.[60] These returns constitute the only consistent, Europe-wide measure of functional literacy in the period. There are some less complete indices of reading, such as book or newspaper production, but nothing comparable in the field of writing. As figure 1.4 indicates, the figures displayed a striking disparity of practice.[61] In the first year, the usage ranged between thirty-eight items per head

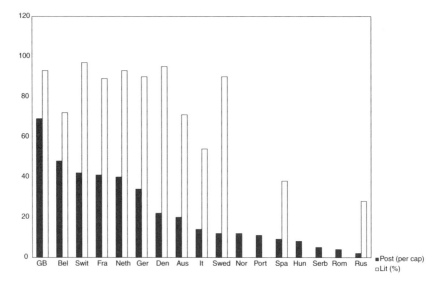

Figure 1.5   European postal flows and literacy, 1890

of population in Britain and one in Russia.[62] Over the succeeding
half-century, the gap widened, with Britain increasing to sixty-nine items
in 1890 and 128 in 1913, and Russia to two and eleven. Between the first
and the last, the other countries of Europe were strung out across the
field, largely maintaining their positions as the years passed. As with the
literacy statistics, the back-markers in the tables showed the greatest pro-
portionate increases during the decades before 1914, but in this context
there was to be no common destination. By the time war broke out, only
Germany and Switzerland were beginning to challenge Britain's ascen-
dancy (on a worldwide basis, the United States had by now taken the
lead), and these three countries were using this form of reading and
writing between five and ten times more heavily than those at the bottom
of the table.

The disparities of performance were particularly striking if compared
to the mere possession of literacy as measured by signatures and census
returns. Figure 1.5 displays the data for 1890, by which time both the
international postal system and most of the national education structures
were firmly established.[63] There was some consonance between the two
indices of communication skills. The higher levels of practice, like those
of possession, tended to be found in northern and western Europe, and
the lower more often in the south and east. However it is evident that
the technical ability to sign a name did not determine the extent of this

form of usage. By the last decade of the century, half the countries of Europe had attained nominal literacy rates of around 90 per cent, but within this group, there was a fivefold variation in the per capita postal levels. Sweden and Norway, with long histories of disseminating reading skills, and high, if recently attained, levels of full nominal literacy, were writing fewer letters per head of population than Italy, which was still decades away from eradicating the problem of illiteracy in the southern regions of the country. Conversely, whilst Russia was at the bottom of both tables, it was proportionately much closer to the advanced countries in possession of the skills of literacy, than in their application.

Correspondence cannot be used as a proxy for every form of practice, but the returns of the Universal Postal Union do constitute a powerful corrective to the impression given by the tables of signatures which have dominated accounts of modern European literacy. By the closing years of the nineteenth century, the history of nominal literacy was almost over for a substantial group of countries. The differences between them were as much a reflection of measurement techniques as actual performance, and were of declining comparative interest. By contrast, it is evident that there was and would remain a wide diversity in the deployment of the skills being taught in the classrooms. If convergence was taking place across Europe, it was a much slower and more complex process than the conventional literacy tables implied. Equally it is apparent that the road from possession to use was far from straightforward. A wide range of social, economic and political factors need to be brought into the equation if the variations in practice are to be understood. Some of these are themselves susceptible to statistical analysis, and will be examined in later chapters.

The calibration of change

Contrasting nominal and functional literacy raises questions of both meaning and explanation. It requires a more sophisticated search for the dynamics of change, and a more measured consideration of its significance. Over the last two decades, the study of literacy has shown a constant tendency to polarization. On the one side there has been the stress on the metamorphic effect of encountering the written word. Learning to read and write in the context of institutional schooling, it is argued, generated a fundamental change in the consciousness and capabilities of the mass of the population. Contemporary scholars have elaborated the claims of the nineteenth-century promoters of education and written communication. Where literacy was viewed as an index of civilization, now it is placed at the centre of the process of modernity.[64] Emannuel

Todd's *The Causes of Progress* sees a cultural revolution based on the democratization of the printed word as the prime mover in the demographic and economic revolutions which swept eighteenth- and nineteenth-century Europe.[65] Many who are not attracted by grand narratives of change would nonetheless wish to stress the transformative element of the final drive against illiteracy. Thus, for instance Roger Chartier claims that 'The progress of literacy and diffusion of reading were major factors contributing to change in Western man's idea of himself and his relation to others.'[66] A function of the historian is to remind a culture which now is excited by a means of communication only if it is attached to a plug, of the sheer thrill of first encountering the printed page. It is necessary, argues Daniel Roche, to return to a world confined by the restrictions of oral communication, and then to perceive how, 'even a halting ability to read could utterly transform the ordinary perceptions and mentality of the popular classes.'[67]

A contrasting perspective has demanded that accounts of literacy be founded on a general suspicion of notions of transformation. There is a constant need to challenge what Harvey Graff has termed the 'literacy myth', the grandiloquent claims of both the past and the contemporary education industry which have been too readily accepted by historians and social scientists seeking to pattern cultural development.[68] The language of conversion reflects the self-promotion of new professions as they struggle to assert their authority over parents and children and appropriate the power and status of traditional agencies of control. It overstates the simplicity of oral means of communication, and over-dramatizes the consequences of learning to read and write. Literacy has always been a metaphor-laden event, with the basic activities of decoding print translated into heightened moral and intellectual categories.[69] If organized religion was the intended victim of many literacy campaigns, it managed, at the very least, to bequeath to the secular education process its vocabulary of spiritual reconstruction. The scholar has a responsibility to interrogate this language and the assumptions which it embodied. At every turn, questions must be asked about what newly educated readers and writers could actually do with their skills within their particular society and economy. Becoming literate will only transform the way an individual thinks if literacy is used in order to think. Practice rather than mere possession is the key to change, and its effects have to be sought in the specific contexts in which it takes place.

The more sceptical attitude to the consequences of mass literacy has gained a great deal of ground in recent years. It appeals to the professional caution of historians faced with the overheated claims of elite groups in past societies, and it accords with the modern questioning of the output of contemporary education systems. The limitations of measures of nominal literacy are now so well established that the case for founding any history on the use to which the skills might be put seems unanswerable. Reading and writing were pre-industrial tools of communication, and as with any hand tool they would become blunt and unserviceable if they were not kept in proper repair and employed with appropriate expertise for a particular purpose.[70] Rather than refighting the battle against what Brian Street termed the 'autonomous model' of literacy,[71] the challenge now is to exploit with more rigour and imagination the implications of the functional approach.[72] If it is seen as a purely critical exercise, there is a danger of the entire issue disappearing below the waves, weighed down with an ever-increasing freight of qualifications and contradictions. If the larger claims for literacy are falsified, if the traditional dichotomies of oral and literate, educated and uneducated, rational and irrational, collapse into a complex series of interactions and relativities, there seems little point in the further study of the subject as a particular domain of human activity.

At the outset, the functional approach needs to be distinguished from the purely negative. Certainly there was much to support a pessimistic verdict. An account of the history of modern literacy has to encompass the multitudes of young children for whom education represented the closure of their powers of communication and imagination. It must accompany the young Pierre Besson as he wanders reluctantly along the road in the early morning:

> what he sees before his eyes dazzles him; mysterious smells invade his brain and intoxicate him. Now and then, a pretty girl swells his heart; he presents his compliments. See how he dawdles and delays; surely he will arrive too late as he takes time to rest. He gazes up to the mountain, towards the woods and the heather, and a whole universe of recollections springs up in his memory . . . at last he arrives. The entrance seems dark, loathsome, the school strict, cold and boring.[73]

Failed hopes littered the final drive to universal literacy, yet it was not only the educators who entertained them. The sense of excitement and adventure associated with the spread of the written word was to be found amongst the consumers as well as the suppliers of mass education. An account also has to sit next to self-educated readers embarking on wild, uncharted voyages of intellectual discovery in gloomy, crowded apartments. 'I thought it possible that by the time I reached the age of twenty four', recalled the shoemaker Thomas Cooper,

> I might be able to master the elements of Latin, Greek, Hebrew, and French; might get well through Euclid, and through a course of Algebra; might commit the entire 'Paradise Lost' and seven of the best plays of

Shakespeare to memory; and might read a large and solid course of history, and religious evidences; and be well acquainted also with the current literature of the day.[74]

It has to endure the numbing boredom of the lengthening school years, but it also has to respond to the moments of intellectual rapture. Here for instance, a young compositor encounters Macaulay for the first time:

Bernard Shaw tells how he could get more intoxication from Mozart and Beethoven than any common mortal could from a bottle of brandy. I was as intoxicated that day far more completely than wine or whisky have ever made me, and intoxicated by literary art, as well as by the pageantry of its historical theme.[75]

And between the poles of tedium and transformation there were the life-long opportunities for quiet relaxation which the printed word afforded ever more numerous members of the European population.

This approach further has to escape the confines of instrumentality. The concept of functional literacy was first articulated during the later 1950s in the context of the development of Third World economies,[76] and has never lost its association with the workplace, despite the more recent questioning of the automatic association between schooling and economic growth, and attempts to extend the concept to engagement in 'all the activities in which literacy is required for effective function of [a person's] group and community'.[77] An engagement with the occupational conditions for gaining literacy and with the material consequences of its acquisition remains a major area of concern. It is no longer possible, however, to measure the purpose and outcome of literacy as if it were a mechanical process which always yielded a predictable return for a given investment. At the very beginning, for instance, it is now argued that the nature of young children's early encounters with reading and writing greatly depends on the meaning they invest in the activities.[78] What they think literacy is for, what kind of event they envisage it as being, will have greater influence on their journey towards a competence in written communication than the particular methods by which they are taught. By the same measure, subsequent encounters with the printed word will require not just the application of technical skills to a set of symbolic representations, but a complex engagement between the meanings brought to the text and those inscribed in it. Literacy is a tool for enabling individuals and social groups to extend their understanding of themselves and their world, and amongst the objects of comprehension is that of literacy itself. In this process, those not yet literate can influence the views of those who are becoming so, just as the construction of illiteracy by the literate can alter the self-perception of those still confined to oral means of storing and reproducing information.

The coming of mass literacy has to be located in the particular ways in which people in past societies lived out their lives. This form of cultural history must embrace the manner in which literacy was made distinct from other modes of daily practice, and yet was embedded in the structures of deprivation and opportunity, fear and aspiration, which conditioned the struggle for existence.[79] It must be sensitive to the specific circumstances of time and place, whilst alert to the more general patterns of cause and consequence in a Europe whose cultural boundaries were through the uses of literacy gradually becoming more porous. Amidst this confusion of contexts and meanings there resides a seeming paradox. On the one hand, the hopes born of the Enlightenment that the spread of literacy would act as a solvent on traditional hierarchies were opposed at almost every turn by what Furet and Ozouf describe as the 'inertia of society'.[80] Inequalities of class, occupation, ethnicity, age and gender were much more frequently reproduced through the schoolroom than challenged by it. The churches of Europe enjoyed a late golden age of influence and responsibility as suppliers of mass education and the governments learned new methods of controlling their populations through the power they gained over the upbringing of children. There was change, and the spread of reading and writing was integral to it, but at many junctures in many societies, the descending graphs of illiteracy were as lines drawn in the sand. The case for transformation on either a personal or a collective scale has everywhere to be demonstrated rather than assumed.

At the same time, the peoples of Europe learned to read and write in this period because they wished to do so. As will be argued in the following chapter, compulsion largely followed rather than preceded the achievement of mass literacy. In village after village, in town after town, we find peasants and artisans arranging an education for their children for reasons which were private to them. The labours of salaried teachers, the investments of religious and public bodies and the exhortations of clergymen and politicians all played a role, but for the most part the critical calculation of cost and benefit was made in the home, not outside it. Nothing was more realistic and rational than the decisions made about the allocation of the resources of a hard-pressed family economy. These labouring men and their wives had a far more sober grasp of the limitations of literacy than those who had devoted their careers to its provision. Yet on an increasing scale they departed from the traditions of their parents and grandparents and sought out an education for their children.

In a sense, the fears of the elites of earlier centuries, that print was essentially an anarchic force best kept from the lower orders, were born out in this period. There was no telling why such people wanted to read, or what they were capable of reading into what they read. The estimation of the value and the potential of the written word must begin with those who amidst all the pressures and constraints of their daily lives, sought out these skills and in faltering, imperfect ways, set them to work.[81]

2
Learning Literacy

The state

Anthony Errington, a Tyneside wagonway wright, sat down in 1823 to write out his life history on loose sheets of paper. He began with his motive: 'The reason of my wrighting the particulars of my life and Trans-actions are to inform my famely and the world.'[1] After brief accounts of his parents and his infancy, he turned to his education:

> I Closely atended school to read. And when I got lorned to speling, One Thos Nosbet and severell others was standen to say spelling, and I sounded the word 'strainger', which he had not done, and I got before him. At 12 Oclock, he struck me and made my nose bleed. On which a batel Comenced, and I proved Conckerror by thirsting him into a Boghole and made him all dirt . . . The Mistress lorned me to wright and shortly after I was put to Wm Yollowly of Low Huerth to [learn] figures in Arithmatick. And haveing bean one month at school, at diner time I went into the Church yard to read the grave stones. And thear being a new digged grave, 4 strong lads took me and put me in the grave, One at my feet and One at my head, when the Other said the buriell sarvice over mee and at the same time with the spade put some Soil upon me. The boys left me their . . .[2]

Not every autobiographer of the period composed so vivid an account of the pleasures and pains of learning to read and write, but almost all felt obliged to dwell upon their education, however brief and inadequate it may have been. In every kind of life history the actuality and potential of instruction in basic literacy was becoming a familiar topic of debate.

At the time of Errington's childhood, public interest in the schoolroom was growing across much of western Europe. The topic was given greater priority by the collapse of the *ancien régime* in France and its turbulent aftermath. In itself, the literacy of the French population was little affected by the course of the Revolution and the rise and fall of Napoleon. The trajectory of improvement which had been visible at least since the death of Louis XIV continued much as before.[3] The continuity amidst the upheavals caused first by political crisis and then by war reflected the scale of the investment by the Catholic church during the eighteenth century, and the depth of the commitment by parents to the value of reading and writing. It owed very little to the structural reforms to schooling in the years after 1789. Laws were passed, but they were either overtaken by further constitutional crises before their ambitious provisions could be implemented, or were doomed to a shadow life as the human and material resources of the nation were diverted into costly wars. The real change was at the level of discussion rather than action. The Revolution and its subsequent export to the neighbouring states of Europe instigated an intense debate about the purpose and organization of elementary education. Whether or not the schools of nineteenth-century Europe generated knowledge, they certainly created information. Manifestos, reports, surveys, curricula, textbooks, draft legislation poured forth from the pens of reformers, and as their proposals began to take on a concrete form, so the educational bureaucracies established the archives without which their continued existence would be neither possible nor justified.

The change was partly in the volume of publications and arguments, and partly in the assumptions upon which they were founded. The terms of the debate shifted from whether to when, from if to what. As before, there was a range of opinion from conservative to radical, with the conflict between them increasingly bitter as fundamental political, moral and spiritual conflicts were played out in the classrooms of the European nations. But the option of ignorance was disappearing. It was no longer possible seriously to argue that educating the mass of the population was intrinsically wrong, that the generations from whom the soldiers and workers of the nineteenth century were to be recruited would be better illiterate than literate. Now it was a matter of who paid for the teachers, and who controlled them, how the children were to be kept at their desks, and how they were to be taught, what the teachers themselves learned and what they transmitted to their pupils. If basic issues of function, authority and pedagogy remained in dispute, no one in authority supposed that teaching a child its letters should be left entirely to the discretion of its parents, or that the child should complete a school career without mastering the basic skills of written communication. One way or another, the process of learning literacy was seen as the responsibility of those struggling for control of the nation's destiny.

The common denominator of every blueprint for reform was the notion of system. Whether the outcome was to be a more disciplined population, or one capable of throwing off the discipline of the old regimes, there had to be order in the process. In 1796, as the Dutch struggled to come to terms to the ideological and military aggression of the French revolutionary state, the newly formed Society for the Common Good issued a report on 'General Ideas on National Education'. Instruction, it argued, should be for all children from every class. Government legislation should establish a framework of control, with a structure of inspection to ensure that every locality conformed to central direction. The training, accreditation and remuneration of teachers should be a matter for the state. In the classroom, 'instruction should be classical and systematic', and the materials used by the teachers 'should be the same for all schools.'[4] Similar plans were being devised and circulated in all the neighbouring countries. Most of the Dutch proposals had already been embodied in French legislation, particularly the Loi Lakanal of November 1794 and the Loi Daunou passed by the Convention on the last day of its existence in October 1795 and implemented by the Directory.[5] Any manifesto on the role of the state had to include a plan for education. It was no longer enough merely to exhort local dignitaries to do more for the poor and ignorant. In the vision of the Society for the Common Good, nothing should be left to chance, and everything should fit together. Attendance should be universal, administration comprehensive, and inspection objective and effective. Those in control of the machine for instruction should be able to select, train and pay the teachers, and ensure that every classroom should conduct the same lessons in the same way.

The ambition was born of the Enlightenment. It stemmed from the conviction that every individual was capable of breaking the shackles of tradition and striding forth into a world made transparent by the application of reason. The process of learning was redefined from reproduction to creativity. It was not about absorbing the patterns of the past, but about equipping the autonomous personality with the skills to create a new future. No manual worker, however brutish and benighted, no peasant, however enmeshed in tradition, was beyond the reach of the liberating influence of education. Each and every one was through a process of intellectual awakening capable of making a contribution to the economic, social and political progress of the nation as a whole. But it followed that the children of the labouring poor could not rely on their parents or on the cultural resources of their communities for the kind of schooling they needed. Those whose only ambition was to transmit the fatalism which corrupted and confined their daily lives were by definition incapable of presenting the new generation with the keys to their mental prison. By the same measure, local elites were either implicated in the preservation of the superstitious outlook, or powerless to overcome its grip on the minds of the surrounding population. The initiative had to come from the centre, and the agents of reform had to be equipped with the methods, with the resources and with the authority to overcome the dead hand of the past.[6]

During the course of the eighteenth century, occasional attempts had been made to implement grand visions of reform. The Prussians had legislated for a system of elementary education in 1717, the Swedes in 1723, the Danes in 1739, the Icelanders in 1744, the Portuguese in 1759, the Estonians in 1765, the Bavarians in 1771, the Austrians in 1774, and the Poles in 1783.[7] Even Russia had introduced a statute in 1786 based on the Austrian model which prescribed a standard curriculum and the division of the school into two classes each of one year, which would teach not only morality but also reading, writing and arithmetic. The closer the legislation was to the aspirations of the Enlightenment, the less likely it was to succeed. The only lasting innovations were in those Scandinavian countries where the systems were operated in conjunction with the churches and with the households in which the children were growing up, and sought principally to create Christians who could read their bibles rather than fully literate citizens capable of rebuilding their societies. Elsewhere, the scale of the ambition served largely to measure the poverty of the achievement, nowhere more so than in Russia where the state apparatus proved wholly incapable of funding the grandiose scheme which it had enacted. Even in Prussia, it now seems that the eighteenth-century achievements were more rhetorical than real.[8]

The intensity of the debate over education in the latter part of the eighteenth century robbed the succeeding era of much of its claim to originality. The ferment of innovation in so many aspects of material and cultural life in the nineteenth century was not matched in the one area which was now seen as critical to the generation of new ways of thinking and behaving. In terms of the organization and methods of instruction, especially at the elementary level, almost nothing was invented during the Industrial Revolution. All the ideas about how to manage an education system, what it was for and how it was to be delivered, can be encountered in scores of private and official publications and initiatives in the years before and during the French Revolution. This did not, of course, prevent all succeeding pedagogical prophets claiming complete novelty for their own methods of teaching literacy to the unlettered poor. But in practice, the palette of techniques was limited, and virtually all of them had been attempted at some point in the centuries since the introduction of printing.[9] As soon as books began to circulate, publishers discovered that there was money to be made out of aids to learning how to read them. An ever-expanding market place stimulated a host of scholastic entrepreneurs, all seeking to elaborate or find substitutes for the basic hornbooks and primers. As early as the beginning of the seventeenth century, consumers in Germany and England had available to them graded vocabulary books with and without illustrations, the beginning of the use of colour, various whole-word and whole-sentence schemes, and methods based on phonics and on the shape of letters.[10] Locke recorded the use of alphabetic dice in 1693, and in the eighteenth century a range of ever more ingenious cards and board games were developed to ease the pain of learning.[11] In terms of pedagogy, the question in the modern period is not one of discovery, but of why one amongst a range of available methods was foregrounded at a particular moment in the development of a school programme. And in terms of the educational system as a whole, the question is not why so much was achieved but so little.

In the more developed countries of Europe, it took about 100 years from the promulgation of a universal and compulsory system of elementary education to its final achievement. The first phase of visionary schemes was succeeded by a more cautious programme of reform in the second quarter of the nineteenth century, in which the state accepted the need to make alliances with alternative providers of schooling, particularly the churches, and then by a phase of renewed ambition in the closing decades of the century when a free, inspected school was made available to every child in every village and urban neighbourhood and parents were finally denied the freedom to determine what education their children received. Thereafter it was a matter of gradually extending the curriculum and advancing the leaving age, and beginning to explore ways of connecting elementary to secondary education. In France the milestones were the Loi Guizot in 1833, which instructed *communes* to establish a school for boys which was neither free nor compulsory, the Loi Ferry of 1881 and of 1882, which made elementary education both free and compulsory, and the Loi Goblet, which consolidated state control over the system and introduced higher primary schools. In England, the state began to subsidize the church schools in 1833 and inspect them in 1846, but elementary education only became universal in 1870, compulsory in 1880, and free in 1886. A narrow bridge to further education and beyond was not constructed until 1902. In countries with a longer tradition of basic provision the sequence might begin a little earlier. Sweden legislated for universal compulsory education in 1842, but even here the state did not take on responsibility for teachers' salaries until 1875 or create links with secondary education until 1894.[12] In regions with no effective tradition at all, the process was correspondingly slower. Either an overambitious law was left on the statute books whilst generation after generation struggled to make it a reality, or one doomed Act followed another into the twentieth century. In Spain the Ley Moyano of 1857 provided on paper a system comparable to the most advanced programmes of her western neighbours,[13] but a century was to pass before its provisions were fully operational, and no further general Act was passed until 1970. In Russia, major laws were introduced almost every decade in the nineteenth and early twentieth centuries, but still the new Bolshevik government found it necessary to issue a 'Basic Decree on the Liquidation of Illiteracy' in December 1919 in order to tackle the problem.

It was in some respects as if Stephenson's *Rocket* had been conceived and designed but left in the sidings whilst the stage coaches plied their trade for a few more generations. The reasons why the dreams of the Enlightenment reformers took so long to turn into a reality had to do with the costs of learning to read and write. It was at once extremely cheap and prohibitively expensive. On the one hand, market forces had brought teaching materials within reach of the many European populations long before governments conceived the ambition of educating them. During the early modern period, distribution networks of small printed books – stories, improvement manuals, religious tracts – had been established across Europe. The *luboks* in Russia, the Bibliotèque Bleue, the chapbooks made reading matter available for less than a day's wage of the poorest labourer, supplying both the incentive and the opportunity to learn how to read. Hornbooks, ABC tablets, *fibeln, lesebrettern* and primers were similarly available at a cost no greater than an evening in a bar.[14] They were amongst the earliest mass-produced items in any European nation's economy, regardless of confessional tradition. More than a third of a million copies of the Slavic primer were printed in Muscovy in the second half of the seventeenth century.[15] In London in the 1730s and 1740s, a single publisher brought out more than a quarter of a million copies of one amongst a range of competing cheap reading books.[16] In Hungary, simple prayer books were available for the price of a broomstick.[17] Irish hedge schools used the most common eighteenth-century primers in the English-speaking world in editions specially produced for sale by travelling chapmen, and supplemented specialized texts with all the usual reading matter of the countryside.[18] Alongside them was the official literature of the religious denominations, accessible in the church and often distributed free to the homes of the parishioners. The Reformation caused the dissemination not just of vernacular bibles but of a host of brief texts which could be attempted by inexperienced readers, such as Luther's *Little Catechism*, which had been translated into many European languages by the middle of the sixteenth century.[19] If few schools and fewer homes had unrestricted access to a sufficient volume of specialized teaching material, it was always possible to appropriate or adapt some kind of text. In France, the parish schools depended on pupils bringing into school any scraps of literature possessed by their parents, and failing that, manuscript deeds or petitions from the family's archive.[20] Writing was a more difficult task and required more specialized equipment, but where the ambition existed, a whitewashed wall and a piece of charcoal would be enough to make a start.

Instruction in basic literacy was an undertaking that could be attempted by any adult who could make out an alphabet. John Jones, born in the Forest of Dean in 1774, was first sent to an old woman

> with whom I learnt my letters and spelling, but I believe I made but little progress in reading. The only person in the village who taught writing at that time was an old man, by trade a stone-cutter, and he only on winter evenings – after his return from his daily labour; to him I went the best part of two winters, and that Sir, was the finishing of my education.[21]

Lessons could take place in any kind of space at any moment in the life of the household. Children might pick up rudimentary skills as they played or worked around adults, and where a more prolonged engagement with a teacher was required, it was not difficult to create a classroom. Russian peasant children could learn their alphabets in *vol'nye shkoly* or private 'wild' schools set up in their villages.[22] In rural France, peasants in villages where the church had failed to make any provision organized classes on winter evenings, appointing the least illiterate amongst them as teacher.[23] Clandestine unofficial schools flourished in late eighteenth-century Paris,[24] and in the towns and cities of Prussia and Austria unlicensed *Winkelschulen* or backstreet schools were set up by underemployed artisans, unorthodox preachers, former soldiers, or women seeking to supplement their family incomes.[25] In the urban communities, it was often possible to find a room which could be rented or appropriated as a school, but in the countryside it was less easy to locate a suitable space. Itinerant schoolteachers worked their way through the Bavarian countryside, setting up *Wanderschule* wherever they could find some temporary quarters.[26] In Ireland, 'hedge schools' were established, sometimes literally behind a hedge at the edge of a field, on other

occasions in purpose-built but extremely impermanent premises.[27] Lord
Palmerston described the transmission of literacy on his County Sligo
estate in 1808:

> The thirst for education is so great that there are now three or four schools
> upon the estate. The people join in engaging some itinerant master; they
> run him up a miserable mud hut on the road side, and the boys pay him
> half-a-crown, or some five shillings a quarter. They are taught reading,
> writing and arithmetic, and what, from the appearance of the establish-
> ment, no one would imagine, Latin and Greek.[28]

The fleeting life of these schools and the absence of any kind of
written contract between the parents and the uncertificated teachers,
makes it impossible to establish a clear statistical picture of their extent.
Where official commentators did notice them, it was always to condemn
rather than describe. Thus, for instance, an Irish reformer reported the
work of the hedge schools in 1832: 'it would be difficult to imagine anything more wretched than those receptacles of rags and penury, in which
a semi-barbarous peasantry acquired the rudiments of reading, writing,
Irish history and high-treason.'[29] Much evidence used by historians takes
the form not of objective descriptions but rather of communiqués from
a long guerrilla war between the unsubsidized, uncertificated and above
all uncontrolled private classrooms and the church and state bureaucracies which struggled for more than a century to put them out of
existence.[30] It was frequently the presence of schools rather than their
absence that stimulated the reformers. In Denmark, for instance, the
mushrooming of unlicensed classrooms around the turn of the century
was decisive in stimulating the first systematic Education Act of 1814.[31]
The slower the official bodies were to go on the attack, the greater the
role played by these informal networks of instruction. In England, the
comparatively high rates of literacy at the beginning of the nineteenth
century, with 60 per cent of grooms and 40 per cent of brides able to sign
their names, owed nothing to the state, and less to the church than to the
efforts by the parents of poor children either to teach themselves or
employ some literate neighbour to perform the task for them. As the
American educationalist Horace Mann observed in 1846, 'England is the
only one among the nations of Europe conspicuous for its civilisation
and resources, which has not, and never has had, any system for the education of its people.'[32] In the 1850s, two decades after the state began to
intervene in the provision of literacy, attendance at dame and private-
adventure schools was larger than that at the subsidized and inspected
church schools. In the nation's capital, private day schools were as late
as 1870 still teaching an estimated 44,000 children under the noses of the

legislators and inspectors.[33] The unofficial teacher was only driven from the field in the closing years of the century by a state machine equipped with an arsenal of regulatory and repressive legal instruments.

The nineteenth-century drive to professionalize the teaching of literacy everywhere overstated the complexity of the process. In terms of the cognitive development of the child, the skills of reading and writing could be picked up at an age when it was incapable of performing most of the tasks necessary to the survival of the family economy. A curious and determined child could construct its own pathway to literacy. 'For me to learn to read', recalled Antoine Sylvère,

> took more than ten years, just by following the mass in my book. For a long time I understood nothing, but when I had learned to distinguish the gospels, I got along by myself. I gained possession of four or five words each time I went to church. I stole some good lessons from the priest, and the so-and-so knew nothing about it.[34]

In the broad curriculum of learning through which boys and girls had to pass as they grew into independent workers and parents, learning how to decipher a simple text or write out a few words was an early and soon completed undertaking. By the same measure, the decision by a parent to find a few moments in the midst of a working day or during a long winter evening to read with a child was not one of the more serious that had to be taken, neither was the payment of a few spare coins to an untrained teacher. Parental involvement in the provision of education is a neglected theme in the history of education in this period, at least in part because of the inability or unwillingness of historians to challenge the limitations of the official record. Everywhere the archives of the educational bureaucrats constructed a narrative which relegated the consumers of schooling to passive onlookers in the process of overcoming illiteracy. In reality, the problem for the educational reformers was not that parents could do so little but they could do so much. Nineteenth-century governments found it much easier to justify and impose a monopoly of violence than a monopoly of instruction. Success in the second endeavour was delayed until the state itself became a learning organization, capable of understanding the specific nature of the service its trained and inspected teachers could perform for the parents of the labouring poor.

Robert Lowe famously defended the Revised Code of 1862 by claiming that the country would have an education which was either cheap or effective. Governments of the nineteenth century everywhere discovered that official schooling was rarely the latter and never the former. If a child might make some progress towards literacy with little cost to its parents, the state was unable to advance the communication skills of the nation as a whole without escalating expense to taxpayers. The sheer scale of the educational enterprise exerted a profound influence on the shape that it took. The task of managing a comprehensive elementary school system demanded an investment in people, buildings and bureaucracies which within the civilian sphere was matched only by the costs of maintaining a national police force and a rail and postal network. Classrooms, textbooks and teachers were amongst the largest items of government expenditure after barracks, guns and soldiers in the century following the conclusion of the Napoleonic Wars.

Despite all the advocacy of the Enlightenment reformers, the proportion of government expenditure devoted to every aspect of education in the early years of peace was negligible. In France it was 1 per cent in 1832, in Belgium 1.5 per cent in 1835, in Britain just 0.1 per cent when the reforming Whig government took office in 1830, and 0.5 per cent when it was replaced by the Tories eleven years later.[35] In those European countries seeking to modernize their institutions in the face of accelerating economic, social and political change, the first priority was law and order. Whatever claims might be made for the disciplinary effects of systematic schooling, it seemed prudent to invest in policemen before schoolteachers. In the aftermath of the revolutionary threats and outbreaks of 1830, France was spending five times as much on law and order as on its educational structure, Belgium four times and Britain eleven. Most of the modernizing states of Europe then settled down to what seems to have been an accepted proportion of national expenditure on overt means of controlling their populations, devoting around 6 per cent of their budgets to their judicial systems right through to 1914.[36] Not until politicians felt safe in their beds did they begin to accede to the demands of the pedagogues. In 1870, the point at which the final drive against literacy was getting under way, the average proportion of public expenditure devoted to schools began to overtake that spent on the police and the courts. As the last illiterates were chased down, the educational budgets continued to grow, costing on average twice as much as the judicial systems on the eve of the First World War.

The state's only other engagement with the circumstances of the less privileged sections of their populations was through various forms of public welfare. Even though a number of countries in northern and western Europe were beginning to invest heavily in their social services in the later nineteenth century, this category of spending was continually outstripped by education. Even Germany, with its admired but rarely imitated national insurance system, was spending more on lessons than on benefits in the early years of the twentieth century. The one category of civilian public expenditure which ever exceeded the growth of schooling in the last third of the nineteenth century was the national rail and postal systems. But whereas the schoolmasters eventually abandoned the ambition of making children pay for the service they received, it proved possible to persuade the correspondents and passengers to do so in ever-increasing numbers. The purchase of stamps and tickets appeared on the other side of the national balance sheet, whereas the return on the investment in literacy did not do so in a way which could be readily recognized. Throughout the period, military budgets normally exceeded any category of domestic spending. The one exception in the available statistics is Finland, whose educational spending had escaped the constraints of its imperial master and was one and a half times greater than its investment in defence in 1910. Elsewhere, the cost of schools was everywhere growing faster than that of barracks, but never overtaking it. Ironically, of the major European powers, the country whose educational spending most nearly matched the army and navy budgets on the eve of the First World War was Germany, whose irresponsible militarism was subsequently blamed for its outbreak.

Viewed from the twentieth century, the nineteenth was the era of large-scale public investment in education. But if we look forward from the plans drawn up by the Enlightenment reformers, the narrative is as much one of expenditure avoided. The growth in most countries in the decades after the defeat of Napoleon was slow and uncertain, the more so where the state ceded control of innovation to the localities. In France, for instance, home of many of the more radical eighteenth-century blueprints, the proportion of national expenditure devoted to all forms of education crept up from 1 per cent in 1822 to 2.3 half a century later, but then quadrupled in the remainder of the period before the First World War. In Norway the percentage had reached 3.9 by 1870, and again more than quadrupled in the following four decades. In Denmark the figure was as low as 3.1 per cent in 1879, but 12 per cent a mere twenty years later. No country followed exactly the same trajectory of growth, but the general pattern was for costs to be held down long after the state formally embraced the ambition of a creating a mass literate society. From at least the time of the Society for the Common Good, it was evident that a fully functioning elementary education system would demand not just a dry, heated, illuminated and furnished schoolroom in every parish, each with its teacher and accompanying materials for lessons, but also a phalanx of teacher trainers, inspectors, attendance officers, examiners and administrators, to say nothing of an expanding industry of textbook writers, publishers and distributors. At best, the small contribution parents might be persuaded to make for a week's schooling would merely offset the cost of this pedagogic army. Yet most of the states lacked the infrastructure necessary to raise and spend the kind of sums which would be involved, or, more fundamentally, were too uncertain of their legitimacy to impose such unprecedented burdens on the taxpaying population. However convincing the reformers, the gains promised by universal education were a great deal less immediate and tangible than those delivered by armies and police forces.

The churches

The only organization in any of these countries with both the tradition of raising and spending large sums of money for the moral improvement of the labouring population, and the experience of managing complex bureaucracies for this purpose, was the church. Since the Reformation and Counter-Reformation, both Protestants and Catholics had wavered in their commitment to teaching the mass of their congregations, but from the late seventeenth century onwards a range of movements on both sides of the confessional divide, such as the Lutherans in Sweden, the Pietists in Germany, the evangelicals in Britain, the Reform Catholics in Austria and the French Jansenists, reinvigorated the educational work of the parish clergy. Instruction in the basic spiritual texts and in the skills required to understand them became both the object and the vehicle of religious revival. By the time the secular authorities began to embrace the goal of systematic education, the churches could invoke a broad experience in the field and could claim much credit for the substantial levels of reading literacy across much of northern and western Europe.[37] Prussia, which became the pace-setter in the drive to universal literacy,[38] owed its head start largely to the work of the clergy and their congregations.[39] In the early decades of the nineteenth century, radical reforms were either still-born or had to be adapted to the work of the religious institutions if they were to survive their infancy. Bavaria, for instance, was one amongst a number of countries which turned to mass education as a response to defeat by Napoleon. But the vision of a complete national system far outstripped the resources of the war-torn state. Issuing a decree did not resolve the problem of how to create and manage the thousands of new schools, and how to ensure that local parents sent their children to them. Only the Catholic church possessed human and material resources in every parish sufficient to make a response to this challenge. And only by collaborating with it was Bavaria capable of preventing its initiative from going the way of earlier paper schemes.[40]

The first two-thirds of the nineteenth century saw many states gradually learning how to work with churches so as to achieve some of their ends without sacrificing all of their powers. Perhaps the most striking example was Prussia, the first European country to display universal literacy in terms of both reading and writing. Frederick II's School Regulations of 1763, and in particular the Prussian General Civil Code of 1794 had formally asserted the authority of the state over nationwide elementary schools, but the Protestant church retained a key role throughout the succeeding century.[41] The *Volksschule* represented a working compromise between the legal power of the state and the practical engagement of the clergy, who, through their control of the school inspectorate and influence over the daily curriculum, ensured that the acquisition of literacy was always associated with confessional instruction.[42] In France, the Loi Guizot of 1833 asserted the right of the state to establish a comprehensive elementary school system (at least for boys) and the responsibility of the *commune* to provide it, but the running of the classroom was left to a partnership between the mayor and the *curé*, with both expected to ensure a strong religious element in the curriculum.[43] The influence of the church in the drive towards universal literacy was further entrenched by the Loi Falloux of 1850, which both extended the scope of elementary education and shifted the balance of power away from the secular forces in the *commune*.[44] The weaker the state, the more overt the role of the religious bodies. In England the government chose to subsidize the church schools in 1833 rather than enter the field in its own right, and inspect rather than directly control the teaching which they gave. Even when it instructed local authorities to start building their own schools in 1870, it was intended that the eradication of illiteracy would remain a joint enterprise.[45] As late as 1862, a third of all Italian teachers were in religious orders.[46] Belgium constructed a dual system in which the church exercised the greater influence, especially in the countryside.[47] At the further end of the spectrum was Russia, where an awakened enthusiasm for the education on the part of the Orthodox church coincided with the increasing anxiety of the tsars about the ignorance of the peasantry. A series of statutes from 1828 onwards culminated in a decree in 1891 which transferred all peasant schools to church control.[48]

Until at least the last third of the nineteenth century, the only certainty that a child had of learning to read and write in any part of Europe without simultaneously being exposed to religious instruction was to use the private market for education, which was despised with equal fervour by both church and secular authorities.[49] Schools retained their confessional identity as the German states united in 1870. The influence of the church in the French elementary schools reached its apogee under Louis Napoleon, ensuring that most of the new voters in the Third Republic had been inducted into the Catholic tradition. Despite the subsequent onslaught on religious teaching, the last nun did not leave the last public school until 1912. The further from northern and western Europe, the slower the erosion of church authority. On the eve of the First World War, four-fifths of elementary schools in Hungary were under the control of religious bodies.[50] In Russia, priests continued to function as teachers after the Revolution until the profession was brought fully under state control in the 1930s.[51] For the churches themselves, the European literacy campaigns ushered in a last golden age of activity and authority. Through a series of government initiatives, they gained new statutory instruments to enforce their influence. States which had long since abandoned trying to compel religious attendance or observance amongst their adult populations were increasingly willing to intervene in the spiritual lives of the innocent young, joining in the churches' ambition of reaching parents through their children. Thanks to subsidies and salaries, church bodies and personnel were in receipt of unprecedented assistance from central and local taxpayers. It was still possible to find senior clergy on the conservative fringes of the Catholic or Russian Orthodox churches willing to denounce the indiscriminate dissemination of the power to decode texts, but for the most part the armies of the Pope and the descendants of Luther and Calvin were united in their determination to exploit their last great opportunity to reach the homes and the hearts of the peasantry and the urban poor. In Prussia, for instance, confessional variation across its wide territories had ceased to have any discernible impact on the distribution of literacy by the time it took control of a united Germany.[52]

The partnership between the religious and secular authorities in the enterprise of creating a literate population rested on both material and ideological foundations. At the outset, the churches offered a bridge between the worlds of voluntary and official endeavour. In the eighteenth century, the local clergyman might have formal responsibility for ensuring that some kind of education was supplied to the parents of the labouring poor, but its actual delivery was often left to a barely literate church servant, such as the parish sexton, who included teaching among a range of duties and lacked any specialized premises, equipment or training. One of the advantages of the churches in the early period of expansion was that they were able to exploit the tradition and machinery of alms-giving within their congregations and also the readiness of newly inspired volunteers to devote part or all of their lives to the provision of schooling on terms and conditions of employment which no professional state employee would tolerate. In Ireland, the Catholic church was so successful in raising money and recruiting to the rapidly expanding lay teaching orders that the British government, fearful of sedition, had to outlaw the endowment of their schools by the local population.[53] The capacity of the European Catholics to meet the challenge of mass instruction in literacy was greatly strengthened by the success of the Christian Brothers who in the early nineteenth century represented the most dynamic element of the church.[54] In France by 1830, 2,370 unordained but trained and supervised *frères* were at work, teaching the children of the poor their letters as part of a broader religious education.[55] In Britain, the National Association for Promoting the Education of the Poor in the Principles of the Established Church, and the rival Nonconformist British and Foreign Schools Society represented powerful combinations of ordained and lay enthusiasm, which, as in the case of the Catholic teaching orders, were capable of developing innovative teaching methods and materials. Without public subsidies these organizations could not expand indefinitely, but the scale of the support they mobilized greatly magnified the impact of such investments as the early nineteenth-century governments felt able to make.

The state was prepared to enter into some kind of financial partnership with the churches because in the aftermath of the French Revolution there existed a set of common objectives. The bitterness of the conflict over secular and religious control of elementary education at the end of the nineteenth century can obscure the history of joint endeavour which preceded it. On the one hand, the Enlightenment concerns for the economic and social progress of the individual were accepted by progressive elements in the churches which saw no necessary contradiction in preparing the children of their parishioners for both this world and the next. On the other, the politicians and their dynastic masters regarded the structures of moral discipline in which the churches' teaching was embedded as the best available protection against the disruptive potential of reading and writing. The Danish founding laws of 1814 stated that the purpose of the elementary school was, 'to educate children to be good and upright persons in accordance with the teaching of the evangelical Christian church; and also to give them the knowledge and training necessary to become useful citizens in the State.'[56] From 1789 through to 1848 and beyond, the outbursts of infidel and republican popular literature associated with revolutionary crises served to strengthen the bonds between all those engaged in the endeavour of systematic training in literacy. In Prussia, the church regained its role in the education system in the 1820s as the ruling order sought assurances that its teachers were not also its gravediggers. The notion of *Schulplfichtigkeit*, or school duty, embraced both secular and spiritual values.[57] The reformed British state began to invest in the church societies in the aftermath of the Reform Bill crisis, which had witnessed an unprecedented outpouring of licentious journalism. The Indian summer of Catholic influence in France was inaugurated by the Revolution of 1848, which ushered in a new authoritarian government determined to retain control of the process of national development.[58]

As in all successful marriages, the partners compensated for each other's shortcomings and were bound together by a set of common anxieties. They were concerned that the reactionary elements in both the church and state who were opposed to any form of popular education would eventually provoke the downfall of all authority. They feared the power of irrational belief systems embodied in what was held to be the inherently superstitious oral tradition. They were for the most part dismissive of the value of domestic instruction.[59] Sweden stood out against the general pattern, its tradition of using the church to police rather than supplant home teaching surviving into the era of state provision, with the decree of 1842 requiring parents to assist their children before and during formal schooling.[60] Everywhere church and state were hostile to the use by parents of the uncontrolled educational market place to meet their demands for basic instruction in illiteracy. They were modernizers obsessed with the consequences of modernity, committed to breaking down barriers of communication between sections of society but fearful that the process would dissolve existing hierarchies of power and privilege. What above all they opposed was the concept of schooling as a purely technical exercise. Literacy in some form was always to be taught but never in isolation. The mechanics of reading, and possibly of writing, should be the means, not the end of systematic education. The loi Guizot of 1833 prescribed that whether the school was run by the mayor or the *curé*, 'moral and religious instruction should hold the front rank' in order to 'penetrate the souls of pupils with those sentiments and principles which safeguard good order and which inspire the fear and love of God'.[61] In Prussia, the Stiehl regulations of 1854 specified that a one-room rural school should devote all but three of the twenty-nine-hours of the teaching week to religion, with reading and writing conveyed through the spiritual instruction.[62] Church and state needed each other to create the system and to control its consequences.[63]

As in many marriages however, the union concealed many tensions, which in some cases would culminate in acrimonious divorce. Everywhere, some kind of compromise had to be maintained at both the national and the local level between two powerful institutions, neither of which wholly trusted the other. There were different ways of achieving this. In Prussia, church personnel were permitted to staff a secular system; in Denmark, elementary schools were overseen by a three-person *Skolekommission* chaired by the parish clergymen with the other two members chosen by the municipality; in England, the activities of the church societies were from 1846 policed by a lay inspectorate; in France a primary school inspectorate was created in 1835 to supplant the supervisory work of local notables and oversee the joint lay and spiritual provision of education in the *communes*.[64] Russia established the post of inspector in 1869, equipped with sweeping but largely illusory powers of intervention. The formal frameworks of control were an attempt to counter the constant trend to inconsistency in the form and extent of provision at the level of individual communities. Too much initiative was left to the variable enthusiasm and resources of religious and civil bodies, and, especially in the rural areas, where most of the task remained, too much scope was left for conflict between the handful of educated dignitaries charged with enlightening the uneducated. At the heart of the problem was the schoolmaster himself, resentful at the growing gap between his qualifications and his pay, and increasingly unwilling to take instruction from either parents or untrained spiritual or lay managers. If common fears tended to confine the tensions within official education, the common problem of the professionalization of teaching tended continually to exacerbate them.

Pedagogy

Money had been made from instruction in literacy for as long as there had been texts to read. Schools had been founded, usually yielding small and insecure livings, and teaching materials had been published, sometimes generating great wealth for those successful in claiming some new technique for instilling a command of the written word in the growing child. But the decision by the civil and religious authorities to wrest control of education from the market place and to embrace the ambition of mass literacy fundamentally altered the nature of teaching as an individual and corporate activity. Initially what changed was the conception rather than the content of method. The lasting influence of the great educational writers of the late eighteenth and early nineteenth centuries lay in the significance they ascribed to the curriculum rather than the substance of their particular nostrums. Enthusiasm for the child-focused theories of Pestalozzi and the monitorial machine of Lancaster waxed and waned. When the visitors to their experimental establishments had gone back to their own countries, when the books had been read and half-forgotten, there was left the conviction that the way in which lessons in elementary schools were devised and conducted could no longer be left to chance. There was a right and a wrong way of acquiring literacy. The instructor could not instruct himself, any more than the child could learn without guidance. The trainers had to be trained, and once qualified, had to exercise command over the classroom and everything that happened in it. In the parlance of the modern education industry, what triumphed in this period was the concept of teacher-centred learning.[65]

The pace of change in the engagement with the printed word in the increasingly inspected elementary schools was relatively slow. At the beginning of the period, England was rare amongst the more advanced European countries in expecting the child to begin work on writing almost as soon as the alphabet had been mastered. The more general pattern was for penmanship to be construed as a distinct and optional motor skill, much as technical drawing might be regarded in a modern curriculum. The two practices belonged to different cultural traditions.[66] Whereas reading was seen as integral to the process of religious instruction, with decoding spiritual texts both the form and the object of classroom lessons, writing was associated with the manual arts, which only those children destined for particular occupations needed to master. It would only be taught, if at all, several years after formal education commenced, and only be learned by pupils whose parents were able and willing to keep at them school well after most of their contemporaries had drifted back into the family economy. As governments began to establish a legislative framework for systematic elementary education, writing was usually given nominal parity with reading. It was made compulsory in Denmark in 1814, in Norway in 1827, in France in 1834, even in Russia in 1864.[67] In the English church schools, most children would be making some attempt at drawing letters when the state began to subsidize them in 1833. Elsewhere, progress towards implementing the newly stated ambition of concurrently learning the first two Rs was uncertain, especially in the countryside. As writing materials were hard to come by in the home, so they were in the under-resourced and over-crowded church schools of the second third of the nineteenth century. It required particular dedication on the part of teacher, parent and child alike to overcome the host of practical obstacles in the way of the profound change in the conception of basic education which the enhanced status of writing implied.

In the early phase of systematic education, the more significant area of reform was in the organization of the classroom. Prior to the nineteenth century, there was a continuum of pedagogic practice stretching from domestic lessons through commercial teachers to church schools. The child received whatever instruction was available on a one-to-one basis. In the home, this would mean gaining a few minutes of a parent's attention amidst the other activities of the household; in the schoolroom the pupil would be called to the teacher's desk to read through the prescribed text, whilst the remainder of the class continued their study as quietly as possible.[68] Most eighteenth-century private or church schools had only one master, and the class was small enough to ensure that during the course of the school week the child could see as much of the teacher as he or she might of a hard-pressed domestic instructor. In the

Hungarian province of Vas late in the century, for instance, there was on average just over one teacher per school, and staff/pupil ratios ranging from thirteen to twenty-five.[69] The ambition of mass education presented a critical challenge to this time-honoured proceeding. What was feasible in a group of ten or twenty children could not, as Horace Mann observed, succeed when a teacher faced a class of sixty or seventy.

> While attending to the recitation of one, his mind is constantly called off to attend to the studies and the conduct of all the others. For this, very few teachers amongst us have the requisite capacity; and hence the idleness and the disorder that reign in so many of our schools – excepting in cases where the debasing motive of fear puts the children in irons.[70]

The immense interest aroused throughout Europe by the monitorial system developed by Joseph Lancaster and Andrew Bell was principally a function of timing.[71] There had been earlier experiments with the synchronized instruction of an entire class of pupils. Hecker had pioneered the simultaneous method in Prussian Pietist schools around 1750, and von Felbiger had followed suit in Silesian Catholic schools. But it fell to the British church societies of the early nineteenth century to find an answer to a question which every educational reformer was now beginning to ask – how to teach large numbers of children both effectively and efficiently. Their solution was the vertical division of the school into separate classes, and the deployment of monitors to engage all the pupils in constant oral teaching. No child would be left to its own devices, and its progress through a carefully structured curriculum would be reflected in its movement from one class to another. The use of more advanced pupils to teach the less was tried for a while in various European countries, including France, Holland and Denmark (though not Prussia),[72] but its sheer impracticality was soon seen to outweigh its wonderful cheapness, and, as Horace Mann noted, by 1846 it had been 'abolished in these countries by a universal public opinion'.[73] What remained was the notion of instruction on a collective rather than an individual basis. The class would function as a single pedagogic unit, and if numbers permitted, two or more of these would be created out of the school population. The classroom teacher would activate the whole machine of learning, ensuring that every pupil was continually engaged in progressive moral and cognitive development.

The shift from individual to collective teaching had a paradoxical effect on methods of becoming literate. A reform introduced with the aim of modernizing and broadening the role of elementary education initially narrowed the range of devices by which reading and writing were taught. The standard approach to the puzzle of decoding print was the alphabetic or synthetic method, which had been in use since at least the ninth century.[74] The child began with the letters of the alphabet, and was next presented with a list of disconnected syllables: 'ba be bi bo bu   ca ce ci co cu' in Thomas Dyche's *Guide to the English Tongue* of 1707;[75] 'ba be bi bo bu   ab eb ib ob ub' in the 1793 edition of Thomas Dilworth's *A New Guide to the English Tongue*, a popular primer on both sides of the Atlantic in the second half of the eighteenth century.[76] The device employed by one of the earliest and simplest teaching aids, the hornbook, whose single cruciform surface displayed the alphabet, some basic syllabic combinations and perhaps a simple religious text, was given intellectual justification by Locke and Descartes, who endorsed the process of learning through assembling fragments of knowledge into larger unities. The child began with what were considered to be the basic elements of language, and made progress by combining letters into syllables and then syllables into words of ascending length. Then came sentences of mounting complexity and finally full literacy.[77] It was further assumed that the sound of a word was built up from the letters and separate syllables, so that by voicing each meaningless fragment the child would lay the foundation for a mastery of spelling as well as reading.[78]

This approach to learning literacy transcended time, space and social status in the early modern period. The system of Dyche and Dilworth could be found in the Slavic primers of early seventeenth-century Muscovy,[79] and in ABCs and instructional texts throughout northern and western Europe. They were produced both for church schools and for the open educational market place, and were consumed by the sons of the aristocracy as they studied with their governesses, and by the children of the labouring poor as they snatched a moment of learning amidst the business of the household or were sent for a few months' schooling at a quiet time of the working year. Rather than rendering these time-honoured devices obsolete, the initial impact of simultaneous teaching gave them a new lease of life. The first page of Henry Innes's *The British Child's Spelling Book*, published in 1835 under the aegis of the newly subsidized English church schools, began 'ba be bi bo bu by ab eb ib ob ub yb'. Manuals which first went on sale before Joseph Lancaster was born remained in print far into the nineteenth century, and were joined by new series produced for the simultaneous method on exactly the same principles. The process of building up words from their assumed constituent elements supplied a ready-made solution to the problem of mass instruction. Method and structure met at the point of classification. The calibration of labour in the new schoolrooms found its analogue in the dismantling of sentences in the old textbooks. The pupil's advance through the curriculum was measured by the transition from monosyllables to lengthening polysyllables. There were eight classes in early model institutions of the British and Foreign Schools Society. The first four progressed from the alphabet to four-letter syllables; the next two mastered one- and two-syllable words; the final two encountered simple religious passages and then brief anthologies of uplifting texts.[80]

The primers, which once had served only to prepare children for continuous prose, were now self-sufficient courses of learning. As we have seen, the growing demand for teaching materials in the eighteenth century had brought forth an ever more inventive range of devices to ease the task of the private instructor. Alphabetic board games, playing cards and puzzles were on sale for those who could afford them, as were an increasingly rich variety of anthologized poetry and prose. Those assuming the responsibility for teaching a child, whether at home or in some form of schoolroom, were free to combine purchased with home-made devices, ingenious new methods with the time-honoured syllabic primers, specialized teaching material with odd fragments of print lying around the home or brought into school by the pupils.[81] Such licence could not be permitted in the systematically organized school. The drive to universal literacy and professional instruction demanded a narrowing of pedagogic options. Such status as the newly trained teachers obtained was bought at the expense of their individual autonomy.[82] Faced with the task of conducting simultaneous instruction in a single, undivided classroom, it was only possible to select one method from the rich menu which was now available. Neither experiment nor improvisation could be sanctioned. The synthetic approach offered the best prospect of maintaining discipline and direction in the process of mastering the printed word.

The same entrenchment of traditional techniques was apparent in the medium of instruction. The schoolroom had never been a quiet place. The individual method had generated a constant burble of voices as the teacher heard each pupil repeat a text whilst the remainder of the class mumbled their way through their own passages in preparation for their next moment of personal tuition. The catechism had long provided both a vehicle and an outcome of learning, the chanted sequence of questions and answers displaying the child's knowledge of the essential religious formularies, blurring the distinction between those genuinely able to decode texts and those capable merely of memorizing them. The transition from individual to collective learning served only to unify the voices. Each child became part of a single chorus, repeating together first the letters and syllables, then prayers, biblical passages and other morally improving passages. The vocal approach to literacy ensured that every pupil marched in step, with the teacher confident that authority was being maintained and that progress was being made towards the twin goals of basic literacy and spiritual discipline. It was a means not only of organizing the lessons but also of publicizing their success. Any inspector or visiting dignitary could hear as well as see that the teacher had managed to overcome the inherent anarchy of the school population and the frequent shortfall in specialized textbooks. The classroom became a congregation, lacking only the music which leavened the formulaic proceedings of the church service.

The official and unofficial structures of learning became separated by the differing application of pedagogic devices which went back to the Reformation. Trained teachers distinguished themselves from the untrained by their willingness to keep rigorously to one method of instruction and by their capacity to orchestrate the pupils into a single voice. In the context of the organized, integrated classroom, the inevitable strangeness of print became deliberately absolute. In the domestic curriculum, and in the ramshackle private classroom, improvisation and adaptation were the key to whatever progress could be made, as they were in the many other forms of learning through which the growing child had to pass. Now gaining of a nominal command of literacy was made to feel alien from every other process of acquiring cognitive skills, nowhere more so than in France, where in the official schools founded in the first three-quarters of the nineteenth century, the pupils moved straight from the alphabet to texts in Latin. From the perspective of those employed in the classrooms, the strangeness performed two necessary functions. Firstly it dramatized their responsibility not merely to improve but to rebuild the moral and mental characteristics of the pupil. The drive to mass elementary education was founded on a dismissal of all that the home could teach the child. Left to its parents, the growing boy or girl would gain the wrong lessons in conduct, and at best an undisciplined command of literacy. The more they were made to feel on entering the classroom that they knew nothing, not even how to learn, the more likely the success of the broader educational enterprise of the church and state.

Secondly it helped to consolidate the professional identity of the increasing number of men and sometimes women who had decided to devote their working lives to teaching literacy. They distanced themselves from amateur household instructors and from broken-down working men seeking a less demanding occupation, by their refusal to adjust their approach to the cultural resources and skills of each pupil. Their commitment to method as the key to outcome was associated with the growing influence of 'normal schools'. These teacher training colleges first made their appearance in Silesia in 1765 and Vienna in 1771. As in the case of the Danish Brahetrolleborg school founded in 1794, there was initially a heavy emphasis on religious education and the three Rs.[83]

By the early decades of the nineteenth century, most western European countries were establishing networks of institutions to train and certificate the staff of the subsidized and inspected elementary schools. Although initially they were capable of educating only a fraction of the total workforce of teachers, they were central to the development of a professional identity. They provided an institutional context for the emergence of pedagogy as an autonomous activity. Whereas the village schoolmasters were faced with endless constraints on their work, the staff of the normal schools had the space in which to reflect upon the nature of teaching as a technical practice and the opportunity to transmit their insights to the best of the next cohort of teachers. Together with the school inspectors, who were more exposed to political or church control, they were the source of most of the new generation of textbooks. Whilst they retained a commitment to the larger moral purpose of education, they were increasingly aware that the teachers needed to be more than just good men (or, as the colleges began to broaden their intake around the middle of the century, good women). It was crucial to the professional status of the new educational workforce, and to the delivery of their responsibilities, that they knew the correct way to teach reading and writing, and how to apply it.

In practice, of course, there can be no certainty that in every classroom of every official school, every teacher ran along the lines laid down by the instructors in the normal schools, and that every lesson met the standards demanded by the growing army of inspectors. There was no in-service training in this period. The introduction of new formal qualifications rarely disturbed the employment of those recruited in more relaxed times, and those who had been properly trained might work on for forty and fifty years with no further change in their practices. In France, for instance, the transition from the individual to the collective method took decades to penetrate the rural schools where teachers and parents alike were at ease with the traditional approach. Despite the attempts to formalize pedagogy, the character of the teacher remained a dominating influence in the child's encounter with education.[84] Few elementary schools in any country had more than two or three teachers, and many were staffed by a single individual. The first instinct of those paying for the institutions was to build larger classrooms rather than recruit more staff. In Prussia, the best-organized system in Europe, class sizes had reached an average of eighty by 1848, and in the early 1880s, the figures were still in their seventies for the Netherlands and Austria, and as high as ninety-two for the United Kingdom.[85] Such ratios placed a premium on an efficient method, but also meant that the idiosyncrasies of the teacher frequently loomed larger than the institutional identity of the school.[86] What the child thought reading and writing meant would be deeply coloured by the brutality or kindness, the weariness or energy of a peasant's son who for decade after decade eked out a barely adequate living in a one- or two-room school far from the training colleges in the metropolitan centres.[87]

The normal schools and the inspectorates thus existed partly to support the endeavours of the ever more numerous professional teachers, and partly to draw attention to their shortcomings. From the outset they were abusive about the work of the domestic and casual teachers, but as the decades passed they became increasingly aware of the sheer difficulty of instilling genuine communication skills into large groups of children within the funded and inspected schools. The initial enthusiasm for the syllabic method conveyed by univocal rote-learning began to wane. Attention was drawn to the distinction between writing as calligraphy, which is what it meant everywhere in the first half the century, and writing as some kind of creative activity. Just as historians have tended to rely on the official dismissal of informal instruction, so also their frequent criticism of the stultifying rigidity of teaching methods in the first phase of inspected elementary education is often drawn from writings of contemporary inspectors and training college lecturers. It is not only the late twentieth-century observer who can identify a bored child, and who can wonder what use he or she could make of the increasingly lengthy period spent in the classroom. By the middle of the nineteenth century, those educators capable of maintaining an intellectual distance from the political and religious imperatives of their masters were beginning to interrogate the success of the techniques which had been appropriated from early centuries.[88] An increasingly self-conscious profession began to demand the right to apply its own criteria of achievement.

Parents

In part this was a matter of laying the foundations for the emergence of modern child psychology, the systematic study of cognitive development as a process apart from the issues of national revival and security which had dominated the first period of systematic elementary education. And in part it was a matter of recognizing that the goal of universal literacy would in the end require not merely the submission but also the active support of the families of the labouring poor.[89] By the middle decades of the nineteenth century, the accumulated reports of the inspectors, and the diffuse experience of tens of thousands of schoolteachers, were supplying increasing evidence of the irreducible importance of parental demand. Once the religious and political authorities had reached some kind of working compromise at the national and the local level, there remained the basic problem of how to get the child into the classroom and then keep it there until it had completed at least a minimum programme of learning. Although Prussia and the Scandinavian countries had introduced compulsory attendance by the 1840s, the rest of Europe did not follow suit until the final third of the century. Austria legislated in 1868, Germany did so as soon as it was united in 1871, and most of the rest of Europe gradually fell in line, with the Netherlands waiting until 1900, Belgium until 1914 and Finland until 1921. Until the Acts were passed (and frequently long afterwards), the final decision whether a child got up in the morning and went to school, rather than joining in the work of the household, lay with the parents. They were faced with an increasing range of normative and physical pressures, but as every teacher soon discovered, they had their own views as to what they wanted for their children, and retained the freedom to exercise them.[90]

For most parents for most of the century, any schooling represented sacrifice. As well as the direct charges, which could mount rapidly if there were a number of young children, there were the foregone contributions to the family economy, and the cost of what the school would regard as adequate clothing. Perhaps the biggest single obstacle to formal instruction in the period was the price of shoes, particularly in rural areas when the school day often began and ended with a long walk.[91] An official survey carried out in the comparatively advanced Italian region of Bologna in 1874–5, where just over half the children were missing from the register, discovered that a fifth of the truancy was due to general poverty, almost a quarter specifically to the distance between the home and school, 27 per cent to the child being at work, and a further 27 per cent to 'negligence'.[92] All the evidence suggested that in this area of expenditure as in any other, the peasants and the urban poor wanted a visible return. Religious instruction came free on Sundays, and they were unlikely to share the official view that their own moral instruction was worse than useless. Employment training would be given by older workers, with the more serious skills not taught until the child was beyond school age.

If parents sought schooling at all it was principally for a basic training in literacy. As Egil Johansson writes of Scandinavia, 'on the whole, the rural population believed that, for everyday use, they did not need much bookish education, literacy being saved for the church and Sunday life'.[93] They could and did teach reading themselves, but it might be more convenient and efficient to have the task performed by a specialist, and writing was certainly more easily learned in a classroom. A teacher would be employed to give a specific and limited personal service. Tolstoy described the classrooms established by Russian peasant demand in

1862: 'These schools exist like the tailors' and joiners' workshops. The people even regard them in the same way and the teachers use the same methods.'[94] A year earlier the Newcastle Commission carried out a thorough survey into elementary education in England and Wales. It set out to discover why attendance was still so patchy despite several decades of investment and reform. Its commissioners were instructed to find out what guided the preference of parents for unofficial instead of official schooling. 'I made diligent enquiry into these matters', reported one of them, 'and found no difference of opinion. Schoolmasters, clergymen, ministers, city missionaries, all told me that the poor in selecting a school, looked entirely to whether the school supplied good reading, writing and arithmetic.'[95] Parents had their own agenda, which teachers ignored at their peril. Either they faced rows of empty desks, or they quietly modified the official curriculum. A French school inspector complained in the early 1830s that, 'parents were content with a little reading, writing and arithmetic, and the teachers conform to this wish.'[96]

More training and inspection represented attempts to control the variations in local practice, but they also provided the evidence of failure. In most countries, compulsion in the face of widespread parental opposition raised major ideological and practical difficulties. The better solution was to attempt some cautious negotiation with consumer preferences whilst maintaining overall control of the delivery of mass education. The more parents could be persuaded to send their children to school voluntarily, the smaller the problem which eventually would have to be addressed by the law. Thus the theorists and reformers began to revisit the wide range of devices for teaching literacy which had been available to parents in the seventeenth- and eighteenth-century educational market place. Amongst the techniques which had been lost from sight in the drive to a systematic curriculum was that of introducing the reader to whole words in short sentences, missing out the long grind through the meaningless syllables and endless word lists. The first official critique of this time-honoured approach had been made by late eighteenth-century German pedagogues, but their insistence that the sounds of the syllables should relate more readily to short words did little to reduce the rigid nature of the practice of instruction.[97] Half a century later, most official classrooms were still using a method by which, as a British former school inspector wrote, 'the pupil learns to read words at sight by mechanically associating certain sounds with certain appearances. He is not embarrassed by any intermediate process but goes straight from the printed form of the word to its enunciation.'[98]

'Look and Say' was under discussion in Britain, Germany, Russia and the USA around the middle of the nineteenth century. The American educational reformer Horace Mann was a notable advocate.[99] In contrast to the syllabic approach, it required the teacher to make an accommodation with the linguistic skills that pupils acquired outside the school.[100] The method built upon rather than undermined the confidence that the child had gained as an oral communicator. Strangeness was no longer seen as an essential pedagogic virtue. 'The first lessons', urged another textbook, 'should consist entirely of words with which the ear of the child is familiar.'[101] Instead of prohibiting guesswork, it encouraged the learner to take a chance on a word. The method held out the possibility of connecting lessons in literacy with the process of experimentation and discovery through which the child learned about the world into which it had been born.[102] In England it received official sanction in 1852, and immediately called forth a new generation of textbooks.

It is difficult to gauge how far and how fast 'Look and Say' spread. In both England and the United States, the new technique failed to put the traditional spelling books out of print. The inherently conservative teachers remained attracted to the superficial logic of the particularist approach, and the inspectors tended to recommend some combination of the whole-word and syllabic methods. Nonetheless, the innovation did signal an important change in emphasis. Slowly, and with much hesitation, the professional pedagogues were starting to negotiate with what parents wanted and what their children knew. The anthologies of secular prose and poetry, which had vanished from official schoolrooms at the beginning of the nineteenth century, began to reappear at the higher levels of the curriculum. Care was still taken with their moral content, but literary pleasure and appreciation were now permitted. In the late 1860s, the French education minister Duruy, frustrated in his ambitions for compulsion by liberal opinion, began to introduce more secular subjects into the elementary school curriculum in an effort to interest the children. Far away from Paris in the Department of Deux-Sèvres a small boy was excited by the appearance in 1867 of History and Geography in the curriculum of his village school.[103] In England, the attempt to respond to demand initially had the reverse effect, with all subjects, including religious instruction, subordinated in the Revised Code of 1862 to the three Rs, which it appeared was what parents wanted for their children. Prussia had similarly cut its curriculum back to basic literacy in 1854. Over the succeeding decades, the secular subjects gradually reappeared for those English children who had gained a basic literacy in the lower classes, but the dominance of the Bible as a medium of instruction was lost for ever. At the same time, questions began to be asked about the relentless emphasis on writing as a mechanical art. Composition first appeared in the inspected English curriculum in 1871. It was only for the 2 per cent of children who reached Standard 6, and only offered guidance in how to use the opportunities for correspondence created by the Penny Post in 1840. But it was a beginning. In the same year the 'General Regulations' for the elementary schools in the newly united Germany found space for composition and the study of the leading national poets.[104] The engagement with literacy no longer required a total destruction of every imaginative and creative instinct the child possessed.

Negotiation should not be confused with abdication. The professional pedagogues had no intention of making themselves redundant. Method was still of prime importance, with every possible innovation requiring public debate, official sanction and yet another set of textbooks. If the child was now occasionally permitted to improvise, the teacher was not. Although inspectors more often stressed the need to arouse the curiosity of the class, and criticized schools which failed to do so, the commitment to teaching as a systematic activity remained absolute. No country's pattern of provision was interchangeable with another's, but across Europe, lessons in reading and writing in official schoolrooms showed less variation between them at the end of the nineteenth century than they had at the beginning. Nonetheless the long, confused and incomplete engagement with techniques of teaching literacy had decisively altered the relationship between the official schools and the two great forces with which they had to make an accommodation in the period, the church and the home.

In several respects, the epic battle between the French Third Republic and the Catholic church over the control of elementary education, was atypical of the general process of change. The Ferry laws of 1881 and 1882 were a product of both the insecurity of the state and the long history of local conflicts between lay and clerical teachers which had been encouraged by the particular French system of joint management. The drama obscured a less dramatic transition which was common to most countries, regardless of their relations with the dominant church. It was partly a matter of resources. In the early part of the century, the state had needed the church's assistance if it was to make any progress towards mass literacy, but in the closing decades the church increasingly needed the state's financial, legal and administrative muscle if the patchwork of provision was to be translated into a truly comprehensive system with a free place for every child. And it was partly a matter of relative priorities. Whereas in the early decades, writing and especially reading had been indeterminate objectives within a fundamentally religious curriculum, now competence in the basic skills of communication was a precise goal associated with a set of less sharply defined moral purposes. It was not a linear process of secularization so much as a critical change of significance. No country, particularly the deeply serious Third Republic or the struggling new Italian state, was prepared to disconnect reading and writing from larger issues of self-discipline,[105] but the classroom morality was increasingly generalized, stressing respect for parents, obedience to masters, deference to social superiors and temperance in all pleasures, especially sex, drink and the consumption of cheap literature. The altered relationship with the domestic curriculum was similarly a question of emphasis. What changed over the period was the initial polarity between two conceptions of education. For the poor man's child, the essence of learning was the absence of boundaries. It acquired the skills, the knowledge, the values necessary to function in the community through watching, imitating, talking, listening and doing. The programme of study began at birth, with each successive stage dissolving into the next. Little meaning was attached to the divisions between play and instruction, home and classroom, study and labour which informed the official school system.[106] The Breton anthropologist Pierre-Jakez Hélias had his feet in the old world and the new. His journey through the French education system of the early twentieth century made him sharply aware of the features of his childhood which had remained unchanged since the Middle Ages:

> I have described, above, how I began my earliest education – by learning to use all the resources of the countryside: the trees, the plants, the stones, the birds, the winds, and water in all its guises; by learning not to waste the slightest thing – for example, not to cut two branches from the same copse to make one stick. I described how I, like the others, took the steps necessary for becoming proficient at doing a peasant's job, which would have been my fate were I not to become a teacher, a postman, a railway employee, or a petty officer second class in the Navy. A peasant's job consisted, above all, in knowing everything about the surroundings, including all the traps that were set, and into which you were bound to fall if you were a novice. It was thus that you adapted yourself to nature and occasionally held it in check at the same time as it satisfied your basic needs.[107]

This complex programme of learning was doubly subordinate to the domestic economy. Much of its content was devoted to preparing children to make a contribution to the material well-being of the household, and the state of the family's prosperity determined whether money could be spent on institutional instruction on any given day or at any part of the year. The early proponents of systematic schooling set out on a collision course with this conception of education. They radically narrowed the idea of a legitimate teacher, rejected the value of most of the informal curriculum, and attempted to override the rhythms and realities of the local economy. The consequence was a long war of attrition, which did not reach any kind of conclusion until both sides had undergone important modifications to their position. On the part of the consumers, the key event was a slow alteration in their economic conditions which rendered the labour of young children less necessary and less profitable. Marginal gains in prosperity in the towns and the countryside eased the material pressures on the household, and legal and technological changes made it more difficult to find work for its younger members. The actual and perceived opportunity costs of sending a young child to school were everywhere in decline. The outcome was a change of attitude towards the regularity rather than the content of education. There had always been a willingness to buy when possible and when available the services of a specialist instructor in one or more of the three Rs. By the final quarter of the nineteenth century, however, there was a greater preparedness in most western European countries to commit a child to a sustained period of attendance over a number of years between about the sixth and the twelfth birthdays.

Schooling and literacy

For their part, the authorities were forced by the relative failure of their initial ambitions to make adjustments to the circumstances and aspirations of the labouring poor. The covert concessions to the local seasonal economy which many a beleaguered schoolmaster had been forced to make were now given formal sanction in the official school calendar. Progressive subsidies to the national school systems culminated in the arrival of free elementary education, together with more specific initiatives in some countries to deal with such obstacles as the absence of adequate clothing or writing materials, or the malnourishment of the more deprived and hence inattentive pupils. In this context, the process of professional reflection on methods of teaching literacy both symbolized and contributed to the wider sequence of change. As they reluctantly began to conform to the requirement that their child must not only enter the classroom but remain there for years on end, parents had an increasing assurance that it would gain the basic instruction in literacy which in the past they had often been prepared to purchase from other providers. And at least the more able children now had the prospect that their lessons might supply them with the kind of imaginative development and discovery which previously had only been available as they listened to family story-tellers or played adventurous games in the local streets and fields.

It would be wrong to overdramatize either the scale or the permanence of the transition which had taken place. All that can be said for the official attendance statistics is that they become less unreliable as the century progresses. At face value, they suggest that by the early 1880s, the more organized European countries had around 15 per cent of their entire populations on the registers of their elementary schools, and up to three-quarters of children aged five to fourteen.[108] In practice, only in the Prussian and parts of the Scandinavian systems did the figures conform to any sort of reality. The only acceptable grounds for non-attendance in Prussia, reported Horace Mann, were 'sickness and death'.[109] In England and France, where the official attendance figures had doubled between 1830 and 1881, parents were still fighting a long rearguard action against regular schooling, and remained capable of forcing local concessions from officials, especially in respect of keeping daughters at home to assist in domestic duties. Elsewhere, compulsion remained a distant aspiration. In Spain, two and a half million school-age children were calculated to be otherwise occupied in 1897, forty years after compulsion was enacted, and one and a half million were still missing from the registers as late as 1930.[110] As far as the state could calculate, nearly half of Russian children aged eight to eleven never attended school in the years immediately before the First World War.[111] In the late 1920s, 10 per cent of the Hungarian school-age population were avoiding any contact with the official system.[112]

At a local level, the opening or closure of a school, whether sanctioned by the authorities or not, could have a discernible effect on the registers of the parish church fifteen years later. But at the national level it is difficult to identify a precise relationship between school attendance and literacy rates. Clearly, investment in the former would have an impact on the latter. Prussia was the leading example of early effective compulsion and rapid achievement of nominal mass literacy.[113] But across Europe as a whole, formal schooling cannot be taken as a proxy for the distribution of reading and writing skills.[114] This was partly because the move to comprehensive, compulsory and free systems in the closing decades of the nineteenth century generated a more homogeneous pattern of provision than was apparent in the literacy levels, which were conditioned by a broader range of forces than the work of inspected schoolteachers. By the 1890s, the school registration levels of countries like Italy and Spain were much closer to their northern and western neighbours than were their marriage register returns. It was partly also because of the failure of the official returns to display the role of the private day school in the decades before the state gained some kind of monopoly in the field. This is the explanation for the striking performance of England in figure 2.1,[115] which compares rates of growth in literacy and attendance in the era of consolidation. It was not that England was unique in Europe in improving its educational provision far more rapidly that its marriage register signatures, but rather that, amongst the more advanced states, it was most reliant on unofficial and hence unrecorded provision during

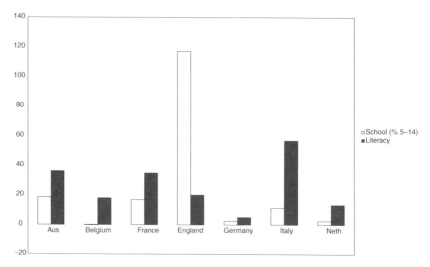

Figure 2.1   Growth in European school attendance and literacy rates,
1875–1900

the period of greatest growth in its literacy levels. Elsewhere, the tendency was for literacy to improve slightly faster than school registration,
which reflects the fact that the major change was not in the numbers of
children who entered the school, but in those who stayed there long
enough to gain some benefit from the lessons in reading and writing.

A final reason why school attendance cannot be taken as a simple
proxy for literacy lies in the quality of the communication skills taught
by the official schoolteachers. The shift from calligraphy to composition
was both late and incomplete. Only the small minority of children who
completed the entire curriculum ever received formal lessons in using a
pen to create knowledge or to connect with the thoughts of others. It is
no surprise, therefore, that the one statistical measure of the use of literacy, the postal rate, is even less closely associated with the attendance
figures than the marriage register signatures. In the early years of the
Universal Postal Union, England had the lowest official attendance
figures of any of her immediate neighbours, and the highest level of
letter-writing. By 1890, the consolidation of the official system had
reduced the discrepancy, but, as figure 2.2[116] suggests, this particular form
of communication still bore only a distant relation to the experience of
schooling. As with other categories of functional literacy, performance at
a particular moment was driven by a range of forces beyond the capacity of the classroom to determine.

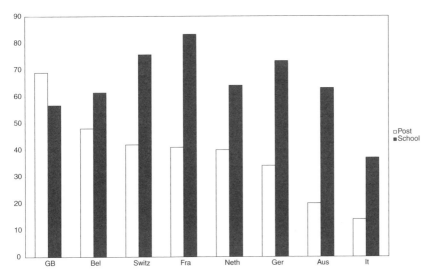

Figure 2.2   European school attendance and per capita postal rates, 1890

There remain two histories in this period: the high drama of pedagogic debate, ideological conflict, and institutional reform, and the quiet but complex narrative of generations of young children in transition from the domestic to the official curriculum. The only members of the European societies whose lives were undoubtedly transformed by the increasing institutionalization of the teaching of literacy were the teachers themselves. Growing numbers of men and women devoted the whole of their careers to the alphabet and the strange fragments of language with which most lessons in reading and writing began in most schools for much of the nineteenth century. The impact of their labours on the serried ranks of children who sat before them was much less decisive. In terms of quantity, formal education and nominal literacy met only at the point of completion. Many localities had demonstrated from the eighteenth century onwards that some combination of high parental demand, gifted teaching or generous external patronage could on occasions lift literacy levels to 70 or 80 per cent. In the western European countries which led the way to universal literacy, legally enforceable attendance was implemented only in the last chapter of a long story.[117] The primary task of effective, compulsory, national systems of elementary education was in a sense a negative one, that of ensuring that no child grew up incapable of demonstrating a minimum grasp of both reading and writing.

Mass literacy may thus be seen as a kind of relay race. In the early laps, the baton was carried variously by parents, older siblings, amateur private teachers and official professionals. Only on the very last lap was it carried by the inspected school system alone, and only because the families of their pupils had finally sanctioned this transfer of responsibility.

In the modernizing societies of Europe, the children of the labouring poor were required to move from learning through living to learning for living. One of the less complex tasks of the domestic curriculum was separated from the rest, and the child was abstracted from the household in order to master it. Childhood became a matter of distinct stages, forcing attention on the novel question of whether there was an identifiable progression from one to another. The professionalization of pedagogy led to the first attempts to tackle issues such as the retention and application of skills in the years succeeding elementary education. In Russia, the European country most systematically aware of its own shortcomings, a series of studies were mounted between 1880 and 1911 to examine the use peasants subsequently made of their schooling. The research concluded that in terms of their ambitions and opportunities, they had become and remained literate. Their reading was less than fluent, their grammar and spelling frequently imperfect, but what had been implanted had survived.[118] In a country still lacking a compulsory system, peasants only sent their children to school to gain the rudimentary literacy which they valued, and the evidence suggested that by and large they were getting a return for their sacrifice. There is no evidence in any European country of the labouring poor demanding a more sophisticated training in the basic skills of communication than the official schools were prepared to provide.

The question for the parents, and still more so for their sons and daughters who had to endure the lengthening periods of attendance, was the kind of connections which could be made between the increasingly fragmented elements of childhood learning. The complexity of this issue is most apparent in the experience of girls. A striking feature of the expansion of elementary education everywhere in Europe was the growing equality of treatment of the sexes, especially in terms of the teaching of reading and writing. The initial public investment was often confined to boys, and large-scale expansion usually aimed at separating the sexes into parallel classes or schools. But learning literacy was not itself a gendered activity. The same methods were used to teach the same words and sentences. Given that the rise in female literacy began later and accelerated faster than the male, the changes explored in this chapter probably had a greater impact on the daughters of the labouring poor than on the sons. The hours they spent studying the alphabet and copying sentences constituted probably the only time in their lives when they underwent the same process as their male contemporaries, and gained the same nominal skills. In terms of the standards applied by the Russian investigators, they emerged from their schooling in the closing decades of the nineteenth century with an equivalent level of attainment. The same could not, of course, be said then or later of the privileged minority who completed secondary or tertiary education.

This realm of equality in the acquisition of literacy is often overlooked by historians anxious to stress the gendered nature of all education. Where the difference occurred was not in the lessons themselves, but in the way in which they were embedded in the rest of the learning experience. In the schools of western Europe, girls were even more intensively exposed than the boys to the moral indoctrination which suffused so much of the early systematic curriculum.[119] They were more likely to attend schools controlled by the church, and were seen as bearing a special responsibility for transmitting moral values to their own homes, and to those they would form as adults. In France in 1866, with the literacy campaign in full swing, 53 per cent of girls compared with just 19 per cent of boys were being instructed by ordained teachers.[120] They were made even more aware of their destiny as manual workers. The attempts at teaching work skills to boys were generally half-hearted and unsuccessful. Parents did not want schools to bother with such training, teachers were poorly equipped to provide it, and public authorities never succeeded in getting pupils to offset the cost of their schooling by productive labour in the classroom. But the lessons in knitting and sewing which filled out the girls' school day transmitted powerful messages about the kind of life the school was preparing them for.[121] Equally the textbooks for more advanced readers in England, Germany and France presented heavily gendered role models for the pupils to embrace.[122] The exigencies of family economies were the most powerful shaping factor in the engagement with learning for all children, but they affected the girls most intensely. Even where education had become genuinely free and compulsory, parents were much more likely to circumvent the regulations to keep their daughters at home to assist in some crisis than they were their sons.[123] For their part, the inspectors and attendance officers were less concerned about the failure of girls to complete the whole of the school curriculum.

The nature of the connections which were made within and outside the schoolroom deeply affected the meaning that was attached to the instruction in literacy. What children could obtain from learning to read and write was conditioned by what they thought the activity was for, and where it stood in the broader process of learning and living. The girls may not have liked the instruction in sewing and domestic economy,[124] but their experience of them taught them lessons about the meaning of their lessons, and in this sense they learned a different literacy. But by the time the systematic curriculum had been established the variations were more those of degree than of kind. Few children escaped the combination of mechanical instruction and tedious moralizing which characterized official schooling, whether controlled by the church or the state, and both sexes benefited from the slow and radically incomplete moves to adjust the method of teaching literacy to the child's broader linguistic development. Similarly, no poor man's child escaped the sense that schooling was subordinate to their past and prospective material condition. For the most part, it was their bodies rather than their minds that went to school, but for girls as for boys it was just possible to find the teaching of literacy opening up possibilities of intellectual exploration, however brief and unfulfilled.

3
Economic Development

Occupation and prosperity

The tradition of associating literacy with economic growth stretches back at least as far as the Enlightenment. The physiocrats promoted the education of the peasantry as a means of generating improvements in agricultural productivity. If the rural workforce could acquire basic communication skills, it would be able to read the increasing volume of publications on new farming techniques, and begin to play an active role in a capitalist market economy. Once a worker could decipher and sign documents, he would be equipped to engage in complex transactions over time and space. More generally, exposure to the printed word would generate a mobile cast of mind, freed from the constraints of custom and inherited ignorance. The literate labourer would be receptive to fresh ideas, and be prepared to experiment with novel ways of carrying out the time-honoured tasks on the land. He and his family would gain a material reward for the time spent in school, and the economy as a whole would see a return for the investment in elementary education. Neither the squire nor the seigneur were capable of freeing the rural worker from his mental prison, and left to its own devices the household alone could merely reproduce errors of former generations. Only the schoolmaster could break the shackles of the past and equip the workforce with the means to create its own economic future.[1]

Historians of economic growth have continued to link reading and writing with the modernization of economies. 'The more literate countries', observed Cipolla in the first standard survey of the subject, 'were the first to import the Industrial Revolution.'[2] Gerschenkron included it as one of the factors constituting a country's level of development.[3] Partly because literacy is one of the most easily quantifiable of cultural goods, it has long featured in large-scale comparative exercises. C. A. Anderson's observation, derived mainly from mid-twentieth-century worldwide literacy data, that 'about forty per cent of adult literacy or of primary enrolment is a threshold for economic development'[4] has been widely cited in studies of modernization over the past three decades. Apparent support for the significance of the connection between how men, and sometimes women, earned their living, and how they communicated with each other, comes from the available statistics of occupational literacy. The era preceding that covered by this survey is summarized by R. A. Houston: 'Across the whole of Europe between the Renaissance and the beginning of the nineteenth century, literacy was intimately related to social position.'[5] Social position here largely means work, and in this sense, the nineteenth century was no different from the fifteenth or the sixteenth.[6] Studies of the *menu peuple* of France in 1858 and 1860 placed shopkeepers, innkeepers and café proprietors near the top of the literacy tables, traditional artisans just behind them, then the new factory proletariat and finally urban day labourers and the rural workforce. In England, the first figures available from the reformed system of registering marriages displayed near-universal literacy amongst the landowning, professional and commercial classes, but spread the labouring classes over a wide range of performance. The table for manual workers was headed by those in the modern 'literate' occupations such as the post office, police and the railways, followed by artisans, various categories of factory workers, semi-skilled labourers, miners and unskilled labourers in town or country.[7] An initial gap of 73 points between the head and the foot of the table gradually closed during the succeeding decades, but not until the early twentieth century did it cease to be visible amongst the young men who went to the altar. Out in the fields and in the streets of the towns there remained plenty of older unskilled workers still unable to sign their names.

Income was by no means the sole determinant of literacy. Amongst many other factors, geography, population density and church and state intervention influenced the overall distribution of marks and signatures.[8] Nonetheless, no other social factor was as commonly correlated with literacy as the broad occupational groupings. The prevailing social order was consistently replicated in the distribution of marks and signatures, and where recorded, in such measures as reading grades and length of school attendance.[9] The literacy of rural workers bore witness to the comparative failure of the Physiocrats' ambitions, although even here there was a marked correlation between the size of a landholding and the level of educational attainment.[10] There are, however, two major difficulties with the conclusion that some combination of supply and demand for literacy lay behind the accelerating growth of the European economies. The most obvious problem is the direction of cause and effect. With the formation of human capital, as with every other factor associated with industrialization, there is an ever-present possibility that growth was the father and not the child of the process of change. As the previous chapter argued, formal instruction in literacy imposed a cost on the family even when it was technically free, and when it was free, it imposed a heavy financial burden on the state. Marriage register scores might more properly be seen as a consequence rather than a precondition of individual and national prosperity. Linked to this issue is the problem of specifying the nature of the causal mechanism. Accounts of human capital formation in this context are not always clear about whether the subject under discussion is literacy as a technical skill, or schooling as an institutional force, nor whether the connection is one of mechanical practice (the actual employment of reading or writing in a specific occupation) or one of attitude or personality (an orientation to work whose effect may be independent of any particular application of the capacities learned in the schoolroom).[11] And in the case of both difficulties, it is not necessarily apparent that a given resolution will apply to all the diverse countries of Europe throughout an era of rapid economic and educational development.[12]

It is best to begin with literacy as a luxury. Deprivation tends always to shorten the list of necessities and increase the number of items whose purchase is optional.[13] A household uncertain whether there will be food on the table at the end of the week, or whether the rent can be paid, will regard all but a bare minimum of consumption as dispensable. Conversely, the more secure the family economy, the more goods and services will be viewed as essential to its basic existence. Direct or indirect spending on education, and even more so, on books to read and paper to write on, was all too readily moved from one column to the other. Schooling was an eminently deferable cost. Unlike modern private education, where only one decision to purchase need be made and the fees must be paid a term in advance, attendance at elementary schools of the nineteenth century, even after compulsion, required constant choice. And unlike the other major investment in the future of the poor man's family, insurance policies against sickness or death, there was no recognized penalty attached to interruptions in payments. Every day that followed initial registration witnessed a fresh judgement as to whether or not a son and especially a daughter could be spared from the essential task of keeping the family afloat. Few parents in the more prosperous European societies firmly turned their face against schooling even in the early period of systematic education, but fewer still escaped the need constantly to review this category of expenditure. Only those already employed in credentialized occupations could be certain enough of the security of their family economies to make schooling an automatic expenditure. Within most households there was no necessary pattern in which child was sent to school or for how long.[14] Hopes and aspirations for individual children were blown this way and that by the winds which continually buffeted the domestic unit, almost literally so in the case of Robert Lowery, whose school attendance was dependent on the fortunes of his father's work in the Peterhead whaling industry. He made a start, but then his father's health collapsed after twenty years of expeditions to Greenland:

> At the commencement of my father's illness I was taken from school at the age of nine, and never had the privilege of returning afterwards. I had passed through the common rules, into Practice, been drilled twice through Lenny – but by rote, and had rather received a desire for, than learned much of Geography and History. The little savings of my mother were soon exhausted and she opened a girls' school, and I went to work after I was ten years old, to pick the brasses out from the coals at the mouth of the mine by which I earned five shillings per week.[15]

Individual literacy should initially be regarded as a function rather than a precondition of prosperity. Le Roy Ladurie examined the physical and cultural characteristics of French army recruits in 1868 and discovered that, 'the illiterate are undoubtedly shorter in stature than those who have received schooling.'[16] 'Can it be', he speculated, 'that schooling, by limiting the amount of physical labour demanded of the young child, has a tendency to stimulate physical growth?', to which the answer must be no. Poor education and low height were alike measures of poverty in childhood. It was no accident that those western countries which approached universal nominal literacy by the end of the nineteenth century were also those which escaped a major famine for the first time in their history.[17] With the bulk of the European workforce still employed on the land, the increasing rarity of total crop failure permitted each succeeding generation to devote small margins of surplus income to non-essential cultural goods. By the same measure, governments began to widen their conception of necessary expenditure, moving out, as we saw in the previous chapter, from the basic areas of defence, central administration and law and order. The contrast between France and her neighbour over the Pyrenees was a case in point. At the end of the nineteenth century, the Spanish budget was still dominated by the armed forces, a reflection of a stagnant economy and expensive colonial wars. In 1900 it was allocating nine times as much to guns as to schools, spending 1.5 pesetas a year per inhabitant on education, in comparison with 5.6 in France.[18]

In broad terms, the hierarchy of illiteracy followed the graph of material deprivation across a nation's workforce. The conclusion of a recent Unesco survey on contemporary literacy has a general application to the period under review: 'Everywhere, illiteracy affects particularly the most under-privileged categories and groups, the most defenceless. Depending on the country, this situation more or less affects persons engaged in unskilled manual labour, ethnic, national, linguistic or religious minorities, nomads, migrants, refugees, physically or mentally handicapped persons, but everywhere it affects the unemployed and those living in remote and inaccessible places.'[19] In some form or another, the capacity to invest in the luxury of literacy was influenced by the nature of the household's participation in the economy. At the heart of the matter was the simple matter of surplus income. Beyond that was the question of the location and the organization of a particular mode of production, which conditioned the availability of schooling and the ability of parents to purchase it. Artisans knew seasonal poverty, but were more likely to work in the concentrations of population which made possible a flourishing market in education and literary artefacts, and to be able to exercise control over the labour of their household members. Unlike unskilled urban workers, they might hope to conduct their domestic economies by the week rather than the day, and contemplate the deferral of a return on their spending.

The wider the range of economic conditions in a given society, the more variable the performance of its literacy tables. Tomasson has persuasively argued that one of the reasons why Iceland was probably the first European country to achieve universal nominal literacy was because of its unusually narrow social spectrum.[20] Elsewhere, the initial impact of industrialization was to widen the gaps between different sectors of the workforce, and hold back the commencement of the final drive towards full literacy. Over the last quarter of a century, support has been given to the thesis originally advanced by Michael Sanderson that the factory system was directly destructive of educational standards.[21] The argument claims that the comparatively high rates of literacy achieved by England in earlier centuries were not so much the cause as the victim of the world's first Industrial Revolution. It is difficult to reach a final verdict on this debate, not least because, in the English example, the damage to which Sanderson draws attention took place before the state required marriage registers consistently to record the occupation of the groom and his father. Once the interval between school age and marriage has been taken into account, the era of destruction moves back to the late eighteenth century, a time when the factory system was in its infancy and systematic elementary education barely conceived.[22] A much later study of Basque and Catalan industrialization, for instance, with more modern factory and education systems, failed to discover any damage to literacy rates.[23] In the English case, further obstacles are posed by uncertainty about whether the harm was caused by the nature of factory production, the characteristics of the early industrial workforce, or the crisis of urban living which the first phase of industrialization provoked throughout Europe.

More detailed work on a wider range of cases suggests that the culprits are the second and third rather than the first of these factors.[24] Examples can undoubtedly be found not only in England but also amongst her industrializing neighbours of raw factory communities in which nominal literacy went into decline for several decades.[25] In Prussia, the acceleration of industrialization coincided with a period of stasis in the aggregate national rates.[26] However, a reworking of late eighteenth- and early nineteenth-century English marriage registers which happen to contain occupational data indicates that the source of the problem was the sudden influx of unskilled and semi-skilled families from the surrounding villages and townships, who often brought with them traditionally low levels of literacy and in the short term diluted the higher standards normally found in well-established urban communities.[27] There is little evidence that the literacy of existing occupational groups in the towns and cities was pushed down by the establishment of factory production. Problems arose either from the arrival of rural migrants, or from the failure of more backward regions to keep pace with the more advanced. The declivities in the rates in central Scotland owed less to the factories and more to the arrival of large numbers of Irish immigrants drawn to the cities by the prospect of employment.[28] In Prussia, the stagnation proves on closer analysis to have been caused not by factories, but by the inability of the poverty-stricken countryside to match the progress of the more developed economic sectors.[29] More generally the initial phases of rapid urbanization threatened to overwhelm every kind of social provision, from churches to public houses to clubs and societies, and there is no reason to suppose that schooling escaped the damage. Everywhere more teachers had to be found, whether private or official, and more schoolrooms had to be established, merely in order to defend the existing levels of provision. As an optional form of consumption, education may well have been interrupted, postponed or never started for the children of the first generation of urban dwellers.

An additional factor here is the nature of migration itself. Education was frequently promoted by reformers and feared by conservatives because of its assumed capacity to generate not just a flexible mind but a mobile population. Literate men and women would be more attracted to new ways of living and working, and more prepared to break free from the villages of their forebears. The introduction of versions of the Penny Post was also justified by the potential impact of cheap correspondence on migration. Families in the countryside would learn of the attractions of the cities from the letters of those who had gone before them, and would in turn be more prepared to take the risk of leaving their family networks because they could keep in touch with them via the postman. Empirical studies offer partial support to these expectations. From the modernizing countryside of western Europe to the newly emancipated serfs in Russia, there is evidence that those who had made some progress with reading and writing were more likely to journey beyond their birthplace than those who had not.[30] The streets of the growing urban communities and the emigrant ships sailing to a new world were full of men and women who had received their education in village schoolrooms. But as in other forms of social behaviour, literacy does not seem to have been a determining factor. If those whose households had been sufficiently secure to give them some kind of education were predisposed to a new life, so also were those whose family economies were in terminal crisis. An empty stomach was as persuasive a factor as a modern mind. There was nothing to prevent an illiterate moving to the town, and for the increasing army of landless labourers, much to attract them.[31] In Marseille, for instance, the immigrant grooms were on average more literate than comparable native-born grooms, but nonetheless 30 per cent of male and 70 of female migrants were unable to sign their names on arriving in the city.[32] It did not take a schoolmaster to tell you that hunger was less inevitable in the urban economies, neither was schooling a necessary passport for travel. There were plenty of occupations inside and outside factories which demanded no formal educational qualifications, and almost all jobs until late in the period were found by word of mouth rather than by printed advertisement and written application.

In terms of literacy, there was no such thing as a standard migrant, any more than there was a standard town or a standard industry. Studies of individual factory communities have failed to identify a consistent trajectory of change. There were examples, such as the Staffordshire Potteries adjacent to the university from which this book comes, of a long period of decline and stagnation in the literacy rates as the factories were established.[33] But equally there were examples, such as the

rapidly growing Normandy city of Caen, of the levels remaining un-
affected by extensive immigration.[34] Adjacent industrializing areas in
north-west England displayed quite different profiles of marriage register signatures.[35] There are perhaps just two generalizations which can be
advanced. The first is that the determining factor was not so much a new
factory or an increase in population, but rather the evolving composition
of the urban workforce.[36] It appears that existing artisan populations in
the industrializing towns maintained their comparatively good literacy
levels. Equally the less skilled workers maintained their traditionally
lower rates. The outcome in terms of the attainments of the urban community as a whole was the local balance of upward and downward forces.
A sudden growth of a basic factory process might temporarily overwhelm the existing pattern of growth in the literacy levels. But industrialization in many instances created new work for skilled men, inside and
outside the factory walls. Where this happened, and where, as for instance
in Caen, the intellectual elite of the surrounding countryside was finding
its way into the city, the traditional educational buoyancy of the urban
society was maintained. The second conclusion is that where industrialization did damage literacy levels, it was usually in the form of placing a
brake on growth rather than driving performance back to the levels of
earlier centuries. And sooner or later the brake was released as urban
communities built new and better social facilities, and the factory workforce began to reproduce itself in a more stable fashion and attain a
higher standard of living.

   Growth was not the necessary enemy of literacy, nor should it be identified as its necessary product. The primary relationship between learning to read and write and the economic endeavours of households and
states rests with the levels of prosperity which permitted investment in
the privilege of education.[37] This does not, however, mean that there was
no place for a second-order relationship in which individuals prospered
because they could communicate in better ways than their parents, or in
which economies as a whole grew because higher levels of schooling
could be afforded. Such possibilities can only be approached through a
closer examination of the precise role of literacy in given occupational
contexts. This task is complicated by the absence of clear gradations in
the levels of communication skill demanded by different jobs. It is difficult to identify more than a handful of manual tasks in the period before
the First World War for which literacy was a formal or *de facto* condition
of entry and practice. The most careful attempt to categorize occupational usage is to be found in Mitch's study of supply and demand in
England. His 'literacy required' level contains a range of commercial
and professional occupations, a few of which, such as teaching and low-
level public administration, were gradually opening up to working-class

children. But the only manual occupations demanding proficiency in reading and writing listed in his table were the police and the prison service.[38] To these might be added other sectors of the uniformed . working class, particularly postal and railway workers, together with printers and compositors.[39] Indeed the bulk of the 'literate' manual occupations of the nineteenth century were those produced by or responsible for the communications revolution itself.[40]

An example of what might be achieved as urbanization and industrialization took hold in the second quarter of nineteenth-century England is afforded by the younger brother of the Lancashire handloom weaver Ben Brierley:

> He had begun to associate with a number of boys who have since made a mark in society. One is now the principal in a cotton manufacturing concern in Ashton-under-Lyne, and is a justice of the peace. Another is his partner; and both are held in high esteem by those who know them. They formed a kind of Mutual Improvement Society among themselves, meeting alternately at each other's homes. I was astonished at the progress my brother made along with his companions. He mastered figures with amazing rapidity, became proficient in phonography, and for a time corresponded with others in a phonetic magazine published by the brothers Pitman. He was a splendid penman; and whilst I was labouring with my cramped hieroglyphics, he could dash off a sentence like the copperplate headings of a copy book. The learning he managed to pick up at this time did him good service in after life. He became 'putter-out' in a silk warehouse; but the firm he was employed by failing, he returned to the loom, and followed the occupation of weaving until something better offered . . . My brother had been married some years, and had a family growing about him. Weaving only afforded them scant fare, and there was little prospect of it ever being better. Through a little influence he got connected with the Oldham police force . . . He had not long been in the force ere he obtained promotion, being taken from the streets, and put to a clerkship in the police office. In this capacity he died, being taken away by a malignant fever at a time when his prospects appeared to the brightest.[41]

It required not merely basic instruction in reading and writing, but a sustained period of further study to create these opportunities, and no amount of talent, ambition and dedication was proof against the rising mortality rates in the industrial communities. Beyond the small number of occupations for which literacy was required, the boundaries become uncertain. Mitch divides the remainder of the workforce into those for whom literacy was 'likely to be useful', those with a 'possible (or ambiguous) use', and those 'unlikely' to use it at all. The first group mostly comprises traditional artisan trades, the second the more sophisticated factory processes and various kinds of shopkeepers, and the third the simpler manufacturing processes, mining and unskilled labour. It is as robust a classification as can be achieved, but is nonetheless a very provisional exercise. There are no fixed rules for allocating jobs between the lower categories, and workers could be found in any of them making a living without needing or being able to employ reading and especially writing. Even those who needed to keep accounts had long discovered ways of doing so without using a pen themselves. A careful study of some Kentish communities in the late 1830s discovered a woman managing a wood-dealing business on behalf of her husband but using her children to make the entries in the books, which she could not do herself.[42] Equally there were, at least in the west European economies, always some agricultural workers or day labourers who might occasionally send a message, sign an agreement, draw up an account, read a street sign or decipher an emigration notice. In local contexts, occupational literacy could develop in ways which defy larger generalization. Domestic servants appear in the bottom division of Mitch's classification, but in Paris on the eve of the French Revolution, almost all men engaged in personal service could sign their names on inventories and about two-thirds of them possessed all the paraphernalia of a man of letters, including not only pens, inkstands and sand horns but also writing-cases and desks.[43] Specific occupational groups in particular geographical locations developed attitudes towards the value of schooling which cannot be reduced to the immediate economic benefits of literacy. All that can be said with certainty is that over time the higher categories were expanding faster than the lower. Mitch calculates that the percentage of men and women needing or likely to use literacy grew by 7–10 per cent in the second half of the nineteenth century. This was scarcely a revolution, and his 'literacy required' sector still only contained 11 per cent of men and half as many women in 1891.[44]

There is a crucial difference between categorizing occupational groups by relative performance in literacy tables, which can be done with certainty in any economy where there are appropriate data, and distinguishing them by their need to use the skills to earn a living. The problem is partly a function of the distinction between the marriage register scores, which divided all occupations below the most literate and skilled into two groups, and the occupational application of literacy, where any given trade might display a range of performance. And it is partly a function of the blurred line between the direct use of reading and writing for a specific task, and the more diffuse application of the skills in a range of contexts associated with a particular position in society. Reformers who were concerned with the potential impact of education on the economy, and historians who have tried to measure their achievements, have alike imposed boundaries which the contemporary workforce would be reluctant to acknowledge. At issue was the culture rather than the practice of an occupation, the bundle of status concerns, indirect economic strategies and recreational activities which frequently were inseparable from the transactions with customers, employers and other workers.

We can, for instance, gain an indication of why the skilled urban trades had achieved high levels of literacy well before the church and the state began systematically to address the issue, by glancing at the memoir of the eighteenth-century French glazier, Jacques-Louis Ménétra.[45] His entire life was infused with the written word. He used it in his business with customers and other artisans, drawing up accounts for his work (and on one occasion helping out a widowed glass wholesaler by forging her signature on papers he had written out for her), and exchanging letters containing news of work opportunities. Everywhere he went he carried with him his master's certificate and a sketchbook in which he recorded new techniques and designs. He gained positions of responsibility in his confraternity which demanded the frequent use of his pen. Arriving in Lyon on one occasion he records that, 'In such a large city I had business almost every day with the arrival and departure of companions or with letters from cities on the tour of France having to do with disputes of the sort than can arise between masters and companions.'[46] Work and his private life were also connected by correspondence, as he kept in touch with his mother and sundry girlfriends during his tour as a young journeyman. On the road and at home with his growing family he read to amuse himself, wrote burlesques and songs, and towards the end his life was caught up in the vigorous propaganda warfare generated by the French revolutionary crisis. Reading and writing traversed and connected his private and his public life, his work and his pleasure, and his real and imaginary existences, both of which informed the composition of an early contribution to the growing genre of working-class autobiography.

For most workers the following century brought a limited growth rather than a transformation in the place of the written word in their occupational existence. Artisans gradually enlarged the range of their economic transactions, and began to formalize their collective activities. Printed documents were being produced by English trade unions by the 1830s, their leaders gradually evolving from correspondents to bureaucrats. Occasional experiments at co-operative production or distribution demanded an active use of all three Rs.[47] Agricultural economies slowly shifted from exchange to cash relations, placing a greater emphasis on the keeping of written records.[48] In the towns and factories called into being by commercial growth the initial demand was for reading rather

Economic Development

than writing.[49] Factory owners posted regulations on walls and disciplined those who failed to observe them, although the workers had plenty of means other than private study to learn the new rules of the game. In some industries, such as coal mining, safety notices became legal requirements, but little attention seems to have been paid to whether recruits could decipher them. Foremen were more frequently expected to be able to read and write, but only in the more advanced industrial processes of the later nineteenth century were the bulk of employees required to employ their schooling in the performance of their routine tasks. Until that point, the factory workforce had only marginally more use for classroom knowledge than the rural occupations from which many had come, and far less effective cultural traditions of functional literacy than the artisans still working in un-mechanized industries.

It is important not to confuse the direction with the scale of change. Taking the period of industrialization as a whole, what is most striking is not how much of manual labour was invaded by the written word, but how little. Recruitment to most occupations was conducted by personal contact rather than formal advertisement. Newspapers did begin to carry more notices for jobs, but these were mostly for specialized positions such as superior servants, and represented only a tiny fraction of the total number of vacancies at any one time. Even modern employers in large-scale industries initially preferred to delegate the search for suitable recruits to their existing workforce, finding family contact a more reliable and a much cheaper alternative to the formation of a specialized personnel department. Where the industrial process demanded real skill, training was still for the most part supplied by the time-honoured practice of imitation and oral instruction, even if the institution of a formal apprenticeship was increasingly under pressure. Employers such as the Schneiders at Le Creusot who not only set up schools for basic literacy in the middle decades of the nineteenth century but also trained the more able pupils in technical knowledge, were the exceptions to the general rule.[50] The only European country to establish an effective connection between elementary and technical education prior to 1914 was Germany, although there is doubt whether employers in the first phase of rapid industrial growth paid much attention to attributes their recruits brought with them into the factories.[51] The consistent pressure for bureaucratizing the European workforce came not from the productive process itself but rather from the welfare system which grew up around it. Amongst traditional artisans, the maintenance of friendly-society schemes for unemployment and sickness benefits represented the most important and sophisticated use of literacy. The arrival of state-provided or -sponsored insurance, first in Bismarckian Germany, and in other advanced economies just before and after the First World War, did much to consolidate in the minds of workers the association between employment and paper. It was not for obtaining or performing labour that the forms had to be filled in and signed, but rather in prospect of losing it through redundancy or injury.

If literacy is seen as a matter of costs and opportunities, it can be argued that completion of a period of schooling would sufficiently enhance lifelong earning prospects to render the initial investment by the child's parents worthwhile.[52] Just how many households made this calculation and acted upon it is difficult to determine. The range of comparatively well-paid jobs from which the illiterate were excluded was perceptibly increasing as the national education systems were established. There were, however, two powerful factors opposing this kind of rational decision-making. The first is that it applied mainly to boys. Few of the advantages anticipated for those who expected to become family breadwinners could be associated with those they would marry. Learning to read and write may have perceptibly increased the prospects of the daughters of unskilled parents finding a husband with better earning potential,[53] but will have done little to enhance their own prospects in the labour market. Teaching, and towards the end of the nineteenth century, nursing and secretarial work, offered unprecedented opportunities for secure and respectable employment to the daughters of the labouring poor, but they were out of reach for all but the very fortunate. Until the post-1945 era, most such careers were terminated by marriage, further qualifying any calculations about the financial return on education. Domestic service, the most rapidly expanding sector of female employment up to the First World War, fell squarely into the category of the possible or ambiguous application of reading and writing.

The second problem was the shifting relationship between the supply of nominally literate workers and the demand for their services. Every European economy witnessing a successful drive to mass education was subject to the basic paradox that the harder the schoolteachers worked, the less positive value their labours had for the bulk of their pupils. In the last third of the nineteenth century, such expansion as there was in paper-based occupations was overtaken by the growth in literacy rates. This applied particularly to unskilled labourers, whose marriage register scores could jump by 40 or 50 points in a generation, far outstripping any conceivable growth in openings requiring their classroom skills. The largest improvements took place in those sections of the workforce, male and even more so female, which were remotest from the career opportunities being created by the modernizing economies. In such households, it was increasingly difficult to make the equation balance. Whatever premium there had existed in the labour market for literacy was shrinking away as the capacity to read and write became the standard attribute of every entrant. The more they sent their children to school, the greater the damage to the economic well-being of the family economy, especially if girls were taken from child-minding; the more they declined to do so, the greater their exposure to fines. By the last quarter of the nineteenth century, non-attendance was second only to drunkenness as a cause of fiscal sanctions by the English courts against the poorest sections of the community.[54]

After a certain point, it was often necessary for parents to reverse the calculation, and focus on the costs for their children of growing up illiterate, rather than the benefits of gaining a rudimentary command of reading and writing. There is some evidence that the sons of skilled workers who failed to learn their letters were in growing danger of downward mobility. But even in this sense, it was not always easy to make the sums add up. Whilst it is impossible to make a precise comparison, the opportunities for illiterates to make a living were declining more slowly in the later nineteenth century than the number of brides and grooms unable to sign the marriage register. There were still plenty of occupations in the interstices of the industrial economy with no kind of formal or *de facto* educational requirements, and numerous illiterate older workers still undertaking them. Indeed it was precisely because it too often appeared a rational choice for households of unskilled labourers not to educate their sons and daughters that compulsion had to be introduced. But as we shall see later, many of these same households were fond of gambling, and indeed were actively using their new attainments in literacy and numeracy to engage in it. There remains the possibility that the time in the classroom was seen in these terms, a throw of the dice which might for the fortunate few provide the means of breaking out of the cycle of inherited deprivation.

Inequality

The odds against success in this competition varied over time and between countries. They were always long, and never more so than during the final drive to universal literacy. Institutional instruction in reading and writing was constructed over a major fault line in the Enlightenment project. On the one hand it was seen as a mechanism for breaking up the remnants of feudalism, replacing ascriptive status with individual achievement and equipping the mass of the population with the opportunity to give their talents full expression. On the other, it was viewed as a means of gaining entry into the households of the labouring poor in order to counteract the tendency of economic modernization to dissolve the structures of inequality and deference which alone guaranteed the social and political order. Literacy itself was an inherently ambiguous skill, the vehicle for conveying or challenging the received wisdom of the ruling order. The more emphasis that was placed on teaching reading and writing in the curriculum, the more acute was the tension between the radical and conservative aspirations. There was no resolution of this conflict during the period under review, or indeed through to the present day, merely a shifting balance between the forces, with the rhetoric of reform rarely coinciding with the delivery.

The uncertainty of purpose was nowhere more apparent than in Prussia, which led the way to mass literacy in Europe. The initial reform of 1806 had embodied the aspirations of von Humboldt for an educational system which would develop the innate human potential for intellectual life.[55] Schooling should disregard vocational training in favour of an induction into the national culture. The subsequent programme enacted in 1819 set up separate *Landschulen* for peasants and *Stadtschulen* for the children of urban workers, but both were to be encouraged to promote their more able and ambitious products to higher levels of education.[56] However, before any of the pupils could set foot on this ladder, it was cut down by a conservative reaction, fearful that unmanageable forces of economic and social aspiration were being fostered by the state.[57] For the remainder of the nineteenth century, it became progressively more rather than less difficult to move upwards through the system. At the time of German unification, nearly 13 per cent of children still had the prospect of further education if they did well in their initial lessons in reading and writing; twenty years later the proportion had been halved.[58] The same drama was played out in a more minor key in Russia. An initial enthusiasm imported from revolutionary France for an integrated education system was halted in its tracks by Nicholas I, who in 1827 specifically forbade universities and secondary schools to admit the children of serfs. The later emancipation of the peasantry did little to alter their prospects. On the eve of the First World War, the entire secondary school system of Russia contained just 30,000 peasants' children.[59]

If the notion of class had any consistent meaning in any industrializing European society it was in the classroom. At best there was just enough possiblity of moving to secondary education to keep alive the myth of the career open to talent, but no more. The general tendency was for the factory and school systems jointly to entrench the division between the worlds of manual and white-collar labour. As they chanted through their alphabets and their readers, the cohorts of pupils learned the limits of aspiration. In France and England there was no legal prohibition on community-wide elementary education but the determination of middle-class parents to use their money to insulate their children from daily contact with those of the lower orders ensured that wholly separate systems were constructed.[60] Where societies were more relaxed about mixing the rising generation in their junior years, the relevance of the schooling for future careers remained sharply distinguished. The more the state invested in teaching literacy, the less the lessons in literacy became a sufficient preparation for occupational advance. During the period in which the modern school system was being constructed, the major exception to the general tendency to closure lay in the personnel appointed to conduct it. Where the economy had yet to modernize, the teaching profession assumed enormous proportional significance. In Russia by the end of the nineteenth century, it was the biggest single category of white-collar employment, outstripping the entire state bureaucracy.[61] The cost-cutting device of pupil-apprenticeships offered some prospect for boys and even for girls of escaping their fate as manual workers, although, partly as a consequence of this mode of entry, the elementary schoolteaching profession enjoyed far less income and reputation than its secondary counterpart, and struggled to gain financial parity with even the poorest of the local clergy. Marooned in their one- or two-class schools, the brightest of the peasant children lacked the prospect of further occupational or geographical mobility. They were freed from the life of back-breaking toil, but would always struggle to earn enough money to keep their family, or enough status to preserve their dignity.

The decision to impose effective compulsion required the state to readdress the material outcome of elementary education. Removing children from their family economies for an unbroken period of time posed in a sharper form the question of the transition from the schoolroom to the workplace. As the moral purpose of learning to read and write became more secular, so the striving for personal advancement was given greater emphasis. Every local economy had always deployed complex informal means of recognizing ability and fitness for employment. Issues such as family background, manual dexterity, physical capacity and occupational temperament had in the past had little connection with the few months passed in the classroom. Now the state sought to establish its own criterion of suitability for the labour market. France, for instance, extended the innovation made by Duruy in the late 1860s of a leaving examination leading to the *certificat des études primaires*, which was intended partly as an incentive to pupils to complete the curriculum, and partly as a service to future employers.[62] As the school system finally became free and compulsory under the Ferry reforms, grades of attainment were introduced, and a lesser certificate of primary instruction was given to those who had merely survived the curriculum. A similar two-tier structure was created in Sweden, with the *avgångsbetyg* awarded by examination and the 'minimum' given for attendance.[63] In England, pupils could give evidence of passing up to six, and later seven grades of competence in the three Rs, and as in other countries, the teacher was added to the local clergyman, doctor and landowner as a source of 'characters' for job applicants.

Performance in reading and writing, and also arithmetic, became the basic unit of exchange between the school and the state, the teacher and the family, and the education system and the labour market. The length of the sentences the child could read without stumbling, the number of words it could write without spelling errors, became the means by which governments could measure the efficiency of their expenditure of tax-payers' money, by which parents could determine that their children were making some kind of progress during the long years in the class-room, and by which employers could discriminate between applicants who could all now sign their names on a piece of paper. Of all these trans-actions, the last was the least significant. Credentialism spread into the world of manual labour at a much slower pace than formal schooling. There were a handful of occupations, such as the post office, where the degree of literacy really was important,[64] but they tended to set their own tests rather than rely on the uncertain assessment procedures of belea-guered, overworked schoolteachers. At best the certificates were sec-ondary evidence of the basic question potential workers had always been asked: did they come from a good family, and had care been taken with their upbringing?

Giving formal recognition to the completion of the elementary cur-riculum brought into focus the boundaries between the levels of educa-tion. The certificate could also stand as measure of fitness to proceed to the next stage of schooling. The first cohorts to be compelled to stay in the classroom were the first to be offered systematic access to study which could provide entry to a wider range of white-collar occupations. Provision either took the form of some kind of higher elementary school, which would introduce the pupil to more sophisticated intellectual or vocational training, or a passport to the middle-class preserve of the grammar school. The *lycée* became a more recognizable aspiration for the children educated under the Ferry laws.[65] England consolidated a drift to schooling beyond literacy through the Balfour Education Act of 1902, which provided for both higher grade schools and competition for a small number of free grammar school places. Sweden established a crack in the door to secondary education through legislation in 1894 and 1909, as did Denmark in 1899 and 1903.[66] The reforms looked both back-wards and forwards. The aspirations which they embodied had been set forth during the Enlightenment, and indeed in many countries there were more opportunities for an able poor man's child to enter a grammar school and even university in the eighteenth century than throughout most of the nineteenth. At the same time the rhetoric of equal opportunity was not translated into anything like a complete system of progression until the reconstruction of education systems which took place throughout Europe after 1945.

For the children emerging from four to six years of elementary school in the period before and after the First World War, the chances of using their competence in literacy as the first rung of a ladder to a new occupational world were very slender, the nominal possibilities serving more often to measure the waste of talent than to give acknowledgement to it. After half a century of supposed opportunity, just 2.6 per cent of baccalaureate candidates in France in 1932 were the children of 'workers' and a further 3.9 per cent those of small shopkeepers. The comparable figures in Germany were 7 and 24 per cent.[67] The opportunities created by the Balfour Education Act of 1902 resulted in only one in fourteen elementary schoolboys and one in twenty girls reaching a maintained secondary school, and just one in 100 boys and one in 300 girls making it to university.[68] At the time of the Fisher Act of 1918, 9.5 per cent of pupils in state elementary schools were able to advance from their basic instruction in literacy to secondary education.[69] In Italy, 5 per cent of university students were the sons of workers in 1911, and only 3 per cent in 1931.[70] Success required not only innate ability and ambition, but also a dedicated schoolteacher and a family able and willing to make the major financial sacrifice which secondary education would entail, even when it was notionally free. It also required the pupil to be male. What was a narrow wicket gate for boys to squeeze through was still almost completely closed to girls. The state felt little obligation to provide secondary education for the clever daughters of the labouring poor, and neither did their parents. Nothing did more to confirm the restricted meaning of their formal instruction in literacy than the obstacles to its further deployment. The most they could hope for was to stay long enough in their elementary classroom to prepare themselves for entry into a normal school where they could be prepared to teach the next generation of poor girls about the limits of their prospects.

A final assessment of the impact of literacy on social mobility must await the outcome of more systematic European comparative research which is still taking place. Interim judgements are partly a matter of perspective. Set against a pure model of the schoolroom acting as a universal solvent of ascriptive characteristics, the verdict is generally pessimistic. The development of national education systems contributed powerfully to the widening divide between the status and material rewards of manual and white-collar labour. Their role in reproducing inequalities of birth far outstripped their capacity to assist the able and ambitious to escape their occupational inheritance. The two most strik-ing findings from the work on European social mobility are the number of literate grooms who had made no progress in relation to their fathers, in spite of their greater educational opportunities, and conversely the number of illiterate young men who had nonetheless managed to travel at least some distance from their origins. Most boys, and an even greater proportion of girls who were now able to write their names, grew up to perform the same tasks as their less literate parents, or even fell in their occupational status.[71] One in six of the sons of skilled workers in Mitch's sample who signed the marriage register between 1869 and 1873 were occupying lower rungs in the hierarchy than their fathers. Learning to read and write offered no guarantees in the world of work, not even against failure. In no European society is it possible to derive a graph of increasing mobility which compares with the steep rise in marriage register signatures and school attendance. The more literate a society became, the more children, in this sense, wasted their education.

By contrast, it may be argued that few of the providers of official edu-cation in the nineteenth and early twentieth centuries, and fewer still of the consumers, ever supposed that learning to read and write would instantly release all the children of the labouring poor from the prison of occupational inheritance. Within the framework of structural repro-duction, modest gains were possible. Absolute mobility was increasing in most modernizing economies, and literacy was implicated in the process.[72] As the marriage registers, which are the principal source of these data, rarely recorded the occupations of brides, it is only the pro-gression of the educated boys which can be calculated. The findings indi-cate that for any sector, those who could sign their names were more likely to have advanced beyond their father's position than those who could not. Two studies of the English registers found that twice as many literate as illiterate sons of unskilled labourers had moved up to the semi-skilled level or above by the time they were married.[73] Those making the crucial transition from the working class to the middle-class world were always more likely to have signed their names than those who, like their fathers, were still earning their living with their hands.

Most occupational movements in this era took place within the working class rather than across the boundary into the bourgeoisie. It is likely that literacy was at its most potent in eroding the significance of parental background within the ranks of the manual workers. In Marseille, for instance, high literacy rates played little part in the occu-pational fortunes of the artisans, for whom education was as much a cul-tural as a practical asset. It was far more important for peasants, for whom a basic schooling could at last enable them to contemplate a move to the city with its far greater range of employment possibilities.[74] In the crowded urban communities, elementary education was integral to the gradual reduction in occupational reproduction. As the cabinet-maker's son sat at the same desk as the street-sweeper's, so the significance of who your father was, which had always mattered as much to the aristocracy of labour as to the nobility, was diminished though far from abolished. The relative prosperity of the home, the aspirations of parents for their sons and daughters, were still of great importance. But in their newly acquired skills and basic qualifications, in their occasional encounters with supportive teachers, some children now possessed additional weapons in their struggle to get on in the world.

By the second half of the nineteenth century, an increasing role was being played by the demand side of the equation, the creation of jobs where literacy was a necessary or desirable attribute.[75] The proportion of the occupied workforce in Britain identifiable as 'white-collar' almost tripled between 1851 and 1911,[76] and inside the working class, trades directly associated with the use of literacy were notably buoyant. Those listed in the paper, printing and publishing trades increased nearly six times in the seventy years after 1841. Not surprisingly, these kinds of occupations proved particularly accessible to the sons of unskilled labourers who had learned their letters. In terms of absolute numbers it was again the openings within rather than beyond the ranks of hand workers which were most significant. The uniformed working class generally offered the most secure and the most pensionable positions in their economies, and these were the jobs most likely to require formal qualifications or entrance assessments. There were 218,592 postmen and related workers across Europe in 1890, and 504,481 in 1913.[77] In the large communication systems the postmen constituted the biggest single employment organization. On the eve of war, Germany had 148,769 uniformed workers delivering letters, and Britain 126,190. Most white-collar jobs demanded qualifications beyond the reach of those whose schooling had finished at ten or eleven, but their growth frequently outstripped the capacity of the existing bourgeoisie to fill them, sucking in a fortunate minority from the classes below. The best prospects were in countries like Finland, where a rapid growth in demand for professionals, bureaucrats and entrepreneurs could not be met from within the ranks of a historically small middle and upper class.[78]

Economic growth

Even if literacy was an uncertain source of prosperity at the personal level, the argument that the growth of the economy as a whole was sustained by the investment in education remains attractive.[79] Nunez finds

a 'significant correlation' between literacy rates and economic development in industrializing Spain.[80] Mironov concludes that in Russia, 'the
net contribution of education to the creation of national income comprised approximately 35 per cent of the total contribution by all factors.'[81]
The time-lag between investment and return in both countries was
around a generation. The evidence across the whole of Europe is
however far from straightforward. Cultural explanations of England's
early industrialisation tend to focus on the informal structures of teaching artisan skills rather than the labours of professional teachers. The
general conclusion is that her lead over the rest of the world was
achieved in spite of the condition of her primary education system, not
because of it.[82] At best, Anderson's 40 per cent literacy threshold oper-
ates only as a negative factor. It may contribute to an understanding of
why countries like Russia and Spain did not begin to move until a
century after the industrial pioneers, but it casts no light on the variable
performance of the western European economies.[83] As Blaug pointed
out thirty years ago, Anderson's figures display no significant correlation
in the range of 30 to 70 per cent literacy rates, which is where most of
the western economies found themselves during the period of industrial
take-off.[84] England's most obvious rival during the period of industrial
take-off was France, where, as Furet and Ozouf have demonstrated, the
literacy levels were one of the few indicators of social and economic
health not to have been seriously harmed by the Revolution and the
Napoleonic Wars.[85]

Connections can only be made by refining issues of chronology and
causation. Sandberg, for instance, has addressed the performance of the
Swedish economy, where reading skills were more widely distributed by
the eighteenth century than in any other country possessing the natural
resources for industrialization. He concluded that a literate workforce
was of little relevance to the performance of the economy until it began
to expand for exogenous reasons.[86] It was when rising international
demand transformed the value of the Swedish forests in the second half
of the nineteenth century that the long tradition of teaching children
their letters gained an occupational meaning.[87] As a sophisticated economic and communication infrastructure was called into being, the workforce could turn their skills to more secular ends. If literacy played a
direct causal role it was via the expanding consumption of paper by the
increasingly educated populations of Europe. Once the economy did
begin to grow, the fact that the state did not suddenly have to divert
expenditure into the creation of a new school system may well have contributed to the speed of the process. Even here, however, a recent careful
reworking of the data for both Sweden and her European rivals has
severely qualified the scale of the literacy effect. At best, the relative

strength of the Swedish (and also Scandinavian) literacy and education rates explained a third not of growth in total, but merely of the 'residual growth after controlling for initial 1870 conditions'.[88] The driving force in the Scandinavian economies remained the international processes of trade, migration and capital flows. The same study found no discernible effect of schooling in the variable performances of the 'European industrial leaders.'[89]

The Swedish case also draws attention to the local nature of any interaction between literacy and economic development. In the fertile south of the country, there was evidence of a different pattern of change. A programme of enclosures and the associated development of market relations on the land in the late eighteenth and early nineteenth centuries was facilitated by the presence of a peasantry already capable of entering into written agreements and engaging in innovative forms of production.[90] It was a two-way process. The more commercialized farming became, the greater the incentive to achieve higher levels of literacy, and in particular to gain fluency in writing as well as reading.[91] However contemporary English agriculture witnessed an even larger process of enclosure without any connection with the literacy of the workforce. When the last of the common fields disappeared, farm labourers were as incapable of signing the marriage register as they always had been. The difference was not the standard of education but the pattern of landholding. The Swedish peasant had something to gain from the arrival of formally documented property rights; the English agricultural worker had everything to lose. French peasants had more sense of proprietorship than their counterparts across the Channel, but the period up to the middle of the nineteenth century brought little opportunity to use any of their communication skills to increase their productivity. Here, as was noted above, the subsequent growth in rural prosperity was a cause more than a consequence of increased investment in education by both families and the state.[92]

There was no single narrative of literacy and economic development either across a national economy, or in related sectors across Europe. Overarching statements can only be made at a very high level of generalization. Investment in literacy has to be measured in terms of educational expenditure, but, as we have seen there was no mechanical relationship between the two factors, and whereas the former was bounded by 100 per cent, the latter could continue to expand beyond the completion of the marriage register graphs. It is evident that richer economies spent more on education than their poorer neighbours,[93] but the interaction between these indices was never constant. More prosperous economies achieved male literacy rates of 50 per cent or above by the beginning of the nineteenth century, and thereafter their gross domestic products grew faster than the measurable output of their formal education systems. In England, the economy expanded three times faster than male literacy between 1820 and 1900, and in France twice. Conversely, the later a country was to industrialize, the greater the relative increase in its educational provision. At the extremes of the spectrum, Germany's GDP expanded eight times faster than its already very high male literacy rates between 1870 and 1900, whereas Russia's literacy levels grew seven times faster than its sluggish GDP in the same period.[94] Italy was somewhere in the middle, with school enrolments rising with economic expansion between 1881 and 1913, but not at the same speed.[95] These disparate ratios reflect the fact that early industrialization required a long period of relative prosperity during which time the infrastructure of a complex market economy, including basic literacy, could be put in place. Thereafter, a continuing increase of investment in education could be afforded in the context of an economy which through its own dynamic was growing even more rapidly. The more delayed the take-off of the economy on the other hand, the less in absolute terms was spent on luxuries such as education, but the heavier the burden appeared in relation to the productive sector, whose growth may have been held back by the need to invest in the nation's infrastructure.

There are two particular obstacles to further generalization. The first is the variable relation between mechanized production and economic activity more generally. It can be argued that the factory system which lay at the heart of the Industrial Revolution neither required nor created a particularly literate workforce in the period of development dominated by Britain. What mattered was a good level of communication skills in all parts of the economy where market relations were developing. However, once the industrial processes evolved from an elaboration of artisan techniques to forms of technical engineering, then the presence in at least some of the factories of workers who could read blueprints and other documents did become more important. This may mean that as with other categories of public intervention, government-imposed education was more relevant to a nation's economy the later it industrialized. It may also mean that states such as Britain which continued to rely on low levels of investment in all levels of education as the modern international economy developed were destined to become increasingly uncompetitive.[96] It does not, however, demonstrate that industrial advance at the end of the nineteenth century and beyond was a direct consequence of literacy levels. Attempts to isolate schooling as an identifiable cause of Germany's Industrial Revolution, which followed Britain's and was technically more advanced, have not been successful.[97] Neither does it mean that there was an appropriate balance between investment in factories and elementary education which all countries discovered. Even in Germany it is possible that at least up to the First World War, its economy was held back by overinvestment in formal technical instruction for workers.[98]

The second obstacle is the continuing uncertainty about the operational relationship between education and economic behaviour. A recent authoritative review of the field concludes that 'both in terms of growth accounting and even more so in terms of the sources of innovation, much more needs to be discovered about human-capital formation.'[99] There remains considerable confusion about the form of knowledge or skill under discussion, and about the nature of its impact on the economy.[100] In terms of basic literacy, a distinction needs to be drawn between the allocative effects – the enhanced capacity of workers to discover and respond to opportunities in the labour market – and the productivity effects – the direct consequence of literacy for manufacturing output.[101] Before the First World War, the extent of secondary education may have been more relevant to industrial performance than basic instruction in the three Rs, particularly where elementary schooling was dominated by religious or nationalist agendas.[102] After 1914, levels of marriage signatures can play no part in explaining the relative performances of at least the more advanced European economies. If there is a consistent relationship between economic development and basic communication skills during the later nineteenth century it is in the use not the possession of literacy, and in overall production rather than factory manufacture. As figure 3.1 indicates, there is a close relationship between the extent of a country's gross domestic product in 1890, and its employment of the postal system.[103] A similar relationship cannot be established for more direct measures of industrialization, such as the production of pig iron.[104] What mattered was the dynamism of the economy as a whole, and it may be possible that the greater variation displayed by the postal figures constitutes a better guide to the sophistication of its operation than the aggregate statistics of gross domestic production.

Advanced economies required well-developed communication systems, and each contributed to the expansion of the other. With the national postal rates in the later nineteenth and early twentieth centuries growing between two and seven times faster than the economy,[105] it is evident that the use of literacy was being driven by more than just the way in which the population earned its living. Equally the development of economic systems cannot be seen as a systematic consequence of the levels of elementary education or marriage register systems. It may be said that widespread illiteracy would hold back an economy, particularly if it was amongst those required to start at a relatively advanced level, but otherwise it is necessary to return to the point of departure for

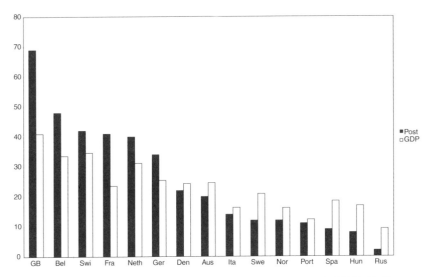

Figure 3.1 European per capita postal rates and GDP, 1890

this chapter, and stress that for both suppliers and consumers, formal education was a relatively expensive good, more needing than determining economic prosperity. In Italy for instance, Barbagli's careful study of the relative performance of schooling and economic growth between 1881 and 1913 concluded that the latter was sustaining the former, although material output was outstripping cultural investment, the gap being filled by an army of uneducated child labourers.[106]

With the human-capital theorists still struggling to identify what they are looking for in terms of the contribution of non-material factors to economic growth in the past, it is difficult to progress beyond a general scepticism about the capacity of literacy to generate the kind of disciplined, flexible, mobile personality which it is considered the modern capitalist required in his workers. At this stage in the debate it is advisable to defer to the judgement of contemporaries. As was stressed in the previous chapter, most citizens of most states became literate because they or their parents valued the skill. There is no evidence that they put themselves to this trouble merely in order to make themselves more deferential employees, and for the most part, they had too realistic a grasp of their prospects to confuse the vision of credentialized mobility with the reality of educational closure. Neither is there much evidence that the capitalists themselves passionately believed in the occupational relevance of mass literacy. They were rarely publicly opposed to it, but they were even less frequently interested in supplying it or directly paying others to do so. There were occasional speeches by industrialists or by politicians who thought they represented them, and here and there experimental workplace schools. But in terms of money raised and time spent, there were a hundred clergy for every one factory owner actively engaged in the creation of a literate European population.

4
Reading and Writing

Oral and written

Benjamin Shaw's formal education began and ended at Peggy Winn's dame school where he learned to read and to knit. It was not until he was nearing the end of his apprenticeship that he began to become actively literate. The transition from reading to writing was triggered by a crisis in his personal life:

> in the Autum of this year, my Sweethart & I quarreled, & after Sometime she detirmined to leave dolphinholme, so another young women and her set of for Preston, but before she went she promised Voluntearly that she would be true to me &c, this was in October 1792. So when she got work which she did at the factory in moor lane, then belonging to Watson & Co She wrote to me, & let me know where she lived &c and envited me to come to see her at Christmas &c – (This was about the time the french convention tried, & condemned their King Leuis the 16th –) at Christmas I went to Preston, with Samuel Winn my cousin, & staid a few days &c She sent me letters by the waggon from dolphinholme, & I frequently wrote to hir – this was the beginning of my writing, for I never went to any school to write in my life – and wanting to send to her I was ashamed to let anybody know my secrets, I set about writing love letters &c, (it is an ill thing that is good for nothing)[1]

Shaw's halting, makeshift journey between different modes of communicating his heart's secrets constrasted sharply with the polarities which informed much of the contemporary commentary on the spread of reading and writing. To educated outsiders, literacy occupied a world of opposites. The tables of signatures divided populations, the graphs measured change between contrasting conditions. The simple pairing of capacity and incapacity belonged to the later nineteenth century as official bodies began to generate the statistics which justified the investment in elementary education. These indices of progress were a shorthand expression of a more profound dichotomy which had shaped the response of educated society to the unlettered since the invention of printing. An 'oral tradition' had been discovered, embracing a large but rapidly diminishing proportion of the rural populations of Europe. In Protestant societies, the association of a mode of communication with a collective mentality had a history stretching back to the Reformation. Catholicism was stigmatized as a non-literary belief system, deriving its authority from the unverifiable spoken word. 'Romish traditions' were contrasted with the divinely sanctioned message of the Bible, which alone could preserve the Christian message across the millennia. This construction persisted long after the Catholic church had embraced the objective of a schooled laity, but by the late eighteenth century the notion of an oral tradition was taking on a broader meaning. Now it represented the dividing line not between religions, but between cultures.

The new delineation was driven by the increasingly acute sense of historical change. Communities which relied wholly on speech to record and communicate their collective knowledge were held to be insulated from the corrosive effects of progress. Their songs and stories preserved intact the values and wisdom of long-dead generations. Observers who sought out and recorded such material could not only protect it from the relentless invasion of the printed word but also gain access to a hidden cultural history of immense wealth and longevity. Just as the emerging science of geology could identify aeons of time in a single rock face, so the folklore collector could locate sedimented layers of custom and belief in surviving outcrops of the oral tradition. The Scottish stonemason Hugh Miller taught himself the science of the rocks upon which he worked, and as he travelled away from his native Cromarty in search of employment, discovered his culture's history laid out before him. 'Some three days' journey into the Highlands', he wrote, 'might be regarded as analogous in some respects to a journey into the past of some three to four centuries.'[2] Thus he became both an internationally renowned geologist, with a fossil named after him, and also one of the relatively few nineteenth-century writers to make a major contribution to the folklore movement from within.[3]

The discoveries had varied significance. The publication of Herder's *Volkslieder* in 1778 set in motion the search for a German national consciousness hidden beneath the artificial political boundaries of the region.[4] Walter Scott's collection of songs for the *Minstrelsy of the Scottish Border* was integral to his creative revival of Scotland's identity,[5] and elsewhere in Europe both the artefacts of oral communication and the language in which they were conveyed were pressed into the service of nascent nationalist movements. The young Hungarian literati of the 1820s, for instance, saw the uncorrupted peasantry as the major source of the linguistic revival which they sought.[6] By contrast, the host of enthusiastic urban collectors who ventured forth into the neighbouring countryside in ever-increasing numbers during the nineteenth century had a more ambivalent attitude to their source material.[7] Some deployed their findings to attack the spiritual and imaginative bankruptcy of contemporary civilization, but most endorsed the necessity of change.[8] They were alert to the loss threatened by the destruction of the networks of oral transmission, but hostile to the irrational and immoral belief systems which had for too long survived amongst the uneducated. They worked alongside rather than against the new race of trained schoolteachers, celebrating their achievements and often recruiting them to the newly formed folklore societies. The songs and the proverbs were for the museums of disappearing cultures, not for the living world of the modern rural society.

The folklore movement contributed to the rise of the new science of anthropology which in more recent decades has challenged the boundaries of conventional text-based historiography and generated much of the scholarship which informs this study.[9] In the course of disciplinary evolution, the fundamental assumptions of the founding fathers have come under scrutiny. The 'oral tradition' is now regarded more as a by-product of European intellectual history than a substantive category of cultural analysis. The most obvious difficulty is that at least in western Europe, communities uncontaminated by the written word disappeared at the Reformation and Counter-Reformation – if ever they existed. Although the Protestant churches had varied in their enthusiasm for an actively literate laity in the centuries after Luther, the commitment to vernacular religious literature had ensured that every worshipper was exposed to the written form of their own language. In the most extreme cases, sustained campaigns of disseminating both spiritual texts and the skills required to read them meant that entire populations possessed and used print a century before the oral tradition was discovered. Egil Johansson reported a survey of a Swedish rural parish in the 1720s, whose 600 families owned 'around 400 ABC-books, 650 to 750 Catechisms, more than 1,100 psalters, 29 Bibles, and about 200 other religious books.'[10] Parish records in Iceland revealed that of a thousand households between 1780 and 1800, only seven were without literature.[11] Even in England, where the state and the established church had been far less active in the field, the drive to mass literacy began rather than ended with books in a majority of homes. Studies undertaken in the late 1830s, just as children were emerging from the first officially subsidized church elementary schools, revealed levels of ownership ranging from 52 to 90 per cent in rural areas, and 75 per cent or more in most towns and cities. Only in areas of acute deprivation, such as an Irish slum in London, did the figure fall below a half.[12] Engagement with print in Catholic societies was hampered not so much by the absence of education as by the persistence well into the nineteenth century of Latin in both church services and the school curriculum. Nonetheless, cheaply produced spiritual works in national languages were finding their way into the homes of the rural poor to be read, remembered or at least preserved as visible evidence of piety.

Much of this literature was supplied not by the churches themselves, but by commercial vendors responding to popular demand for both worldly and spiritual reading matter. Pedlars travelled out from urban centres to the surrounding countryside during the early modern period, carrying in their packs devotional texts, tales of wonder and imagination, and practical guides to living, at prices affordable by all but the most destitute peasant families. The chapbooks and the *Bibliothèque Bleue* found their way into the farthest recesses of the English and French countryside as the road systems improved in the seventeenth and eighteenth centuries, as more slowly did the *pliegos de cordel* in Spain and the *luboks* in Russia.[13] The hawkers who trudged from hamlet to hamlet were supplied by publishers and wholesalers who were pioneers of large-scale, standardized production and marketing. The London firm of Charles Tias held 200,000 unbound sheets in 1674, and enough bound chapbooks to supply one in 44 families in Britain.[14] In 1722 there were one and a quarter million sheets of *Bibliotèque Bleue* pages in the Garnier warehouse at Troyes. Unlike modern newspapers, which in some respects they represented, these flimsy productions were read and reread for years until they finally disintegrated. At the very least, they ensured that in the villages of western Europe, and in those of the east within reach of the scattered towns, the populations already knew the meaning of print before the salaried, inspected schoolteachers arrived to tell them in the nineteenth century. Even if they had to borrow both the texts and the skills to read them, they were familiar with the task of decoding the marks on the page and with the consequences for their spiritual, imaginative and practical lives.

Only in exceptional cases would a labourer's household possess a rudimentary library, and even in the precociously literate rural communities of southern Sweden, the bulk of cultural life was conducted through the spoken word and associated forms of ritual behaviour. However it is now apparent that the characteristic artefacts of the oral tradition, the folk songs and stories which so excited the middle-class collectors, were themselves contaminated by the world of texts. It has been estimated that of the material painstakingly recorded from elderly traditional singers in remote corners of Britain in the late nineteenth and early twentieth centuries, as much as four-fifths had once appeared in printed broadsides.[15] Similar flows from formal to informal reproduction have been traced in Germany and Ireland.[16] Furthermore the singers themselves were not always as reliant on their capacious memories as educated outsiders liked to suppose. They too were concerned lest they forgot the songs, or failed adequately to convey them to the next generation, and had no compunction about making manuscript copies where they possessed the ability to do so. The assumption that the written tradition stood to the oral much as the railway engine stood to the stage-coach was in some respects the reverse of the truth. Creativity had been a more promiscuous process than the folklorists liked to suppose. Printed songs and stories gradually merged into the oral resources of the community as they were performed and repeated to new audiences, reinvigorating the existing local repertoire and for ever compromising the purity of the folk tradition. By the same measure, transmission over time was by no means as secure a process in pre-industrial settlements as the nineteenth-century rural romantics imagined. Aside from intermittent disasters of war, pestilence and famine, the constant realities of early deaths and short-distance migration continually threatened the chain of communication between generations. The handwritten versions passed from hand to hand, and in countries where print was in short supply, became an important addition to the cultural archive. In Ireland in 1857 it was observed,

> how large manuscript collections . . . for the most part written by professional scribes and schoolmasters, and being lent to or bought by those who could read but had no leisure to write, used to be read aloud in farmers' houses on occasions when numbers were collected at some employment, such as woolcarding in the evenings but especially at wakes. Thus the people became familiar with all these tales.[17]

Only when the collections began to appear between hard covers was there a sense of a tradition being embalmed rather than sustained.

Just as the oral forms of communication had depended on the written, so also the reverse was true. Performance was sustained by written forms, and in turn the dissemination of print was assisted by singers and story-tellers. In any community of the labouring poor, both before and during the drive to mass literacy, there were always more people seeking access to the content of books and documents than were able to own or decipher them. The solution was to read them out aloud. Societies where only a small handful of the population were technically literate nonetheless were able to incorporate print and writing into their daily lives through private or public performance. In Hungary for instance, where literacy rates were in single figures before the nineteenth century, prayer books, passports, contracts and letters were deployed in rural areas by means of borrowing the skills of the handful of neighbours capable or reading them.[18] The notion of audience which has become a feature of modern readership studies was literally appropriate to the reception of a large proportion of literature until well into the twentieth century. Most printed words found their way into the minds of most of the populations of the past through their ears rather than their eyes.[19] In this form of consumption, as in all others, deprivation encouraged co-operation. Those who could not afford the cost of an education or reading matter sat at the feet of those who could. In the fireside gatherings known in France as the *veillée* and in Germany as the *Spinnstube*, the contents of chapbooks were read or recalled by one of the company whilst listeners carried on with household tasks.[20] In Iceland, where the nights were the longest of all, the whole sequence of engaging with the written word, from learning to read to reading aloud to discussing the texts was conducted on this collective basis.[21]

The rising graph of literacy brought no corresponding decline in the use of the human voice. Children emerged from schools with their ears ringing with the noise of print. The first generation of inspected teachers aspired to harmony rather than silence in their lessons. Only in the more advanced schools of the last quarter of the nineteenth century were pupils permitted to spend part of their lessons quietly reading or writing. Out in the streets, they encountered the vendors of the new forms of cheap literature, who bawled and sang their wares to passers-by.[22] The broadsides and song sheets, which were the transitional forms between the traditional chapbooks and ballads and the later newspapers and cheap periodicals and novels, were sold as they were bought, as vehicles more for performance than for private perusal.[23] The arrival of popular journalism only added to the clamour. 'The penny newspapers, "*Daily Telegraph*", "*Daily News*", "*Globe*, sir?", "*Standard*, sir?" assail our ears at every hour in all our leading thoroughfares', wrote an observer of London in the mid-1870s.[24] Every city had its own cries, although contemporary Berlin was held to be quieter than most on account of strict by-laws against street-sellers.[25] The newspapers might be read quietly at home, but the tendency for interest in their contents constantly to outstrip the ability to buy them caused a further extension of the time-honoured means of consumption.

In workplaces where machinery had yet to drown the human voice, artisans took turns to read aloud the contents of a collectively purchased paper. The practice began as political journalism escaped the confines of polite society during the revolutionary crises of the late eighteenth century,[26] and continued until the arrival of cheap mass-circulation daily papers in the years before the First World War. A young handloom weaver in Carlisle was able to develop both his literacy skills and his political consciousness as his workshop responded with keen interest to the mounting Reform Bill crisis:

> I well remember how the weavers at Newtown used to club their pennies together to obtain the London newspapers, and with what anxiety they were wont to anticipate the arrival of the mail coaches that brought them. The *Weekly Dispatch* was a great favourite, because of the accounts it furnished of the rick burnings and reform meetings, while *Bell's Life* kept us fully informed of the doings of the 'Fancy.' Our great paper, however, was the tri-weekly *Evening Mail*, published by the *Times*. It gave a *resumé* of the previous two days' news, with many of the leading articles from the 'Thunderer.' At the height of the reform agitation it was common for the men in our shop to gather round the fire about nine, and with me in the middle as reader, go through the debates until long after midnight. Thus with corrections from one and another, I learned to read, and thus likewise, at fourteen, I became somewhat of an advanced politician, known among my playmates as the Chancellor of the Exchequer.[27]

Where conditions of labour discouraged such behaviour during the working day, public consumption of the press became a feature of sociability in the evenings, as for instance, in the case of the cafés of Provence: 'A centrepiece of many such gatherings was the reading aloud by one of their number of the newspaper to which the *patron* or perhaps a prominent (and slightly wealthier) member of the society subscribed. Such readings were often lengthy affairs, whole articles being read out with care, often accompanied by a commentary from the reader, his audience or both.'[28]

The long history of translating the written word into forms which could be used by those without the skills, money or time to read it themselves severely qualified the meaning of the columns of marks and signatures. The simple bifurcation of the literacy tables was not replicated in the realm of cultural practice. Preachers, street-sellers, workplace and fireside readers engaged the illiterate in the world of print.[29] The towns became texts as shop-fronts and vacant walls were covered in increasingly elaborate signs, posters and advertisements.[30] 'At seven I had so far profited by her teaching', wrote the Coventry ribbon weaver Joseph Gutteridge of his dame school teacher, 'as to be able to make out the contents of the local papers, and I derived much pleasure and knowledge from their perusal. Another means of learning that I made use of was the sign board literature of public-houses and shops.'[31] This material combined print with visual images in ways which drew into the world of codified language the barely literate or those yet to be educated. The various forms of cheap literature themselves made every concession to those who would fail the tests of the schoolmasters. The texts of the chap-books, broadsides and early cheap novels deployed formulaic repetition or memorizable verses which spoke to the conventions of oral transmission.[32] They were adorned with illustrations ranging from the crude woodcuts on the covers of the wares of the chapmen and *colporteurs* to the elaborate lithographs on the pages of the newspapers and periodical fiction of the later nineteenth century, which provided points of entry for those unable to cope with the accompanying lines of print, and clues or confirmation for those still uncertain of their abilities. It may indeed be argued that the hybrid forms of popular print provided not only an incentive to learn the alphabet, but far more effective primers for the barely literate than the specialized textbooks which the professional pedagogues were producing for the official elementary schools.[33]

The category of the oral tradition was a means of discriminating between different sectors of the population living in the same chronological moment but belonging to separate eras of development. Those believed to rely exclusively on the spoken word were separated from the literate not just by their specific communication practices but also by the way in which they thought, or rather failed to think. Groups of the European population, particularly those labouring on the land, who still comprised the majority of the total workforce as the mass literacy campaigns commenced, were consigned to the timeless, ancient cultures, in contrast to the temporally conscious, progressive world of readers and writers. The distinction between tradition and modernity was central to how the educated understood their historical identity, and to the way in which they justified the continuing exclusion of the uneducated from political power and economic privilege. The contrast was captured in the catch-all concept of superstition, the joint enemy of the church and the Enlightenment.[34] The term came from without rather than within the language of the uneducated. It referred most frequently to beliefs in magic, but in various contexts embraced a wide range of customary practices which conflicted with the precise and purposeful calendars of contemporary economic and social relations. There was a continuum of outlook and behaviour which stretched from the employment of witches and wisemen to casual drunkenness and violence.[35] Superstition was constituted and preserved by oral transmission and associated ritual forms, and could be attacked most effectively by schoolteachers and the capacity for rational thought and behaviour they instilled in their pupils.

At the heart of the concept was a judgement of what was real. Superstitious beliefs embodied a false sense of time, a false view of the supernatural, and a false estimation of the limits of human agency. As Eugen Weber has written, 'superstition was the religion of others: other credulousness about beliefs we do not share.'[36] Yet as contemporaries were often embarrassed to discover, both the printed word and the agencies which promoted it were deeply implicated in this irrational universe. The church and state educators were motivated by a concern not just with total ignorance but also with the wrong kinds of attempts to instruct the young. The problem was encapsulated by the record left by a Prussian pupil of an unofficial school taught by a working man: 'Once a year, on Shrove Tuesday, it was the custom for the teacher to whip all of his pupils with a fresh birch stick, the local belief being that such beatings had the effect of preventing the farm animals from contracting worms.'[37] This tendency for indigenous instructors to entrench rather than erode traditional belief systems justified the investment in training and inspection, but it remained extremely difficult to control the use made of even the most innocent of books. Everywhere, writing and the written word was interpreted as a physical power.[38] If there was a single core text upon which the European elementary school system was founded it was the anthology of psalms which provided the first and frequently only sustained reading matter for pupils in every denomination and language. However, as a study of the Moscow provinces discovered, 'There are certain superstitions surrounding the psalter, namely that he who reads it from cover to cover forty times is absolved of certain sins, and that it serves as a means of divining, particularly in those cases where the perpetrator of a theft of property is to be found.'[39]

Although such maltreatment of the word of God may have persisted longer in what were held to be the more backward nineteenth-century countries, there was no sense in which the interdependence of magic and print was confined to the European periphery.[40] Joseph Lawson evoked the dense structure of oral and literary authority for the beliefs which permeated his native Yorkshire village in the 1820s:

> Such was the superstition at the time of which we speak, that the whole atmosphere was supposed to be full of good and bad spirits, on errands of mercy or of mischief; the latter mission always preponderating – the evil spirits mostly prevailing over the good. Let us imagine ourselves in Pudsey as it was sixty, or even fifty years ago, on a dark and stormy winter's night, sitting by some fireside, with or without the dim light of a dangle; a few

neighbours – men, women, and children – sitting together. The children both dread and like to hear what are called 'boggard tales.' They ask the older people to tell them some tales they have heard before, or a new one. ... At this time all those who deny the existence of boggards are called infidels and atheists. The Bible even is referred to as a proof of the truth of witchcraft; also the great John Wesley's Journal.[41]

Witches and sorcerers in western societies rested their authority in part on their privileged access to printed or manuscript books of spells and mysteries, and the trade in popular print had long laboured to make this material available to a wider readership. French country booksellers sold newly-educated peasants *Livres de sorcellage*, illustrated pocket-books containing formulas and incantations.[42] These claimed to be based on obscure ancient sources, but the genre of do-it-yourself magic was capable of adapting itself to the times. In Britain the creation of a mass readership brought forth a variety of handbooks, including the 'penny dreamer', a guide to the interpretation of dreams, and to ciphers and omens for foretelling the future.[43] 'One of the most important articles in the literature of that day, recalled Lawson, 'was a "dream book" explaining their meaning, and giving interpretations. There was no end to people's infatuation on the subject of dreams. To dream of fruit out of season meant grief out of reason, etc. Young women who ate the first egg of a pullet before going to bed would dream of their future husbands.'[44] One of the most successful of these publications was associated with a much more recent focus of power. *Napoleon's Book of Fate* was supposed to have been found in the library of the emperor, and was now on sale to all who had benefited from the extension of the school system.[45] Superstition was embedded in the form and the content of print. At one extreme, documents and books were used for magical purposes by those whose awe for their contents was deepened by their inability to read them.[46] At the other, the guides to fortune-telling were models of inter-textuality, referring to other printed and manuscript sources, and demanding of their readers that they engage in various forms of further reading or writing.

If the notion of an oral tradition tells us more about the prejudices of the educated than the practices of the uneducated, the question remains of how to categorize change in the application of reading and writing during the coming of mass literacy. The written word may have thrust its roots deep into the soil of peasant cultures, and the spoken may have been entwined with the printed as the graphs of signatures rose in the nineteenth century, but transformations did take place in what was read and how it was consumed. A more complex model has to be deployed, which can encompass both the continuing exchange between the two modes of communication, and the diverse layers of meanings and material conditions involved in the rapid increase in the use of literacy. This can be best achieved by identifying a series of transitions which occurred in this period, few of them beginning from nothing, and few if any completed by the time the bulk of the European populations had gained a nominal ability to engage with the world of print. At the heart of the movement was movement itself. Literacy was a means of making connection with other ideas and knowledge over space and time. Its application altered the user's relationship with the immediate and local discourses sustained by oral modes of communication. Reading and writing promoted motionless mobility. The association between education and physical migration was not only inconsistent but also of limited significance.[47] The key journeys were made in the mind. Alexander Somerville, a young farm-worker growing up in the Lammermuir Hills, made his first great journeys without leaving the fields in which he laboured:

> The next book which came in my way, and made an impression so strong as to be still unworn and unwearable, was *Anson's Voyage Round the World. Gospel Sonnets, Burn's Poems*, old ballads and self-made doggerel, everything gave way to admit the new knowledge of the earth's geography, and the charms of human adventure which I found in those voyages. I had read nothing of the kind before, and knew nothing of foreign countries . . .[48]

He was able to use the fragments of schooling he had received to take his fellow labourers with him on his travels. After a morning's work, he recalled,

> I remained in the fields, and lay on the grass under the shadow of the trees and read about the *Centurion*, and all that befel her. When the afternoon work began, I related to the other workers what I had read; and even the grieve began to take an interest in the story. And this interest increased in him and in every one else until they all brought their dinners afield, so that they might remain under the shadow of the trees and hear me read. In the evenings at home I continued the reading, and next day at work put them in possession of the events which I knew in advance of them.[49]

The nature of change was dramatized by the growth in correspondence. As we have seen, what Chartier properly describes as 'an ordinary kind of writing',[50] had grown rapidly during the course of the nineteenth century. Benjamin Shaw's early attempts at epistolary courtship were increasingly supplemented by mass-produced valentines, which by the middle of the century were second only to Christmas cards in Britain as a seasonal peak in the annual postal flows.[51] The governments which reformed their postal systems from 1840 onwards were driven by the desire to democratize the practice by making it cheaper and more accessible, and by the intention of transforming the relationship between communication and space. The flat-rate, pre-paid systems were designed to make the state a single cultural entity, and with the formation of the Universal Postal Union in 1875, this ambition was given an international dimension. The first article of the organization stated that there should exist a 'single postal territory',[52] which even at the outset covered 37,000,000 square kilometres and 350,000,000 inhabitants. The concept of a global village was born and given institutional substance almost a century before the phrase was coined. The Universal Postal Union was conceived as both a physical and a moral achievement. It displayed the rationality and power of states in that they could organize complex, large-scale flows of mail within and across their frontiers, and at the same time the ever more elaborate and extensive webs of written exchange would bind together dispersed family members, hostile classes and competing nations into a single, harmonious whole. As the network of contacts became ever more dense, so mutual understanding and dependency would grow, and the ignorance and self-interest which underlay all domestic and international conflict would decline. The UPU was seen by its founders as 'an intimate association of the civilized countries of four parts of the world, upon one of the most important fields of action of the intercourse of nations.'[53] If the more utopian rhetoric was checked by the outbreak of the First World War at a time when the flow of correspondence between and beyond the states of Europe had reached 5,000,000 items a day, the basic features of the organization survived to become the model for the series of international bodies which were established after 1918 and again after 1945.[54]

   The central issue of movement was highlighted by the close association between the postal and railway networks. Mass correspondence was facilitated by the revolution in physical communication. Britain introduced the first flat-rate postal charges immediately after it had laid down the first mainline railway system in Europe. The speed and security of this new mode of transport encouraged the postal reformers in their ambitions, and in turn the ever-increasing volume of mailbags supplied the fledgling railway companies with an important source of revenue. The uniformed employees of the two services systematically penetrated the remotest corners of their countries, linking the capital to the provinces, the countryside to the towns. The scale of the interdependence is confirmed by the statistics which the communication bureaucracies began to produce. As figure 4.1 indicates, there was a close affinity between

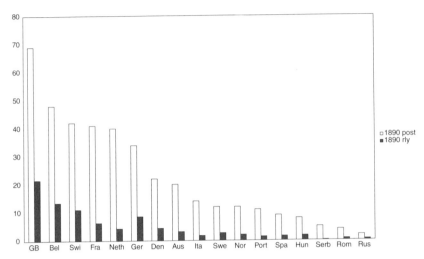

Figure 4.1   European per capita railway passengers and postal rates, 1890

railway travel and correspondence.[55] Across the nations of Europe, the hierarchy in the per capita usage of the two systems was almost identical, as was the proportional relationship between them. In both modes of communication, the key was use rather than possession. It was not the length of the national rail networks which mattered, but the number of passenger kilometres travelled, just as it was the application rather than the distribution of literacy. Furthermore the relationship was dynamic over time, with both modes of communication expanding at the same speed, country by country, as the era of mass literacy took shape between 1890 and 1913.

   Of all the statistical measures of progress which might be connected to the spread of reading and writing, the association between trains and correspondence was the closest. Taking postal flows in 1890 as the standard factor, the correlation with primary school pupils was 0.44, with literacy 0.61, with gross national product 0.93, and with railway passengers 0.94.[56] The near-perfect fit reflected a common enterprise. The figures suggest that the history of mass communication in Europe may have had its own internal dynamic, connected to other material and cultural factors but never reducible to them. By no means every letter was carried by train. The rapidly improving road systems were pressed into service, particularly in countries like France, where broad areas of evenly populated countryside had to be connected to the railway stations; and where geography so dictated, the letters travelled by water, most notably in Norway, where half the mails were carried by boat in 1890.[57] But the *voies ferrées*, as the UPU's tables described them, symbolized, more than any other mode of transport, the speed, the punctuality and the defeat of distance which the postal networks embodied. Contemporaries were convinced that the machinery of communication would do more to encourage the acquisition of literacy and to magnify its consequences than all the exhortations of clerics and politicians.[58] Whilst most children still travelled to school on their feet, the structure of funding and inspection in which their education was now embedded was dependent on regular employment of both correspondence and trains.[59] The interactions between the transfer of people and of information were complex, but both were working to loosen the bonds which tied the mass of the population to the physical and mental surroundings into which they had been born.

Communal and private

Amidst the sense of accelerated movement, it is possible to identify four areas of transition. The first and most obvious was from the communal to the private. The consumption of print encouraged and facilitated a process of withdrawal from collective forms of cultural activity.[60] The process, as we have seen, was far from unilinear. Material deprivation and print scarcity either delayed for long periods or reversed the direction of change. With only thirty printing firms in the whole of Russia in the late eighteenth century, provincial elites were still dependent on reading circles to gain regular access to literature.[61] When newspapers, for instance, began to reach the newly literate, they were usually too expensive to be bought and consumed by a single purchaser. They were read aloud in pubs and workplaces, or, as in the case of early nineteenth-century Belfast, left at houses for a penny an hour.[62] Silent reading, which predated the invention of printing as a mode of engaging with the written word,[63] was dependent on a certain level of prosperity. It required physical space such as a study, a (with)drawing room, or a bedroom occupied by only an adult couple, in which uninterrupted concentration was feasible.[64] It required, particularly in northern Europe, personal access to artificial heat and light. Such levels of comfort themselves promoted forms of domestic sociability in which reading frequently featured.[65] It was not that reading was hostile to communal behaviour amongst the more prosperous classes, but rather that the increasing availability of both books and space increased the possibility of choosing how to encounter the world of print. Further down the social scale, the option was much more difficult to exercise. Readers had either to turn their backs, sometimes literally, on the life of the household, and abstract their minds from the activities going on around them, or retreat from the home altogether and find solitude, when the weather permitted, in the fields surrounding the towns and villages.[66] The solution was the public library, which gradually became a feature of western urban life during the second half of the nineteenth century.[67] Here, instead of a private endeavour which opposed noise, a collective provision imposed silence.

Surplus income bought the possibility of private consumption, and also the physiological capacity. Spectacles still await their historian, but enough is known to suggest that it was not until after the Second World War that the bulk of the 40 per cent or so of any population which requires glasses were enabled by the new welfare states to acquire them as they were needed.[68] Before then, inherited defects or slow degeneration could only be countered by picking through the frames on market stalls in the hope of finding an affordable clarity of vision. Prosperity, combined with the falling price of print, also permitted the more idiosyncratic engagement with print characteristic of the withdrawal from collective forms of consumption.[69] Story-tellers, whether working from memory or a text, imposed their own rhythm on the audience. The individual listener could not out of interest or boredom slow down or accelerate the narration. But once the story had become a personal possession, whether owned or borrowed, then issues of speed and even direction became matters of personal discretion. The transition from dearth to relative abundance in texts has been represented as a move from intensive to extensive reading.[70] The prayer books were construed to be repeated, the chapbooks were pored over until they disintegrated. There was a sense in which the spread of literacy and cheap literature in the nineteenth century represented a shift for the bulk of the population from rereading to reading.[71] It became acceptable for the first time to throw print away before every word had been perused. Yet undisturbed study permitted its own form of intense engagement with a text. The issue once more was one of individual choice. The same reader might now skim a newspaper on the way to work and spend an evening on a single paragraph of a precious book.

The direction of change becomes clearer if the notion of privacy is properly understood. Its central characteristic was not isolation but control. At one level it was the increasingly asserted right to determine what the outside world knew of your thoughts and actions; at another it was the freedom to make your own connections with that world.[72] The figure of the private reader or writer was alone but not enclosed. The issue was dramatized by the post. As with every other aspect of the encounter with the written word, the long journey from limited to full literacy imposed collective practices, as letters were read to or written for the nominal correspondents. Nonetheless, the function of the activity was to engage in communication which could be hidden from the household and the neighbourhood but could connect the individual to family and strangers in other locations. It freed privacy from the constraints of space and time. Letter-writers could exercise control over conversations with chosen individuals who might never be met. Their sense of community was no longer limited by face-to-face relationships in the immediate locality. Correspondence implied not a reduction of social interaction, but a reformulation of its boundaries at the will of the writer of the letter and the addressee. However much the contents of the message might be discussed within a household as it was composed and subsequently read, its transmission required a form of secrecy.[73] Once it had been sealed, or from the 1840s onwards committed to a ready-gummed envelope, it was to be concealed from the gaze of all who handled it. The sheer fragility of the letter, the contrast between the domestic or commercial sensitivity of its contents and the vulnerability of a folded piece of paper, highlighted the issue of trust which was central to written communication. The post could only operate on the assumption of self-restraint on the part of the letter carriers and the governments which employed them. Correspondents escaped the prying tongues of their neighbours but were exposed instead to the threat of theft and espionage.

The major cities of Europe had been connected by postal networks since the sixteenth century. The increasing use of correspondence for commercial, professional, administrative and recreational purposes had been integral to the growth of the domestic comfort and public presence of the middling orders of society. There is evidence that during the eighteenth century, the practice had spread down at least as far as the urban artisans. The irrepressible French glazier Jacques-Louis Ménétra sustained both his business activities and his often complicated private affairs through frequent use of both the *petite poste* of Paris and a rudimentary but apparently reliable national network. As was the case with his better-educated superiors, the two aspects of his life were commonly entwined in the same letter. 'I immediately grabbed a pen', he recalled of a crisis with his fiancée, 'and wrote in a few words that I was giving up the shop if she thought she was better off with the new fellow who had been introduced to her and I had no intention of standing in the way of anybody's inclinations.'[74] The mass mobilization of armies during the Revolutionary Wars further broadened the practice as governments on both sides of the conflict sought to maintain the morale of their conscripts by providing them with the means and sometimes the skills to keep in touch with the families left at home. The introduction of flat-rate, pre-paid postal systems was in part a response to the increasing level of demand, which was imposing strains on the traditional method of calculating distance and demanding payment from unprepared and often reluctant addressees. It represented nonetheless a qualitative shift in both the accessibility of written communication, and the privacy with which it could be conducted. The provision of letter-boxes in doors and post-boxes in the streets (289,934 in Europe in 1890, according to the indefatigable statisticians of the UPU) made possible a new level of anonymity in the practice. No longer was dispatch or receipt a matter of public negotiation with the letter carrier or the post office. Only the household need know a letter had arrived, and no one need discover that one had been posted.

Standardization

The expansion of correspondence was closely associated with a second transition, the move towards standardized forms of cultural practice. The process was most transparent in the consumption of time. Eighteenth-century popular literature already had little local input, and in its fictional forms had only a distant relation to the current moment.[75] The coming of mass communication systems furthered the spatial integration of the market place, but narrowed the time-frame of production and consumption. The most obvious victim of change was the tradition of parochial timekeeping. The growth of surfaced roads and fast mail-coaches in the decades before the coming of the railway had placed a strain on the tradition of setting each church clock to the sun as it was overhead at a precise moment in the day, but the problem could be circumvented by carrying locked timepieces, so that each journey was completed within its own temporal bubble.[76] But as soon as it became necessary to compile integrated rail timetables, and co-ordinate complex postal networks with their published times of delivery and collection, the infinite variation in the hour between east and west became unmanageable. If community wished to connect with community, it would have to sacrifice control of its clocks. For a while the rail and postal authorities struggled to maintain enclosed temporal regimes whilst most of parish life went on at its own pace. Greenwich Mean Time, originally defined as an aid to the early railway companies, was embraced by the British Post Office in 1857, but even so country post offices were permitted to observe local time 'for certain purposes' for another fifteen years.[77] However the construction of the telegraph lines alongside the railway tracks made it possible to transmit a single time pulse to the eastern and western boundaries of a nation, and gradually the co-ordinated discipline of the communication systems spread into other areas of society and the economy.[78] As in education, compulsion followed rather than created popular behaviour. Only when the concept of a single zone had gained broad acceptance did governments intervene, setting out the modern division of European time in a series of enactments from 1880 onwards.

The standardization of the hour reflected a more general assault on the local sense of time. As in other aspects of pre-modern culture, it is important to retain a sense of perspective. There is a tendency to oppose the clock discipline of trains, schools and factories to a timeless pre-industrial countryside, where only a general sense of the diurnal passage of the sun was possible or necessary. In reality, every farm labourer employed in a team had always paid heed to the church bells throughout the working day, and every child assisting the family economy had learned many lessons of punctuality before it ever reached the classroom.[79] Nature itself made its own demands; few forms of factory discipline were more insistent than the task of milking cows. One of the attractions of the new urban centres was the availability of occupations, such as small-scale shop-keeping, which represented a welcome escape from the unavoidable routines of rural labour. Nonetheless, the spread of literacy and its artefacts was implicated in a profound shift from a particular to an abstract sense of time.[80] At a most basic level, writing almost always meant engaging with the formal calendar. Those who could inscribe their name or attempt a short letter, would need to set down numbers as well as words. Legal documents demanded at least the year, letters by convention were begun with some statement of the day and month, even the marriage register signature, the simplest expression of literacy, was accompanied by a date. In eighteenth-century rural Hungary, by contrast, almost none of the uneducated deponents in court proceedings located their accounts by reference to days or months, preferring instead the local calendar of festivities, the cycles of agriculture or, very occasionally, market days.[81]

The more diffuse practice of reading also brought with it an increasing exposure to the official calendar. The chapbooks for the most part had only a distant relation to chronology. Their point of origin was left vague, their contents, where they evoked history, disregarded boundaries of fact and fable. They were never new, never obsolete. The repeated consumption of a single item distanced them from a particular moment in the reader's biography. Print merged with rather than opposed the local sense of time. However the topical broadsides and canards which reached this market from the late eighteenth century onwards depended for their effect on a quite specific association with a public history, whether of kings and queens or recent robberies and murders. Narrative became infused with dates, meaning with a common measure of time. This transitory form then split into two categories of popular reading, each bearing a yet more precise notation. Imagination was sold in numbers, the weekly serial not only dated, but requiring a planned engagement with the future if the entire story was to be read. Fact was sold as newspapers, further anchoring reading to the formal calendar, although for most of the labouring poor up to the First World War, it was only Sunday that was identified in this way. Perhaps the most intense engagement with the national calendar came not in the occasional eruption of wars and revolutions, but in an increasingly profitable subsection of journalism, the sporting press. During the final quarter of the nineteenth century it combined the achievements of electronic communication and mass instruction in literacy and numeracy to create a betting industry financed by myriads of poor men simultaneously investing their hopes and their money in the outcome of timetabled horse races taking place far from their own neighbourhood.

The association of literacy with a new sense of clock time was dramatized by the official curriculum. The ambition of allocating each minute and hour of the school day to a purposeful activity was conceived by Pietist educators in mid-eighteenth century Germany and Austria, and was subsequently embodied in the curriculum of every inspected elementary school.[82] The shapeless lessons in which children spent a few minutes at the teacher's desk and the rest of their day working at their own speed were replaced by blocks of time, beginning and ending at a set moment, within which the pupils collectively undertook a specific task without pause or interruption. Whereas the unofficial teacher was pleased enough to greet a pupil and accept his or her fee at any point in the week, now punctuality became both a moral and a practical objective in its own right. Pupils were punished not only for failing to learn, but also for not doing so at the required time, irrespective of the existing rhythms of the household and the local economy. The length of the lessons were determined not by the content of the task or the interest of the teacher and the pupils, but by the relentless sounding of the school bell, which served also to distinguish periods of work from those of play, before, during and after the school day. The extent to which not only the length but also the content of each lesson was standardized by the government varied across Europe. Not every country was enraptured by the French vision of a million children learning the same words at exactly the same moment in a given year. Local school administrations might be permitted to set their own timetables, but none were allowed to instruct without them.

The parallel between the clock discipline of the school and of the factory was as clear to contemporaries as to later historians. What is more difficult to assess is the impact of this temporal regimentation on the cohorts of new readers and writers who were finally released from the classroom. On the one hand they had been made acutely aware at a most impressionable age that external chronologies were both more moral and more powerful than their own instincts for periodizing the day and the week. On the other they had endured endless lessons which seemed not so much infused with time as emptied of it altogether. The problem was less the sounding of the bell but rather the mounting fear that it would never sound at all. Whilst some did indeed walk out through the school gates and in through those of a factory whose routines of clocking on and off seemed all too familiar, most of the male school-leavers in nineteenth- and early twentieth-century Europe moved into occupations where the daily or seasonal demands of nature or the structured interactions of the workforce still influenced the rhythms of the working day. The closest affinities between the temporal regimes of school and work were probably experienced by the increasing number of girls who went into domestic service, where the clock always rang for them before the rest of the household was awake. School was only ever an exact microcosm of life for the pupils who themselves became teachers. For the rest, the classroom taught many lessons which needed to be unlearned, not least that it was possible to read or write and not be endlessly alert to the anxious minutes and hours.

Those responsible for inculcating a new temporal discipline through instruction in literacy were themselves exercised about the use that might be made of the new skills in the life after school. Their concern in this context was with the particular literature of time which was to be found in the packs of all the travelling pedlars and booksellers of early modern Europe. After the various religious publications, the almanac was the most commonly available item of print to be found in the households of the labouring poor.[83] In Prussia, its circulation increased with the labours of the schoolmasters, with about one almanac for every three households being published around the middle of the nineteenth century.[84] Its illustrations, charts and hieroglyphs made it accessible to those who could not read at all, and its cornucopia of zodiacs, calendars, phases of the moon, weather predictions, historical dates, proverbs and wise saws provided nourishing fare for the literate and those who listened to them.[85] In one sense, this temporal document was anything but parochial. The almanacs supplied national and indeed cosmic timetables. They did so, however, in a way which subjugated the registers to the cultural traditions and material needs of the communities which bought them. The moon and the stars were brought down to the fields and homes of those who toiled with their hands to make a living. Through the medium of print, the long-established local devices for manipulating time were given strength and precision. This applied most obviously to the interlinked issues of the weather and the cycle of planting and harvesting.[86] The planetary and lunar tables, interpreted by the light of oral wisdom about the climate of the area and the nature of its soil and crops, imparted an apparent authority to the necessary task of anticipating the future. It needed no education to read the weather from the skies or other natural indicators, but there was always a gap between prediction and outcome which the additional claims of the texts could help to close. There was a continuum between collective experience and the information on the page. The almanacs empowered rather than undermined the inherited skills and beliefs of the locality.

By the end of the eighteenth century, polite society had become disenchanted with prophecy, although it remained a staple element of popular print.[87] Astrology, whether related to the crops or to other aspects of human affairs, was construed as an irrational, non-scientific engagement with time. The component parts of the almanac were separated from each other. The proverbs and local wisdom were consigned to folklore collections, the planetary charts became the province of the rising science of astronomy, and the temporal material was issued as calendars, which were purely statistical documents, compiled by objective measurement and immune to appropriation by local belief systems. A rapid decline occurred in the circulation of almanacs claiming official status, but the genre itself proved difficult to expel from the literary market place. There was a continuing need for its information, nowhere more obviously than in the desire to predict the weather. During the first half of the nineteenth century, scientific advance in this field as in many others was largely destructive. It cast doubt on claims that the climate could be foretold months or years ahead on the basis of natural or planetary observations, but offered no reliable alternative. However the spread of the electric telegraph across Europe from the late 1840s onwards permitted the systematic collection of meteorological data and the production of synoptic maps firstly of current weather systems and then of changes which were likely to occur in the immediate future. The source of much of the information was innumerable measurements by amateur naturalists, but it was processed and given authority by an increasingly self-conscious profession of meteorology, which during the third quarter of the century evacuated from its procedures the last vestiges of astrology. In 1873, two years before the formation of the Universal Postal Union, the International Meteorological Committee was founded to co-ordinate the collection and interpretation of data.[88] After several false starts, newspapers commenced publication of what in

1889 came to be termed 'forecasts', covering up to forty-eight hours ahead.[89] Each community now became the passive recipient of nationally and internationally produced information syndicated through metropolitan or provincial dailies. The meteorologists were capable only of recognizing rather than explaining weather patterns.[90] Knowledge beyond the narrow temporal horizons of the scientists was still dependent on local strategies of prediction, but these were increasingly bereft of textual support as the almanac was exiled to the margins of astrology.

Print was not simply a centralizing phenomenon. It would be more accurate to describe the arrival of mass literacy as furthering the spatial focusing of cultural practice. Almost everywhere the countryside lost out to the towns, but both the production and the consumption of print were integral to the growth of vigorous urban identities which neither replicated nor were controlled by the capital cities. Whilst the development of steam printing from 1812 onwards and the arrival of mechanized composition half a century later favoured the capital-intensive mass manufacture of newspapers and books, the simultaneous proliferation of cheap iron-frame presses made every urban community a location for the production of every kind of text. The growth of the provincial newspaper and the associated development of new kinds of public sphere will be examined in the next chapter, but some sense of the trajectory of change can be glimpsed in the route taken in the north of England by the popular almanac. As the prophetic dimension lost authority, the remaining function of sheer entertainment was translated into a form which satirized the astrological claims of the genre and celebrated the new patterns of living which were emerging out of the disorder of the first phase of urbanization. Local dialects were retrieved from the contempt of the oral tradition and manipulated into written forms through which the new calendars of work and leisure could be expressed. At the heart of many of the fabricated customs was education itself. Day and Sunday schools developed their own rituals of anniversaries and celebrations. For the young French shepherd Paul Besson *la fête de l'école*, when all the pupils paraded in new clothes, was much the warmest memory of his schooldays.[91] Outside the classroom, the imposition of the academic year began to influence the timing of local excursions and holidays of the community as a whole.

Control

The publication by newspapers of weather forecasts and of other practical information and services was integral to a third transition, that from restricted to expansive control over the circumstances of life. Print enlarged the intellectual resources of the locality, supplying instrumental knowledge which challenged the limitations of everyday experience.[92] It was a matter of disseminating the specialized advances of natural and social scientists, and at a more humdrum level of pooling the information previously trapped within enclosed speech communities. The issues ranged from advances in medicine or production to assistance in locating employment or lost relatives and possessions. The early modern market for cheap literature had always contained a small but flourishing genre of practical manuals, and with the coming of mass literacy, the volume and variety of useful print available to poor readers increased dramatically. Assessing the consequences of this growth is complicated by the way in which those who assumed the responsibility for informing the new readers conceived the nature of their task. Knowledge embodied in oral forms was held to be not only irrational but also passive. It represented a fatalistic view of the universe which was fundamentally at odds with the optimistic and interventionist mentality of modern society.[93] In reality, the complex bodies of inherited wisdom and practices manifested a determination to take arms against a sea of troubles whatever the chances of success. Ignorance and resignation were not interchangeable conditions, and indeed Durkheim managed to demonstrate that across Europe, in Protestant and Catholic countries alike, the illiterate were statistically less likely to commit suicide than the literate.[94] If belief systems condemned as superstitions or magic were a product of poor communications and inadequate command of the resources for living,[95] they were also an indication of the refusal to accept such conditions. Change was not a simple process of empowerment, but rather a complex engagement between intensely active strategies of survival.

As the printed word became more commonplace, so books themselves became less mysterious. An increasing proportion were on purely secular subjects, and their growing variety encouraged a more discriminating engagement with their contents. If more texts on magic were published in the nineteenth century than ever before, the idea of the text itself gradually became less magical.[96] However, a critical response could well cause the reader to return to older forms of intervention. The key was the perceived consequences of the inscribed intervention, nowhere more obviously than in the central matters of life and death. The advice and information began in the classroom as teachers mounted a sustained attack on the supposedly irrational beliefs that pupils brought with them from their homes. The teaching of literacy was held to be obstructed by the superstitious attitudes of parents to the value of education, and in turn the lessons in reading and writing were designed to equip their children with the capacity to emancipate themselves from traditional ignorance.[97] It was a matter of instilling a respect for book knowledge and for the authority of those most qualified in it, and also of beginning to inform those who would become the parents of the next generation of the basic principles of health and hygiene. As mothers were held to bear a special responsibility for the health of their families, so it was the girls in the classrooms who were exposed to the most sustained instruction.

The extent to which the lessons bore fruit depended on how far the claims for the power of scientific rationality were perceived to be justified. The struggle was particularly prolonged and incomplete in Russia, where the eradication of superstition had been proclaimed an official objective of education as early as 1803.[98] An increasingly assertive medical profession mounted campaigns against, for instance, the lethal custom of distributing to other families as 'gifts in memory' the clothing of children who had died of contagious diseases, but was constantly frustrated by what it dismissed as the ignorance of the illiterate.[99] There were, however, several rational grounds for maintaining a sceptical view of the official pamphlets, lectures and advice. In the first instance the networks of relatives, experienced mothers and unofficial midwives, which the professionals saw as the enemy of scientific progress, remained the source of critical moral and practical assistance in the fraught practice of child-rearing.[100] Whatever the source of their knowledge and skills, women could do more for women than the occasional well-meaning outsider. Linked to this was the inescapable presence of material deprivation, which sustained both the high levels of illiteracy and the stubborn rates of infant mortality. Poverty instilled a realistic pessimism against which the optimism of the highly educated could make only slow progress.[101] Conversely, rising living standards and declining infant mortality made the claims of the schoolteachers suddenly rational.[102] Finally, the claims of the doctors were themselves a kind of superstition. Advances were being made in the understanding of infection and in other aspects of preventative medicine, such as inoculation against smallpox. But these were slow, often contested within the profession, and fell far short of the transformative role associated with modern science in popular propaganda. Throughout the campaign for mass literacy in Europe, doctors remained incapable of curing the bulk of life-threatening illnesses of either children or adults. They could diagnose with increasing precision, reduce the spread of some diseases and alleviate the symptoms of others, but for the most part they could no more prevent acute pain and death than the traditional remedies and unqualified practitioners the uneducated were condemned for employing.

The consequence was the persistence of a tangled pluralism. What the illiterate and newly literate resisted was not official medicine itself, but the oppositional discourse which accompanied it. The acceptance of a new procedure did not imply the rejection of all that had been learned from earlier generations, nor did a visit to a clinic or doctor forbid the further employment of local wise women or midwives. The most obvious cause of rejection of the monopolizing pressure of the book-trained professionals was the simple issue of expense. Only the skilled, regularly employed, male workforce in some of the more advanced economies of Europe could arrange free access to doctors whilst the campaign against unofficial medicine was at its height. Thus poorer households developed a two-tier approach, employing home-made remedies for an everyday problem, and only risking the cost of the doctor and his prescriptions when the condition became serious. When in turn the professional intervention failed, uneducated and educated alike would turn back to any source of assistance whose efficacy could not be convincingly disproved. At such times, the twin forces of literacy and commercialization were the enemies rather than the agents of what the medical profession viewed as progress. The interdependence of print and proprietary medicine long predated the coming of official education. Remedies were sold alongside or through the pages of popular print in the eighteenth century. As the proportion of the population capable of reading advertisements was increased by the church and the state, so the manufacture of unauthorized medicines became more capital-intensive, and the sales techniques more aggressive. At the bottom end of the market, those suffering from shameful conditions employed their newly acquired skills to correspond with the blackmailing vendors of abortifacients and cures for venereal diseases.[103]

The tendency for the teaching of the schools to diversify rather than displace existing cultural resources created what Laura Strumingher describes as a 'crazy-quilt pattern' of knowledge in the communities of the newly literate.[104] The lines between the traditional and the modern, the irrational and the scientific, were continually blurred as households struggled to exercise any kind of control over their circumstances. In the midst of this confusion stood the clergy, as hostile to 'superstition' as the lay professions, and as vulnerable to change as the purveyors of oral wisdom. Their charge against the magical mind was that it conflated the spiritual with the material, and the human with the supernatural. It misconstrued the power of man, and invaded the province of God. 'Natural religion' was immune to the discipline of the churches, and through its tendency to spiritualize any inanimate object, prevented individuals from comprehending what was within and beyond their sphere of influence.[105] As we saw in chapter 2, Protestants and Catholics alike had accepted by the beginning of the nineteenth century that a victory over heterodox belief systems required the eradication of mass illiteracy. The scale of their human and material resources enabled them to play a leading role in the growth of elementary education, and also to intervene in the dynamic market for cheap literature. In the face of the impending deluge of licentious material, voluntary societies were formed which combined moral purpose with entrepreneurial vigour. The traditional fare of bibles, psalters and saints' lives was supplemented by a cornucopia of tracts and periodicals embodying all the journalistic and technological advances of the time. The market was segmented, with publications directed specifically at children, women, the newly literate and urban families with recreational time on their hands. Capital was raised to subsidize production, and the churches' communication networks were pressed into service to ensure that the material was available for sale or free distribution in every village and in every street of the expanding towns.

Institutional religion tried to overwhelm its enemies by sheer volume. Although the Catholic church retained the apparatus of censorship, it no longer believed it possible to exercise control through prevention alone. Together with the Protestant denominations, it accepted that the forces of the age must be fought with its weapons. In the middle decades of the nineteenth century, six-figure circulation figures were claimed for weekly religious periodicals in France, and still larger numbers of spiritual texts were given to captive audiences in day and Sunday classrooms or handed out to their parents as they went about their daily lives.[106] By 1850 the largest British organization, the Society for the Promotion of Christian Knowledge, was issuing about 4,000,000 items a year.[107] Purely commercial publishers maintained extensive religious lists, whose sales generated large profits.[108] The ambition was to invade the realm of natural religion with more powerful weapons of instruction and entertainment than were available from the oral sources, and at the same time to arm the emancipated citizens against the temptations of infidelism and immorality. The effort invested in the multiplication of God's word was immense, and when the production of new texts was associated with the invention of new festivals or shrines, major inroads were made into the local, semi-pagan calendars of events and devotions.[109] The development of Lourdes, for instance, publicized by written and visual propaganda all over Europe, helped to bring the pilgrimage business firmly under the control of the national church.[110]

There were, however, mounting obstacles to the fulfilment of the hopes entertained for the printed word. The most obvious was that commerce would always outrun religion. It was a race the churches could not win. The more they published, the smaller the proportion of literature in households that was even remotely connected with religion. Signs that the domination by spiritual texts of private libraries was on the wane were apparent well before the eighteenth century ended.[111] It is difficult to calculate the shifting balance with any precision, but we may take as an example an unusual long-run survey in Estonia, far from the centres of commercialization in the west. Between 1700 and 1850, the religious works accounted for a steady 52 or 53 per cent of the total volume of printed matter in the country, before declining to 28 per cent by 1900, and to 17 per cent by 1917.[112] As in the case of education, the established resources of the churches gave them an early advantage in the race to take charge of the revolution in mass communication, but gradually other forces gained the upper hand. It was a matter partly of increasing consumer expenditure on an ever-widening range of secular material, and partly of the development of new kinds of sociability in which neither the spoken nor the written word of God was present. Cafés and clubs ran on alcohol and print. Informal gatherings centred on readings from newspapers too expensive to be bought individually, and the more structured self-help organizations inculcated the newly literate into the mysteries of agendas, minutes and official correspondence. In the home the symbolic turning point was when the former pupils of the first generation of inspected elementary schools began to purchase Sunday newspapers, and sat on their doorsteps reading of bloody murders whilst the church services began without them.

The process of change must not be compressed. More religious literature was consumed by more Christians in nineteenth-century Europe than ever before. In the rural regions of modernizing societies, devotional texts maintained a large presence in the tiny libraries of those who could read.[113] In countries such as Russia where the inroads of education and commerce were particularly slow, the relative decline did not gain speed until immediately before the First World War. Through their involuntary presence in day and Sunday schools, unprecedented numbers of European children acquired at least an outline knowledge of Christianity. But even as the illustrated periodicals, holy cards, spiritual manuals and exemplary biographies poured from the presses, the message was diminished.[114] The indiscriminate distribution of religious literature was tending to cast the word of God into the gutter, often literally in the case of the free tracts. The psalters and prayer books which had formed the mainstay of the tiny libraries of early modern readers had been venerated as objects of faith. Perusing them had been itself a salutary activity.[115] Hungarian peasants had employed the words reading and praying as synonyms.[116] Now much of the material was as disposable as yesterday's newspapers. To Catholic critics, always more alert to the desacralizing tendency of print, the widespread sale of guides to indulgences in the later nineteenth century raised the spectre of the abuses that had provoked the Reformation. The self-taught intellectuals who used the freedom of the literary market place to interrogate the basic tenets of

Christianity at least took seriously the doctrines they were attacking. The real threat was not disbelief but disrespect, a reduction of the sacred to the commonplace.

Literacy was a double-edged sword. It was a vehicle for carrying the teaching of the churches into areas of popular culture which they had never previously penetrated. The provision of schools and reading matter gave all the denominations a sense of progress. Not only was their sphere of activity visibly expanding, but they were consciously embracing the instruments of modernity. The promotion of the skills and artefacts of mass communication demonstrated the social utility of religion, but at the same time exposed the churches to competition from alternative suppliers of such goods. Just as civil and professional bodies could challenge their control of the school curriculum, so also the commercial publishers could outbid them in the market place. At best, organized religion was adapting to the times, enabling belief to be practised as private choice rather than community obligation.[117] At worst, it was placing itself at the mercy of wholly secular narratives of utility. However slow and incomplete, the promotion by print of the possibility of enhanced control over the circumstances of life threatened the claims of transcendental authority. The heyday of religious influence in the growth of literacy was in the period when the claims of the Enlightenment were most blatantly contradicted by the reality of the lives of the urban and rural poor. But as mass famine receded into folk memory for an increasing number of European societies, as reading became not a consolation for powerlessness but an expression of growing command over the household economy, so the written word was increasingly divested of the remnants of its sacred identity.

Specialization

The final transition was towards a more specialized set of cultural practices. The change was apparent at the level of personal status. Where information and entertainment were conveyed largely in an oral form, there was an imperceptible increase of authority with age. The old had heard the most and had the most to tell. As they became less physically active, so they had more time to talk to those with the most to learn. The literacy campaigns of the nineteenth and early twentieth centuries both segmented and inverted the traditional hierarchy. Now there was a marked difference in levels of command of increasingly vital forms of communication. The literate began to acquire pieces of paper to prove their achievements, and could gain access to bodies of knowledge and imagination far beyond the mental resources of their grandparents' generation. As noted above, periods of rapid growth in literacy rates accentuated the gulf between the old and the young, upsetting the usual relationships of dependency. Whilst children might be read to if a parent was literate, they might equally find themselves reading to household members born too early to benefit from the expansion of the education systems. They wrote letters for adult members of the neighbourhood, and dealt with the first tentacles of official bureaucracy as they thrust their way into the homes of the poor.[118] Where literacy brought a new language, they could find themselves the only members of their household able to communicate with significant elements of the outside world.[119] Just as the role of the priest was threatened by the arrival of the schoolmaster, so the status of all the older members of his congregation was at risk.[120] If fears about the wholesale collapse of parental authority were exaggerated, there was a loss to seniority which could never fully be regained. Conversely, where the literacy revolution was stalled, as in late nineteenth-century Russia, the mainly uneducated village elders retained their authority, continuing to take all the important decisions in relation to both individuals and the community as a whole.[121]

The task of story-telling fell to the old of either gender. In certain contexts women might take on more of the task of inducting the young into the unwritten archive of the family and neighbourhood, particularly when supervising small children or combining domestic tasks with narrative performance.[122] But the young sought out voices wherever they could find them, listening to men as they laboured with them in the fields and workshops, or sat with them at the end of the working day. The drive to mass literacy both standardized and differentiated capacities. On the one hand, the wide gaps in formal attainment were closed and even reversed as the marriage register scores moved towards 100 per cent. On the other, the possibilities for applying the lessons learned in the classroom became more diverse and in many respects less equal. The slow process of secularization affords a glimpse of this process. The cafés and voluntary associations which supplied alternative forms of sociability where the skills of reading and writing could be sharpened into effective tools of communication were largely male preserves in the nineteenth century. Wives and daughters were more likely to have been exposed to denominational schooling and found that the church congregations remained one of the few gatherings in which they had a place, however lowly. Self-improvement was rarely undertaken alone; but when reader sought out the company of reader, the networks were formed by men. The masculinity of intellectual exploration was a function partly of convention and partly of control of such surplus cash as the household possessed. And, as we have seen, it was the boys and not the girls who first began to find ways of connecting success in school with subsequent career advancement.

The extent of differentiation was greatest at the time when female literacy was growing fastest. Economies in which universal literacy had finally become a reality began to increase the opportunities for bright schoolgirls to do something with their skills. Older women, who had missed their one opportunity for schooling, could still look forward to little except growing isolation. Between the wars the wealth of their memories mocked the poverty of their engagement with the modern forms of mass communication. Their daughters and granddaughters, by contrast, found it slightly easier to move beyond passive literacy. Not only was there a slow growth of credentialized occupations for women, particularly nursing and secretarial work, but levels of domestic comfort gradually improved, particularly for the families of securely employed workers in the towns and cities. Wives could occasionally spend a little money on their pleasures, and with their homes mostly free of manufacturing activity, could find odd moments of peace in which to read or write. In the outside world, it remained difficult to break into the male preserves of collective organization. As trade unions consolidated their presence in the industrializing economies, the main pathway from classroom to functional literacy was kept largely under the control of men. The best hope of practice for their wives was in the field of recreation.

As readers became more differentiated, so also did their texts. Popular literature in the era of restricted literacy had never been completely homogeneous. It is possible to classify the little books carried through the country roads of Europe into various kinds of instruction and entertainment, and the key spiritual works always occupied a separate place in such tiny libraries as could be accumulated. Nevertheless poor readers subsisted on a narrow diet of literary forms, only occasionally scavenging crumbs from the progressively better-stocked tables of educated consumers. The arrival of mass literacy signified a transformation not only of volume but also of genre. In one sense it was a matter of poor readers gradually gaining access to the fare of their educational and social superiors, as novels, travellers' tales and other eighteenth-century innovations came within reach of limited budgets. Here the discrimination was maintained in the dimension of time, as the products of the new elementary schools were restricted to the literature of the preceding generation of middle-class readers. The youngest readers began with the tales which had been moving between oral and printed forms for centuries. John Clare listed the material which he encountered as he learnt his letters in his Northamptonshire parish as the nineteenth century commenced:

> About now all my stock of learning was gleaned from the Sixpenny
> Romances of 'Cinderella', 'Little Red Riding Hood', 'Jack and the bean

Stalk', 'Zig Zag', 'Prince Cherry', etc and great was the pleasure, pain, or supprise increased by allowing them authenticity, for I firmly believed every page I read and considerd I possesd in these the chief learning and literature of the country.[123]

Advancing skills increased his appetite, but not his capacity to impose order on his taste, or bring it up to date:

> I fancyd too that I was book learnd for I had gotten together by savings a quantity of old books of motly merits . . . I will reccolect some of them there was the yong mans best companion Dilworths Wingates Hodders Vyses and Cockers Arithmetic the last was a favoruite with me and I kept it Bonnycastles and Horners Mensuration and Wards Mathematics Leybourns and Morgans Dialling Female Shipwright Robinson Crusoe Pilgrims Progress Martindales Land surveying and Cockers land surveying Hills Herbal Balls Astrology Culpeppers Herbal Rays History of the Rebellion Hudibras some Numbers of Josephus Parnels Poems Miltons Paradise Lost Thompsons Seasons Sam Westleys Poems Hemmings Algebra Sturms Reflections Harveys Meditations Wallers Poems Westleys Philosophy Thompsons Travels Lestranges Fables of Esop A book on Commets Life of Barnfield more Carew The Art of Guaging Duty of Man Watts Hymns Lees Botany Waltons Angler Kings Tricks of London laid open The Fathers Legacy or seven stages of Life Bloomfields Poems.[124]

Not until public libraries began to be established after the middle of the nineteenth century could the self-educated begin to read in the same literary moment as the well-educated,[125] and not until the paperback revolution of the mid-twentieth century was it possible simultaneously to own the best and the latest that was being written.

Traditional categories were pushed downmarket in respect of both status and age. Tales of giants and witches, once enjoyed by readers in every sector of society, were increasingly seen as fit only for childish minds in terms either of the young or the barely schooled. They survived in their original form well into the nineteenth century, but their only long-term future was in an enclosed world of children's literature, available to those who could afford to treat the junior members of their household as separate consumers. Alongside and rapidly in place of the chapbook form emerged a range of new range of literary artefacts. As the market expanded, so it was segmented. Fact was more sharply distinguished from fiction, and both were published in an ever wider range of mediums. News emerged as a specialized concept and form, inheriting an appetite for extraordinary events and heightened prose from older categories of street literature, but laying fresh claim to accuracy and topicality. The proliferating cheap newspapers were directed to more sharply differentiated markets.[126] The flow of genres was upward as well as downward. The dynamism of consumer demand stimulated innovation which embraced every sector of the reading public. The two most significant developments were the weekly or monthly serial and the periodical miscellany. Fiction published by numbers could be cheap enough to be afforded by almost any reader, and could contain almost anything from formulaic melodramas to instalments from the leading authors of the day. The thirst for fragments of information was visible in the earliest newspapers, but it was not until the closing decades of the nineteenth century that the abundance of sources and the restriction on reading time were combined into publications devoted entirely to the brief and the ephemeral.

Each European country had its own variations on the emerging forms, and each its own rate of expansion. Everywhere, however, the market was moving in the same direction. The best evidence comes not from purchasing but from borrowing. Libraries were like postal systems in that they not only facilitated but also recorded the use of literacy. 'By the late nineteenth century', concludes Robert Darnton,

> ... patterns in German, English and American libraries had fallen into a strikingly similar pattern: seventy to eighty percent of the books came from the category of light fiction (mostly novels); ten percent came from history, biography and travel; and less than one percent came from religion. In little more than two hundred years, the world of reading had been transformed.[127]

The first French public libraries established during the Third Republic reported an overwhelming preference for fiction. On railway bookstalls and in street kiosks newspapers, periodicals, specialised items like timetables, still outsold bound fiction. Non-fiction sales of history and travel in the increasing number of specialized bookshops expanded rapidly. Demand was diverse, but those seeking to make a profit from the multiplying number of readers, and those commentating on the outcome of mass literacy were in no doubt about where it was centred. There was no significant difference by social class or gender. Commercial circulating libraries recorded the same pattern as those open to the penniless public. Male and female readers both took pleasure in works of imagination, although there was some evidence of higher consumption by the latter, and amongst the specialized forms appearing before the First World War was the so-called 'woman's novel'. The taste for fiction was evident in the most literate of European countries,[128] as in the least literate. In Russia, the failure to make serious inroads into the poor educational standards of the countryside meant that both the traditional forms of popular reading, such as the *lubok*, and the standard categories of religious literature persisted longer than in the west. Nonetheless, as commercial publishers expanded their business towards the end of the nineteenth century, it was again works of fiction which sold in largest numbers to poor readers.[129]

It is unhelpful to label such material as escapist. In different ways, histories, travellers' accounts or scientific works were devices for abstracting readers from their immediate circumstances. Conversely, works of imagination were means of replaying the realities of daily life. What most concerned observers was the disjunction between the ambitions of the educators and the intentions of the educated. The churches which diverted so much spiritual energy and resources to the early promotion of mass literacy, the governments which persuaded their more prosperous citizens to pay increasing subsidies to schools for the poor, had not done so merely in order to generate large profits for a branch of the leisure industry. Yet as the lives of the labouring population themselves became more segmented, with growing divisions between work and recreation, between the home and the street, between domestic morality and religious observance, so the practice of their newly acquired skills of communication seemed increasingly concentrated on the least serious categories of the printed word.

A similar trajectory is visible in the most salient use of writing. The initially costly flat-rate postage systems which had spread through Europe from 1840 onwards had been introduced with the highest of motives. Not only would they facilitate commercial transactions over distance, they would also promote mobility of labour without destroying the increasingly crucial structures of domestic authority.[130] Children would be encouraged to leave home in search of work, and through correspondence, parents could continue to supervise their moral development. In practice, the early beneficiaries of the reduced costs were the middle classes. Businessmen welcomed the opportunities not only of increasing the geographical scope of their activities, but also of engaging in new forms of marketing, including the mass distribution of circulars and samples. An innovation which in some countries was costing the national exchequers far more than elementary education was directly responsible for the invention of junk mail. Meanwhile their wives occupied their leisure time corresponding with relatives and friends. Those emerging from the official elementary schools were, by contrast, still too hesitant in their command of writing skills to put pen to paper except at times of family crisis. It took half a century for the bulk of the population to begin to take up the opportunities which had been created for them. Between 1890 and the outbreak of war, one item of mail grew much faster than any other. The number of picture postcards circulating throughout Europe, and being sent to and from other parts of the world, increased by 565 per cent, exactly twice the rate of letters. Helped by a change in the rules by the Universal Postal Union in 1897 which permitted the circulation of privately manufactured items,[131] the volume of these most simple of messages had reached five billion by 1913. The growth coincided with the development of holidays for working-class families. It was now feasible to travel to resorts for a day or even a week, and not difficult for the newly literate to inscribe a few words on half of one side of a card.

The journeys from the overcrowded towns and cities to rural beauty spots or seaside resorts were in most cases made by train. The picture postcard united the two forms of communication. It partly explains why the growth of railway travel and the practice of writing were so closely associated during the coming of mass education. More generally there is a sense in which trains can be used as a proxy for literacy. Whereas we have only fragmentary evidence about the essentially private activity of writing a letter, we are better informed about the identity and intentions of those who exploited the much more public mode of connecting people over distance. The first railway journeys were too expensive for all but those on business or accustomed to travelling for enjoyment. Except in domestic emergencies and occasional family excursions, the impact of the new form of transport on the rest of society was confined to the provision of comparatively well-paid jobs for which literacy was a *de facto* requirement. Cheap fares, the occasional use of railways to get to work and the large-scale employment for recreation had to wait until the very end of the nineteenth century. So it was for the skills that the schoolteachers laboured to instil in their pupils. Although stamps cost less than railway tickets, the inadequacy of the grasp of the newly educated on the task of writing, as distinct from copying, similarly delayed their exploitation of the delights of mass communication.

The letter in its flimsy envelope, the postcard with its brief inscription, conveyed much of the nature of change in the spread of reading and writing. As with the engagement with the printed word more generally, correspondence was not the invention of the era of mass education, but it did undergo a qualitative and quantitative change as the volume of potential users multiplied and technical innovations were made in response to growing demand. A new dimension of privacy was made possible as individuals transmitted their secrets to each other over long distances, and families established lines of contact beyond the confines of their villages and neighbourhoods. A new element of standardization was introduced as the labouring poor were required to conform their communication practices to the temporal and procedural disciplines of the post office. The postcards home celebrated a new sense of control over the realities of life as an increasing proportion of the labouring population were able to abstract themselves from the struggle for existence and devote themselves to spending marginal surpluses of cash. And the use of this specialized form of correspondence reflected both the growing variety of applications of literacy and the unpremeditated appropriation of the labours of the teachers for the pleasures of the poor.

5

The Boundaries of Literacy

Authority

During the eighteenth and the nineteenth centuries, literacy moved from the periphery to the centre of the political process. The modern nation state saw the creation of an educated society as both an expression and a condition of its authority.[1] The provision of mass schooling was a measure of its capacity to reach into the home of every inhabitant, and the work of the schoolteacher would ensure that every member of the rising generation would identify with the new order. The pattern of reform and reaction varied from country to country as spatial and ideological frontiers were drawn and redrawn during the upheavals set in motion by the Enlightenment and the French Revolution. Increasingly, however, instruction in the basic skills of formal communication became a common cause. The shifting balance of power between reformers and conservatives, and between secular and religious forces, affected the scope of the curriculum and the mode of its delivery, but after 1815, it was almost impossible to find any agency engaged in the struggle to control the emerging societies that was indifferent or hostile to the ambition of mass education. Indeed the more vigorous the reaction to the revolutionary era, the greater tended to be the concentration on the essentials of reading and writing, learned through and in preparation for the literature of spiritual improvement. The constant factor was the topic itself. Modernity was not so much about education as about arguing about education.

At the centre of the debate was the desire to deploy the skills and artefacts of literacy against the fissiparous tendencies of the age. Mass communication was seen as the most effective means of overcoming the divisions which had crippled nations in the past and the obstacles to national integration which the future threatened to create. Ruling elites came to believe that if they were to defend or enlarge their external boundaries, they must pay systematic attention to the boundaries within their countries. The walls were constructed in different ways. In the countries seeking to rebuild themselves after humiliation by Napoleon's armies, it was the rigidities of feudal and corporate powers which needed to be dissolved.[2] The caste-like structures had to be broken down and through a controlled programme of instruction a new order established which would be fluid yet hierarchical. The better-educated elites would be integrated with the national enterprise, and those receiving more basic instruction would share in the cause of their superiors. In countries where the encounter with Napoleon had been less traumatic, there was an equally urgent search for a means of preventing the forces of change from erecting new barriers against spiritual and secular authority. Movements for reform still resonating with the clamour of the French Revolution and gaining fresh strength from increasing economic and social dislocation threatened to deepen the chasm between the rulers and the ruled. Religious and political leaders had a common interest in finding new ways of reaching the minds and the hearts of the common people. As we saw in chapter 3, church and state for most part played complementary roles in a joint enterprise during the fraught decades of the early nineteenth century.

Mass literacy and the modern state existed in a relationship of mutual dependency. If it seemed increasingly impossible to establish the infrastructural power of the ruling order without a population that had learned to read and write, so also the provision of systematic education required the creation of a stable and integrated national bureaucracy. A case in point was late eighteenth-century Poland. The annexation of substantial territory by her neighbours in 1772 provoked a determined campaign to educate the population in order to promote cohesion and patriotism in what was left of the country. All the school reforms, however, were wrecked when the country lost its independence altogether in 1794.[3] Belgian literacy was similarly set back by the territorial disruption of the Revolutionary Wars.[4] It is possible to identify a range of countries which expressed the same determination as Prussia to promote mass instruction as a defence against future external threats. From the Iberian and Italian peninsulas in the south to the Baltic states and Russia, voices were raised in favour of national regeneration through the classroom, but in most instances internal divisions were too deep and central authority too weak to permit the full realization of such ambitions for a century or more. There was indeed something of a knock-on effect across nineteenth-century Europe. Just as the larger German kingdoms overhauled their education systems in the aftermath of defeat by the centralized French revolutionary state, so their subsequent growth and integration provoked reaction amongst envious or apprehensive neighbours. Denmark, for instance, renewed its commitment to universal instruction as tensions increased on its southern borders in the 1860s.[5]

The diversion of national resources to the creation of a literate society was a powerful but at the same time indirect and indeterminate exercise of central authority. The most optimistic reformer had to accept that the consequences of innovation would not be visible for decades, and that the vehicles of progress had to be the citizens themselves, not their masters. In the short term, integration through literacy represented a shift from adults to children as the principal focus of public engagement with the attitudes and behaviour of the population at large. The increasing tendency to insert overt patriotic messages into the ABCs and primers supplied to inspected schools constituted both an advance and a retreat by the state.[6] The hope that the pupil would internalize values which would guide its footsteps throughout the remainder of its life was accompanied by a recognition that an immediate, effective intervention in the outlook of the current adult population was beyond the capacity of government, no matter how determined. In revolutionary France, where many of the modern educational aspirations were codified, if not implemented, the enthusiasm for schooling increased as support from the citizens diminished. From 1794 onwards the microcosm of the classroom supplanted the totality of society as the laboratory for the future.[7] It was hoped that the pupils would grow up freed of the superstition and ignorance which had constrained their parents' generation, but there could be no guarantee of success. In an era in which profit was everywhere coming to be dependent on patient investment, the elementary school represented the longest of all the gambles on the future.

The combination of assertion and withdrawal, of optimism and anxiety was reflected in the confused development of controls over the ways in which the newly literate made use of their skills. The successors of the French Convention, whether republican or royalist, liberal or conservative, retained a dual commitment to education and censorship. The Revolution itself had been summoned into being by an explosion of unlicensed and licentious journalism, and subsequent governments took care to ensure that the increasing number of trained readers could not enjoy the same opportunities for political freethinking. A Napoleonic decree of 1810 limited the number of authorized newspapers and printers in each Department. Paris was allocated eighty printers, which remained the figure over the decades as mass literacy was established. The Restoration broadened the field of book censorship from political to more general social and moral issues, and although there was some relaxation under Louis Philippe, the full panoply of restriction was reintroduced by Napoleon III in 1852.[8] Even the declining race of *colporteurs* was once more harassed, required now to seek authorization from the prefect to sell carefully vetted reading material to peasant readers.[9] In this aspect of the spread of literacy as in others, the secular and spiritual authorities reinforced each other's efforts, with the Catholic church receiving protection from the state's censors, and further extending its own index of banned literature.

The Third Republic waited until it was secure in its existence before it finally swept away the edifice of controls in 1880 and 1881, just before elementary education was made fully compulsory. A similar reluctance to trust the product of the official classroom was commonplace in nineteenth-century Europe. Few governments were wholly at ease with the implications of their commitment to universal literacy. The more authoritarian regimes took care to ensure that controls over reading matter encased the slow growth in the numbers able to read. Nonetheless it may be argued that the belated cessation of censorship in France was more representative of the direction of change than the cycle of repression that preceded it. In this respect, the British state was the harbinger of the future. It too was initially reluctant to permit an already substantial reading public to engage freely with the printed word in the fraught aftermath of the Napoleonic Wars. Just as the first serious proposals for establishing a national system of elementary education were being discussed, it passed a Publications Act which imposed security bonds on printers and increased the tax on newspapers in a further attempt to price them out of the hands of poor readers.[10] It was advisable to 'deprive the lowest classes of all political information', argued the Lord Privy Seal, for he 'saw no good to be derived to the country from having statesmen at the loom and politicians at the spinning jenny'.[11]

However, printing presses were now too widely available to be properly controlled, and radical politicians too immersed in a tradition of free speech to be intimidated by laws which juries were often reluctant to enforce.[12] James Watson, born in the last year of the eighteenth century, at a time when 'there were no cheap books, no cheap newspapers or periodicals, no Mechanics' Institutions to facilitate the acquisition of knowledge.'[13] As a young man he moved to Leeds, and was immediately immersed in the clandestine world of the unstamped press:

> It was in the autumn of 1818 that I first became acquainted with politics and theology. Passing along Briggate one evening, I saw at the corner of Union Court a bill, which stated that the Radical Reformers held their meetings in a room in that court. Curiosity prompted me to go and hear what was going on. I found them reading Wooler's *Black Dwarf*, Carlile's *Republican*, and Cobbett's *Register*.[14]

Evading the punitive tax rendered the press both the vehicle and the object of political protest. The journalists and compositors were endlessly resourceful. Watson's shop sold its illegal items 'by clockwork' whereby purchasers moved a hand on a dial and the invisible vendor dropped down the newspaper as if by machine. The police were always too slow, the magistrates never punitive enough. Despite numerous court appearances and three spells in prison, Watson continued to meet the rising demand of an increasingly militant readership. The struggle reached its climax during the Reform Bill crisis when a campaign of disobedience against the legislation not only led to an outpouring of radical commentary but also provided a rallying point for the forces opposed to the crumbling old regime.[15] The reform of the franchise which took place in 1832 led to a reconsideration of the state's relationship to mass communication. A year later it made its first investment in elementary education, and in 1836, as Watson later recorded, 'after sending 600 persons to prison, they were compelled to reduce the price of the stamp from fourpence to one penny.'[16]

The introduction of the Penny Post at the end of the decade was a further sacrifice of public revenue in the cause of increasing the use of literacy and the demand for the services of the schoolteachers. The decision to abandon overt controls reflected three considerations. Firstly, the middle classes had been secured to the constitution by the first Reform Act, and thereafter governments were less exercised about the prospect of revolution, despite further outbreaks of violence before and during the Chartist movement. Secondly, the costs of 'taxes on knowledge' had been discovered to exceed the benefits.[17] They made the radical press not only the medium but also the cause of insubordination, dramatizing the repression and the impotence of governments and dissolving the divisions of interest and outlook amongst their enemies. Thirdly, market forces were found to be a natural ally of the political order. Whereas the French state looked initially towards parallel hierarchies, such as the Catholic church, to help it contain the consequences of mass literacy, the world's first industrial nation turned to capitalism.[18] If the appetite for news could be satisfied not by small groups of politically motivated journalists but by large-scale entrepreneurs, radical writers could be disciplined and radical readers diverted towards less seditious pathways. The task was to direct the curiosity about the wider world into a culture of consumption rather than protest. This was achieved through the development in the middle decades of the nineteenth century of the Sunday newspaper, which combined national and international news with the sensational and salacious reporting of crimes and natural disasters which had long formed the staple of street literature.

In the British tradition of policing the consequences of literacy, the epochal event took place just after the final abolition of the newspaper stamp in 1855, when Edward Lloyd, founder of the largest-circulation newspaper of the second half of the nineteenth century, paid £10,000 for the country's first rotary press. The state correctly calculated that no proprietor would imperil so large an investment by courting prosecution for treason or blasphemy. 'Capitalists', observed a Parliamentary Select Committee, 'will not embark on an illegal proceeding.'[19] The papers, particularly Lloyd's rival publication, *Reynold's News*, might be critical of governments, but from within a liberal consensus. Journalists were controlled by their semi-monopolistic employers, who in turn were constrained by the acceptable sanctions of the libel and bankruptcy laws. Furthermore, mass circulations would permit a safer mode of consumption. The inflation of price by taxation had forced collective purchase, turning every act of reading into a seditious meeting.[20] With the market free to drive costs down towards the pockets of individual working men, the papers could be perused in the privacy of the home. Distance was placed between one reader and another, and between deciphering and debating the news. Whatever its content, information absorbed at the kitchen table or on the front doorstep during the more sharply defined leisure time was less inflammatory than when it was read aloud to the company of a public house or artisan workshop.

Even in countries where the concept of free speech had to be imported like the steam engine, reluctant moves were eventually made towards the market as a disciplinary agency. Spain's systems fluctuated wildly between freedom and repression as regimes bearing liberal ideas were established and overthrown in the nineteenth century.[21] In the more consistently authoritarian Russia the early engagement of both the church and the state with the reading practices of the mass of the population was everywhere repressive. A centralized Chief Administrator of Censorship was established in 1828 to assert authority over both the content of newspapers and books and the mechanics of publishing.[22] The Orthodox church fulfilled its long-held ambition of censoring all publications for their spiritual content in 1839, and public censors imposed pre-publication controls over journalism and *luboks*. But between 1865 and 1905 there was a gradual relaxation of interference in material produced for the small but growing number who could read to themselves or their neighbours.[23] As elsewhere, it was partly a matter of the increasing physical difficulty of policing a market continually enlarged by the labours of the schoolteachers, and partly of a growing confidence in the responsibility of publishers, reinforced by the penalties of the civil courts. The state slowly and often inconsistently recognized that it was not strong enough to censor with adequate efficiency, or to risk permanently alienating the progressively self-conscious entrepreneurs of print. Across Europe, the sheer volume of mass communication posed increasingly difficult questions to the ruling order. As the official classrooms trained more and more readers, overt controls appeared either impractical or counter-productive or both. The most direct application of reading and writing illustrated the problem. In the unsettled years after 1815, every government opened the mail of suspected subversives as a matter of course. Even Britain engaged in epistolary espionage, although unlike most of its neighbours it was too embarrassed to give formal recognition to its practices.[24] But as versions of the Penny Post were introduced, so comprehensive surveillance became impossible. On the eve of the First World War, twenty-five billion items of mail a year, or fifty thousand items a minute, were circulating within and across the boundaries of Europe.[25] The readers and writers were outrunning the censors. Only in time of war would the state be empowered to revive all its former controls.

The Bolshevik seizure of power during the First World War was in this context as in many others both a throwback to the late eighteenth century and a precursor of a new twentieth-century aspiration of total control. The embattled regime shared the Jacobins' dream of the classroom as the crucible of a new society. Lunacharsky, the commissar of education until 1929, subscribed to the words of the last great product of the Enlightenment, Karl Marx: 'On the one hand, a change of social circumstances is required to establish a proper system of education. On the other hand, a proper system of education is required to bring about a change of social circumstances.'[26] The increasing dependence of the last tsarist governments on economic development to sustain educational growth and contain its disruptive effects was thrown into reverse. Popular commercial literature was banned, and stocks left over from the pre-revolutionary era were destroyed.[27] Lenin, the son of a school inspector, lacked ideological and practical confidence in the capacity of the market to deliver the didactic discipline the revolution now required. Instead, in the midst of total national dislocation he embarked on the twin paths of complete censorship and immediate mass instruction. The

Decree of Illiteracy of 19 December 1919 imposed criminal sanctions on any illiterate up to the age of fifty who refused to study, and on any literate who refused to teach. The following June the All-Russian Extraordinary Commission for the Eradication of Illiteracy was established to oversee the campaign.[28]

The immediate consequence of attempting to transform the educational system in the midst of a civil war was to depress the levels of attainment well below those being achieved during the later years of the tsarist regime.[29] As had happened in the 1790s, expectations of instant transformation were everywhere frustrated by administrative disorder and widespread material shortcomings. During the 1920s, however, a new model of popular instruction and communication emerged. The aspiration of a cultural transformation of every peasant household was crushed between the need of the Kremlin for political coercion and the hostility of parents and professional teachers to the abandonment of traditional methods of dictation, memorization and rote learning.[30] The outcome was the least imaginative pedagogy allied to the least liberal use of such literacy as was acquired. Stalin finally managed to force all children into school at just the moment when he stamped out the last vestiges of free expression. At the same time he began to perfect the techniques used by Lenin to such effect in the civil war of deploying non-literary modes of mass propaganda.[31] The Bolsheviks, soon to be followed yet more effectively by the fascist regimes in Italy and Germany, learned how to use the inventions of the new century to solve the problems of the old. The dark forests of oral communication, which nineteenth-century governments had sought to open up with the written word, were now invaded by devices which bypassed print altogether. As some kind of peace was achieved, so the technological developments of the era, especially the cinema, were pressed into the service of the totalitarian state.

In the field of politics, as in every other, it is far easier to delineate the hopes for mass literacy than to identify the consequences. And it is much less difficult to recognize the failure of aspiration than to locate its success. The only citizens of the developing states whose outlook was clearly transformed by popular literacy were those employed to disseminate it. Schoolteachers rapidly gained a sense of professional identity which became an influential presence in the long struggle to construct an effective system of instruction. They curtailed the freedom of politicians to remake at will the curriculum of the inspected classroom, and increasingly resisted the attempts of parents to intervene directly in the conduct of the lessons. In countries where the lower reaches of the middle class were still excluded from the political nation, their collective grievances spilled over into direct action, most notably in the continental revolutions of 1848 and in the movements which led up to the Russian

Revolution in 1917. In 1849, the Prussian monarch Frederick William blamed 'all the misery of the past year' on a profession which was the most advanced and hence the most troublesome in Europe.[32] The teachers had become and were to remain marginal figures in the modernizing societies, operating, as Seregny writes of Russian schoolmasters, 'within the cramped interstices of traditional power and privilege'.[33] Their status as credentialized public officials contrasted sharply with their pay as skilled artisans, leaving them straddling the increasingly well-defined boundary between mental and manual labour.[34] The older professions looked down upon men, and still more so upon women, whose education had only lasted two or three years longer than that given to those they were now teaching, and whose prospects of financial advancement were negligible. At the same time, the communities from which the pupils were drawn regarded with suspicion the newly elevated peasants' sons and daughters whose authority was derived from a distant central bureaucracy.[35] As a result the teachers were both committed to the bureaucratic state and deeply resentful of its failure properly to reward those who were supposed to be central to its creation.[36]

Once the focus moves from the teachers to the taught, the picture becomes less clear. Those on the left were no less guilty than those on the right of oversimplifying and overestimating the impact of learning to read and write. On the one hand it became apparent that systematic instruction conveyed through an increasingly explicit body of patriotic literature did not necessarily deliver the docile and deferential populations that had been anticipated. 'The history of Europe', concludes A. K. Pugh, 'would seem to suggest that even functional literacy is not a very effective instrument of control, at least not if that means conserving the old order.'[37] Nowhere was this more evident than in Germany, where the subordination of literacy to nation-building was most transparent, and where the challenge from organized Marxism was eventually most powerful. The only direct connection between the schoolrooms and the authority of the state the lay in the armies which achieved unification between 1864 and 1870. Napoleon had been the first to discover that literate recruits made better soldiers, and his revengeful enemy was the first to embody that insight in a fully educated fighting force.[38] At the same time, the belief that endowing the mass of the population with the tools for critical inquiry would erode every structure of inherited privilege was also frustrated by experience.[39] Neither across Europe nor within any given country was there a simple correlation between rising literacy rates and increasing political militancy.[40] The only common terminus of the mass literacy campaigns of the later nineteenth century was the First World War, where entire armies on both sides of the conflict could read why they were dying for their country. It might be noted that the least literate combatant, Russia, was the first to disintegrate, although the critical factor was the weakness of the state, which could neither educate its population, nor feed and equip its troops in the field.

The problem for the historian is that literacy was everywhere present in the development of modern democratic processes, yet nowhere acted as an autonomous agent of change.[41] The outcome of the education systems which were supported in different ways by both poor parents and increasingly affluent governments must be sought not in terms of stability versus revolution, but rather in the ways in which the boundaries of political action were redrawn in this period. From the perspective of those investing public funds in elementary schools, simple indoctrination could never be effective. However explicit the textbooks on national identity and history, the huge classes of inattentive young children were unlikely to absorb messages powerful enough to counter every other lesson taught by their family and neighbourhood, and permanent enough to guide their footsteps throughout the remainder of their lives. Instead, change was effected as literate adults engaged in narrower and more disciplined forms of interaction with their rulers. The shift from oral to written modes of discourse widened the gap between street theatre and electoral participation, between recreation and citizenship and between one voter and another. The goal was the individual political consumer, who communicated only with the information written and disseminated by educated superiors. Attitudes were formed in private, away from the influence of conversation and debate, and were expressed in the silent ritual of the ballot.

In 1865, Napoleon III proclaimed that, 'in the country of universal suffrage, every citizen should be able to read and write.'[42] In France, as was to be the case in most European countries, the vote had been granted before literacy had become universal. Even in Germany, where the signatures of grooms were approaching 100 per cent when Bismarck established a form of democracy, there remained older voters who displayed the shortcomings of the educational system in earlier decades. The same was true in Britain, which delayed universal manhood suffrage until 1918, just after the illiteracy scores in the marriage registers had fallen below 1 per cent. At the outset of the Second Empire, more than half the men entitled to vote could not write their names.[43] Napoleon III sought to rectify the problem, but he had no intention of ceding genuine power to the products of the elementary schools. The aspiration of the democratizing ruling classes is conveyed in the distinction between Robert Lowe's much misquoted injunction as the Second Reform Act was passed to 'educate our masters', and his actual words to his fellow MPs, 'I believe it absolutely necessary that you should prevail upon our future masters to learn their letters.' His was a deeply patronizing vision, which sought not a single political culture, in which all participants were equally equipped to challenge each other's authority, but rather a mass electorate with just enough command over the written word to receive the messages transmitted to it. The spoken word retained its place in the form of the public meeting, but this event was now encased in print, which both advertised and reproduced the orations. The audience listened rather than participated, and read the speaker's words, not their own, in the next morning's papers.

Protest

Amongst those seeking to challenge the established order, the lines of demarcation were more complex, but no less real. The particular impact of mass literacy on forms and outcomes of protest depended on interactions between multiplying categories of formal communication and a wide range of political, commercial and structural forces. There can thus be no simple argument that the lessons in the classroom were a precondition of incorporation or of rebellion, that they necessarily promoted either accommodation or alienation. The continuing need to share the scarce resource of print sustained forms of sociability throughout the long struggle to obtain democratic freedoms. Newspapers continued to be read and discussed in pubs, clubs and cabarets. Even where nominal literacy was becoming commonplace, audiences had to be addressed more by the spoken than the written word. No aspiring leader could succeed without at least a basic grasp of the skills of oratory. But increasingly it was impossible to make a career in any kind of collective body without a sophisticated command of the techniques of written communication. For much of the nineteenth century, trade unions were more bureaucratic organizations than the companies they struggled against. However opposed some political movements were to the consequences of industrialization, they were as dependent on the technological infrastructure of the modern economy as any sector of the ruling order.[44] Although correspondence and occasional documentary records had played a part in the eighteenth-century artisan organizations such as friendly societies and *compagnonnages*, the bulk of their activities had been conducted through ritual and various forms of conviviality. At the centre of the institutionalization of protest during the following century was the expanding and diversifying employment of the pen. In order to entrench and extend their influence, men sat down to write, and where necessary print agendas, minutes, financial accounts, rule-books, membership forms, blacklists, contribution and claim forms, placards, public addresses and collective agreements. Members were kept in touch with each other and with conditions of trade through regular newsletters, and where possible, newspapers were started to extend the organization's sphere of influence. And always there were letters. The Scottish miners' leader Alexander Macdonald calculated that he wrote 17,000 over a seven-year period in the late 1860s.[45]

The culture of print embraced every member of these organizations. Once a grouping of artisans moved beyond a handful of workshops, once a political movement survived the initial burst of energy, then all those involved had to develop some kind of relationship with the printed word. A common activity was the formation of libraries for the instruction, and frequently entertainment, of the members.[46] The nascent social, political and industrial bodies themselves became agents of the ideology of literacy. This was of particular importance in more developed European countries during the second third of the nineteenth century, when the state had yet to achieve either an acceptance of its own legitimacy or a monopoly in the provision of schooling. Teaching young workers their letters seemed in every sense a practical contribution to the realization of the wider aspirations of movements organized from below. In Prussia, for instance, the *Arbeiterbildungsvereine*, or working men's education clubs, played an increasingly important role in elementary instruction during the formative period between the 1830s and 1860s. If they did not themselves determine the trend of rising literacy, their periodic surges of militancy had a discernible impact on variations within it.[47]

Beneath the attempts at mass instruction, there was an increasing division of labour. If large-scale, long-term organization was dependent on the spread of literacy, the command of reading and especially of writing possessed by school-leavers fell far short of the kind of skills required to operate these bureaucracies. A new figure emerged, the organizational secretary, at first part-time and unpaid, and later permanent and salaried. This was an individual who partly through natural aptitude but mostly through industrious self-education succeeded in crossing the divide from nominal possession to assured practice. Twentieth-century labour organizations eventually became credentialized employers with formal examinations to determine entry and promotion. Their more primitive forerunners relied instead on the traditional apprenticeship model, with the aspiring official learning by imitation and experiment, beginning with simple tasks such as brief letters and committee minutes and culminating in sophisticated and nuanced literary engagements with employers, fellow workers and the general public. In their competence and confidence in formal communication they were separated from most of those on whose behalf they were working. These self-improving, self-sacrificing officials were critical to the maintenance of protest over space and time, but as their organizations grew in size and lengthened in history, so there was a constant tendency for them to place the demands of print and paper in front of the immediate interests of their members. The maintenance of communication systems became ends in themselves, absorbing increasing funds, and diverting energies away from more direct forms of confrontation. As with the state, so with its enemies, the written word was an agency of centralizing control, privileging those with access to printing presses over those without, prioritizing formal agitation over spontaneous protest.

The writers of minutes and agendas were also set apart from the female half of the labouring poor, whose marriage register scores were moving rapidly towards parity wherever national school systems had been introduced. Nothing did more to differentiate functional literacy between the sexes than the fact that through their conditions of employment men found it so much easier than women to create the organizational contexts in which the shortcomings of elementary education could be overcome. The union meetings and political committees were an extension of workplace sociability, combining alcohol with the written word, including those who could adapt to the more formal ways of collective behaviour, excluding those whose interactions were confined to oral intercourse in the household and the street. There are few recorded instances of husbands and wives giving each other the confidence to experiment with their half-learned, half-forgotten literary skills. Lovers might exchange valentines or even correspond when separated, but marriage was rarely conceived as a process of mutual intellectual instruction. The structures of support and encouragement lay outside the home, and for the most part, a full-time job was a condition of entry. Even those few married women who found regular work in the industrializing economies were unlikely to have the surplus time or energy for extracurricular reading and writing. They were still required to manage the domestic arena whilst their menfolk went out to enlarge their public domain.

The most likely prospect of the entire family engaging with literacy and protest was when the developing organizations succeeded in integrating a more sharply defined sense of the political or the industrial with the full literary appetite of the recently educated. Even at times of revolutionary crisis, such as France in the late 1780s, or England and Germany in the 1830s and 1840s, newly activated writers and purchasers moved endlessly between news, polemic, satire, sensation and fiction. However as the media of protest gained a permanent identity, so they had to respond to the entrepreneurial publishers seeking to exploit the same expanding market by means of the same technologies of mass communication. Either the journalism retreated to the narrow interests of political bodies and trade unions and lost what prospects it had of monopolizing the attention of their own membership and of making any appeal to wider audiences, or it exposed itself to direct competition from better-resourced and often better-written commercial papers.[48] Only in particular circumstances, such as Imperial Germany, did a combination of strength and persecution permit the creation of a mass-circulation press which broadly responded to the recreational life of its readers without debasing the substance of the political struggle.[49]

It was a paradox of print that it was deployed to give stability to protest, but that only at times of crisis and repression could the fissures threatened by the use of literacy be fully overcome. When all kinds of writing were by definition an act of rebellion, then the gap between communication and protest, and between the communicators and the protesters, disappeared. As working men succeeded in exploiting the potential of mass literacy to institutionalize their resistance to other centres of power, so the dangers of overspecialization of function and communication increased. Time was both the prize and the penalty of the formalization of collective activity. The more manual workers learned how to use their education to make permanent their protest, the greater the prospect of inward-looking officials and the larger the opportunity for commercial forces to translate politics into a form of consumption. Yet if the most vibrant relationship between literacy and protest occurred in short-lived periods of intense persecution, it was then that the power of print was at its most fragile. The less certain the state was of its future, the more imperilled were its enemies, whose past thoughts and activities were stored in documents. The anonymity of oral agitation was a strength as well as a weakness. The trail of signed articles and handwritten papers was easier for the police and courts to follow. In Spain for instance, those of the rural poor who were prevented by material deprivation from gaining an education could not play a full part in the revolutionary movements of the early twentieth century. But when the battle was lost, they were protected from the full vengeance of Franco by the fact of their illiteracy.[50]

Language

The transition from spoken to written modes of discourse everywhere raised the question of language. Across much of Europe, the intervention by the state in the provision of mass literacy was driven by an ambition to overcome the linguistic divisions within their territories. In the eighteenth century, dialects and subaltern languages had been objects of intellectual fascination rather than a political danger.[51] From 1789 onwards however, the way in which populations spoke, the medium of their reading and their writing, were increasingly seen as integral to the development of the modern nation. Not only was it no longer acceptable to have a German-speaking monarch of Britain, or a French-speaking king of Prussia, it was also now critical that every peasant, every street-sweeper, was capable of communicating with every other peasant and street-sweeper within the country's borders, and with all those in authority over them. Under the influence of Fichte, language was coming to be seen as the highest manifestation of human rationality and the prime responsibility of the political structures which were emerging from the turmoil set in motion by the termination of the French *ancien régime*. A common tongue at once facilitated and justified the emergence of the modern state.[52]

As with other aspects of educational reform in Europe, the ambition was first codified by the French revolutionary governments, although, as with their school programme in general, little more was achieved than a recognition of the problem. The main source of information was the official survey undertaken by Abbé Grégoire in 1790. This established that most of the population of France spoke and read in tongues other than French.[53] Only about one Department in six was fully conversant with the language of the shifting cast of rulers in Paris. Six million men could not understand French at all, another 6,000,000 preferred to use one of at least four foreign languages and thirty distinct dialects, and probably no more than 3,000,000 used the language of government in their daily lives, of whom no more than a half could write it.[54] The persistence on the periphery of the country of Celtic, German, Catalan, Italian and Flamand, together with Occitan in Provence and all the versions of patois, was seen to be an obstacle to the destruction of the pre-revolutionary system of inherited privilege, and to the creation of a cohesive and powerful national culture.[55] Tolerance for linguistic diversity declined as the Revolution progressed, until finally in 1794 the Law of Second Thermidor decreed that all public and private acts within the boundaries of France must be conducted in French.

Elsewhere in Europe, the same difficulties were encountered. In this respect, as in the provision of literacy in general, the Scandinavians showed a precocious concern. The 1686 Church Edict of Sweden, the earliest effective piece of school legislation, was promoted in part as a means of standardizing speech in former Danish territories.[56] In turn, the Danes pushed their language into the areas which they continued to control.[57] As the boundaries of much of the rest of the Continent were drawn and redrawn during and after the French Revolutionary Wars, so the same aspirations were formulated. Prussia was one of the first of the emerging states to integrate language with national identity, and from

1830 onwards embarked on a vigorous campaign to spread German throughout its territory, especially at the expense of Polish.[58] The government in Vienna also attempted to promote German throughout its vast domains, but eventually was forced to accept the predominance of Hungarian in the east.[59] Once it escaped the direct control of Austria, the government in Budapest embarked on its own campaign of forced Magyarization at the expense of the minority languages under its control.[60] The result by 1890 was that the Magyars, together with German-speakers, had the highest levels of literacy, with other national groups trailing in their wake, the small Ruthenian minority not yet able to reach double figures.[61] Of all the states called into being during the nineteenth century, Italy faced the greatest difficulties. At unification in 1870, no more than 2 or 3 per cent of the population could understand the Italian of the Tuscan region, which became the new country's official language.[62] An official campaign to unite the regions and diffuse the skills for communicating between them made slow progress.[63] Forty-five years later, the illiteracy rate in Calabria was still twice the national average, and remained a presence in the countryside into the 1950s.[64]

The chosen instrument of linguistic integration was the elementary schoolteacher. The failure of the French Revolution's attempt to achieve uniformity through decree was an indication of the limitations of direct control. However insistent a state was on the language in which its affairs should be conducted, adult men and women were not going to abandon overnight the ways in which they spoke to each other. Governments could best reach their populations through the youngest members. The only alternative captive age-group were the young men conscripted into the armies of nineteenth-century Europe. The newly united Italy went so far as to compel recruits who failed to learn to read and write to undergo a further five years' military service.[65] The pedagogy of literacy everywhere stressed interrelation of reading, writing and reasoning. The mode of communication was intimately related to its content. Nothing would do more to dramatize the break from the culture of the home and the street than a reconstruction of the child's language. As instruction in reading and writing was largely conducted through speech, how the child sounded its letters was an immediate concern of the school. Even in England where the issues were ones of accent, syntax and vocabulary rather than complete dialects or languages, teachers were from the outset trained to pay close attention to pronunciation in literacy lessons. Children who merely reproduced the speech patterns of their parents would remain trapped within the moral and intellectual environment of the family and the neighbourhood. 'Hence the necessity', explained an English textbook in 1834, 'that individuals conform in their habits of speech to the rules prescribed by general usage, or, more properly speaking, to the custom of the educated and intellectual classes of society.'[66]

If France was the first modern state to define the ambition of homogeneity, it was also the first to measure its frustration.[67] A series of surveys carried out during the nineteenth century charted the resistance of old tongues to new methods of instruction. In 1863, three decades after Guizot had established the basis of a national education system, French was still a foreign tongue for a fifth of the population.[68] A third of all conscripts in 1867 did not normally express themselves in the language of the country for which they were required to lay down their lives.[69] Outside the enclaves of Brittany or Languedoc or the Pyrenees, patois still retained its hold across broad areas of the country, with pupils paying at best lip service to the demands of their teachers before resuming their accustomed modes of discourse as they went about the real business of their lives. As late as 1893, with the elementary school system a model of centralized control, French remained a minority tongue in as many as a quarter of the *communes*.[70] The problem was not confined to the older generations whose schooling was now a distant memory. A century after the original revolutionary edict, out of 4,000,000 children aged between seven and fourteen, 500,000 spoke no French at all, and another 1,500,000 could manage some conversation with their teachers in the official language, but were unable to write it.[71] France was unique only in its calibration of the problem. Nowhere in Europe was it possible to translate the rising graphs of nominal literacy into increasing levels of linguistic conformity.

The persistence of the barriers to communication was a reflection of the widespread gap between the *histoire événementielle* of educational reform, and the *longue durée* of cultural change. It was partly a matter of generational lag, as the investment in a cohort of children took decades to show a return across the adult population as a whole. It was partly a matter of the plasticity of pupils, who were perfectly capable of humouring the teacher's obsession with how they spoke in the classroom and ignoring it altogether once outside the school gates.[72] In the Hungarian Empire, for instance, the children from minority nationalities were compelled to parrot fragments of Magyar which were never used or usable.[73] It was partly a matter of the slow spread of complementary communication systems, and the persistence of functioning regional economies where the native language remained a necessary qualification for advancement and where local variations in employment patterns and prosperity continued to influence the spread of schooling.[74] And it was partly a matter of the latent capacity of parents and their communities to obstruct the intentions of reformers and bureaucrats in distant capitals. The mother's tongue remained the mother tongue, no matter what the curriculum prescribed. In regions where the task of national integration was most urgent, literacy and linguistic conformity were opposing rather than complementary objectives for much of the nineteenth century. The more the state insisted on instruction in what was for the pupils a foreign language, the lower were the levels of attendance or of successful learning.[75] Whereas the schools rarely flourished in spite of indigenous hostility, a well-resourced minority could often promote its difference through informal mechanisms of elementary instruction. In areas of northern Sweden for instance, where the local language was Finnish, the official measures of literacy in the later nineteenth century significantly understated the capacity of the population to read and write.

The passive resistance of parents and pupils became much more effective when it was allied to broader commercial and educational forces. During the first half of the nineteenth century, the Russian government managed to impose effective censorship on Finnish-language publications, but after the Crimean War, the local newspaper industry took advantage of the high levels of reading ability in Finland and burst through the restrictions. Thereafter an indigenous press became the vehicle for national self-assertion, propelling demands equally for full literacy and full independence.[76] It was no more successful in its Polish territories. Such resistance was strengthened when it was allied to older forms of cultural transmission. The Catholic church in France initially welcomed the revolutionary drive to conformity, but as its educational ambitions revived in 1815 it began to give support to local languages which clearly were not about to disappear. Elsewhere, the religious engagement with elementary instruction became the focus of more overt opposition. In Wales, for instance, the Nonconformist denominations promoted both literacy and a national literature in the face of the English Anglican establishment, not only defending but for a time actually enlarging the hold of the Welsh language, which was still the native tongue of over half the population in the 1890s.[77] The Prussian government set out to Germanize its Polish possessions through its new school system, but abandoned the project in the early 1840s in the face of local non-cooperation.[78] At unification language was the single most significant variable in the distribution of literacy.[79] In response, the new state once more deployed the *Volksschule* as an agency for assimilating the Poles into the German language and culture. The attempt provoked mounting hostility, culminating in widespread school strikes in 1906. The demands of parents that their children be taught in their own language were given added weight by the support of the Catholic church in Poland. As had been the case in France, it was concerned that the systematic attack on the children's accustomed communication skills would leave them unable to read the key devotional texts or prepare themselves for communion. It was better to produce fluent Polish Christians than halting German citizens.[80]

In many instances, the state succeeded in entrenching rather than dissolving boundaries. Through the institutionalization of mass instruction, modes of communication increasingly separated nations by class as well as by region. Not only were minority languages downgraded, but the speech patterns of entire sections of the population were stigmatized. Pierre-Jakez Hélias understood the complex emotions of parents as they required their children to learn their letters in the alien French language:

> There was another reason for our parents' resolute desire to have us learn the language of the bourgeoisie, even if it meant being humiliated by 'la vache' and, to a certain extent, repudiating our mother tongue. It was that they themselves were humiliated because they knew nothing but their mother tongue. Every time they had to deal with a city civil-servant and every time they ventured into a city, they were exposed to sly smiles and to jeers of all kinds. They were called 'straw-choppers,' for example, or 'gorse-grinders,' since their language seemed uncouth to those who didn't understand it. Or else they had to put up with charity in the form of pity, which was still more insulting; or they were simply told to go to the devil until they could talk like Christians. Because of that incapacity, the Breton-speaking Bretons were considered simpletons or retarded by tough guys whose intelligence quotient was lower than their own.[81]

Dialect became a measure of exclusion, a vocal representation of the deeply fissured education systems of the period. Successful resistance to linguistic imperialism was frequently bought at the expense of status and opportunity. Children went to school only long enough to learn to be ashamed of the way they and their parents spoke, and returned to communities whose capacity to engage with the proliferating opportunities of the printed word was diminishing by the year. The entrenched illiteracy of the southern Italian countryside, for instance, exacerbated the historic disadvantages of the rural poor, whose only hope of advance was to gain an education for themselves or their children from the American school system.[82] The issue of language gave added resonance to the significance of being 'educated'. Far from integrating society, it deepened the divide between high and low cultures.[83] Whereas governments were frequently forced to give *de facto* or *de jure* recognition to local tongues at the elementary level, they were much more successful in enforcing their policies in secondary and higher education, thus further raising the barriers to upward social mobility. In Belgium, for instance, French ceased to be compulsory after 1830, but children who were taught to read in Flemish found themselves in an educational dead end, cut off from further study in their own language, and from the careers which required formal qualifications.[84]

Remaking boundaries

The attempts to force those learning their letters to join the speech and print communities of their social superiors raises the more general question of how far the spread of mass literacy can be viewed as a one-way process of cultural integration. The most forthright case for this construction of change is made by Eugen Weber in the closing lines of his classic study of the modernization of the French peasantry. Schooling, he concludes, together with a general acceleration of intercourse between town and country, instilled a new rationality in the minds of the rural poor, eradicating the engagement with the supernatural which up to the beginning of the nineteenth century had increasingly separated them from educated society:'by the end of the century, the nature of the magic, and the authority on which it was accepted, had profoundly changed. People still took their cultural norms and assumptions from others; but popular and elite culture had come together again.'[85] Over the last two decades, however, this conception of modernity has been subjected to mounting criticism. The first difficulty, identified in an early response to Weber by Charles Tilly, concerns the portrayal of the enclosed, preliterate rural community.[86] It can be argued that the agrarian societies of the early modern era were neither as isolated, nor as immobile, nor as irrational in their relations with the natural world as nineteenth-century educators and twentieth-century historians have so often supposed. As was stressed in earlier chapters of this survey, the notion of an 'oral tradition' illuminates the mentalities of the literate more than the illiterate. On closer scrutiny, both the communities supposedly untouched by the written word and their associated states of mind dissolve into much more complex structures of communication and belief.

Other analytical building blocks have followed the oral tradition into the dustbin of historiography. An argument most closely associated with Roger Chartier challenges the possibility of any fixed relationship between the printed word and the basic social or economic categories of a population. Distinctions of employment or status cannot organize cultural practice.[87] If the notion of a folk culture defined by the absence of print is untenable, so is that of a popular culture constituted by the absence of control over the means of production.[88] By the same measure, the concept of a single mass culture, defined by the pervasive influence of the capitalist production of consumer goods, conceals more than it illuminates.[89] There are three strands to this critique. The first is the sheer fluidity of cultural practices, nowhere more so than in sections of society where material deprivation imposed a constant need to appropriate and improvise.[90] Daniel Roche captured this world in his characterization of the autobiographical Parisian glazier: 'Ménétra's culture is the culture of everyman: active, syncretic, porous, composed of borrowed and imitated materials. Quilts are not the only example of patchwork art; they are a cultural model.'[91] Eclecticism was at once a necessity and a virtue for the reader of limited means.[92] Nothing and everything fitted. Little was owned but by one means or another, contact could be made with most forms of print, engagements could be made with most categories of cultural production. As with their stomachs so with their minds, poor readers were, to use de Certeau's term, lifelong poachers. Accordingly, quantification in this category of historical research can have only a limited role. Not only are the raw materials of the literacy tables open to question, but so also are the uses which were made of the labours of the schools. Statistical tables of print runs and prices, categorizations of forms and genres, are at best points of departure for an understanding of what was read and by whom.

The second strand lays stress on the indeterminate nature of the reader's response to a text. The notion of appropriation, which is central to this critique, has a double charge.[93] It refers both to the annexation of objects and practices and also to the derivation of meanings from the printed word. The act itself took place in multiple contexts. 'Like writing', observes Roche, 'reading is an act of mediation susceptible to infinite modulations, and nothing in notarial records tells us how to distinguish between fluent reading which presupposes the regular handling of books, the irregular, infrequent deciphering of print often linked with pictures, or reading aloud, shared among several people, which may have been an act of friendship, even love, or sociability.'[94] And even where a given book can be associated with a certain reader in a particular space and time, it is impossible to determine the meanings which will be derived from the words on the page. That language is not an innocent mirror of meaning is scarcely the discovery of the modern age. Ben Brierley, the weaver who became a leading champion of the Lancashire dialect, published in 1881 a dictionary in the name of his fictional alter ego, Ab'O'Th'Yate: 'LANGUAGE', he wrote. 'A thing to screen yo'r thowts at th'back on. A ready means o' tellin lies, and tryin to deceive yo'r Makker.'[95] Neither the intentions of the author nor the interpretation of the reader were transparently represented in the text. The writer could not expect to control, and neither can the historian hope to specify all the material, emotional and imaginative experiences which were brought to bear on the printed word. The mental frame of reference was constructed by many hands and by many practices, amongst which the official teacher and the inspected lesson were rarely dominant.

The third strand concerns the variety of shapes which the quilt of culture might take. To the conventional dichotomy of popular and elite must now be added a range of competing and overlapping boundaries. At various points in this survey, stress has been laid on distinctions of gender, generation, religion, space, and, in the preceding paragraphs, of language within and across frontiers. Some of these oppositions were declining in significance as nominal literacy spread throughout populations, but the trajectory of change was far from uniform. Care must always be taken not to confuse some distant destination with the reality for any temporal cohort of a population, and not to assume that movement could only occur in one direction. In some instances, such as gender, a convergence of marriage register returns masked a widening in significant areas of practice. Elsewhere, as with age, eras of rapid change opened up gaps which remained a reality at least until the Second World War. The relationship between literacy and language was particularly volatile, with the endeavours of state schooling allied to other homogenizing forces in some cases carrying official languages into regions which they had never before penetrated, and in others provoking modern forms of national awakening which scored new lines across territorial maps.

The history of literacy can never again rest comfortably on the monoliths of popular and elite cultures.[96] There is now an agenda of research which concentrates on the varied strategies of appropriation, related but not reducible to the complex inequalities in economic, social and political relations.[97] The boundaries of these strategies shifted over time as the market in print developed, as the distribution of communication skills changed, and as the larger structures of power and opportunity were reconfigured. At every point there were dialogues of meanings. What the newly literate thought they were doing as they took up a book or a pen was neither controlled by nor independent of the purposes designated by authors and educators. The iterations between the inscribed and prescribed significance of using literacy can only be recaptured by a patient historical identification of contexts and responses. But as the old boundaries are reduced to ideological constructions, there remain problems of scope and causation. The move to distance cultural practices from institutionalized inequalities of economic and social power reflects a particular emphasis of concern. The contemporary critique arises from a preoccupation with texts and their consumption. It is alert to the stratified world in which the readers lived, and concerned always to understand how material pressures shaped and constrained the formation of meanings and practices. But the reverse process, how ideologies of literacy may have influenced the development of basic structures of authority, tends not to be addressed with the same energy. As Scribner observes, 'too often the material conditions and the relationships which constitute the basis of human subsistence have been ignored, possibly because they appear too mundane or perhaps for fear of falling into a reductive materialism.'[98] In part this is merely a matter of a research agenda. Historians of the book have a spacious field of study, and cannot be expected to pay full attention to matters such as social mobility, occupational learning, and the constantly shifting relationship between the home, the schoolroom and the workplace. But if the implicit economic determinism of some earlier treatments of popular culture is no longer tenable, neither is the fond assertion of many nineteenth-century ideologues that the world of books represented a mental playground in which rich and poor could disport themselves as equals, without implication for the structural inequalities of industrial capitalism.[99] Some attempt has to be made to understand the full range of interactions, and in particular to clarify whether the relative autonomy of the meanings of literacy varied over time.

The point can be made in the context of the churches, which, as this survey has stressed, were a vital presence in much of the drive to mass literacy. The language and the moral sensibility of religion permeated the discourse surrounding the consequences of reading and writing. The notions of orality as a subordinate system of communication, of self-improvement as a conversion experience, of learning letters as a moral exercise, were directly or indirectly derived from the texts and teachings of the denominations. The more the state fought against the influence of the churches in this field, the more it legitimized the conceptual architecture of pastors and bishops. Literacy became fully secular only when secularization ceased to be a preoccupation of pedagogues and politicians. But church and state shared more than an overlapping frame of reference. By the end of the Napoleonic Wars they had forged a joint aspiration of removing the teaching of literacy from the domestic curriculum, and of separating elementary from further education. During the subsequent century their ambitions were given legislative and institutional forms which exercised a profound influence on the range of meanings and uses which poor readers could attach to their new skills.[100] The dissemination of literacy in modern Europe cannot be separated from the way in which ideological constructions of mass communication were entrenched in systems for reproducing the labour force. As Richard Biernacki has argued of this era, 'culture exercised an influence *of its own* but not completely *by itself*. The power of culture arose from its inscription in material practice.'[101]

It was of course the case that parents and pupils everywhere subverted the intentions of the official curriculum, and that uses were made of the investments of the churchmen and the politicians which confirmed many of their worst fears. Yet in the inescapable matter of earning a living, the victories of the new readers and their families were mostly negative. Absolute control was resisted, but alternative structures of power and opportunity were rarely constructed. For most boys and almost all girls, the first encounters with the written word had no perceptible relevance to their occupational futures, and as adults, a determined programme of reading and writing was usually an escape from, rather than an encounter with their struggle to maintain their family economies. Much the most common encounter with print by the newly literate was in the realm of fiction.[102] This fact has directed the attention of historians to the breakdown of the division between oral and written, and between popular and elite cultures, and to the significance of the indeterminate responses to the written word. But the boundary between fiction and non fiction, between literacy for play and literacy for work, was itself a consequence of an institutionalized and deeply divided conception of the function of literacy. In this sense the old dichotomies lingered long into the twentieth century, not so much shaping as disabling the possibilities of written communication. Not until the systems of occupational progression and recruitment began to become linked with all levels of education, not until poor readers started to find the time, space and money to become independent consumers of literature, could the real potential of reading and writing for eroding inherited inequalities of wealth, status and power begin to be realized.

Notes

Chapter 1   The Rise of Mass Literacy

1 The organization was termed the General Postal Union at its foundation, but was renamed the Universal Postal Union at a second congress in Paris in 1878, and has retained this name to the present day (the official title was usually rendered in French – L'Union Générale des Postes, L'Union Postale Universelle).

2 Standard accounts of the organisation are given in, G. A. Codding, *The Universal Postal Union* (New York, 1964); M. A. K. Menon, *The Universal Postal Union* (New York, 1965). On its foundation, see POST (Post Office Archives) 29/519, 326R/1891, *A Brief Account of the Formation of the Universal Postal Union, its Gradual Extension to the Various parts of the British Empire and the Reasons which have hitherto Deterred the Australasian and South African Colonies from Joining the Union* (London, 1886), pp. 3–5; 'The History and Constitution of the Postal Union', *Times*, 15 August 1891; F. E. Baines, *Forty Years at the Post Office* (London, 1895), vol. 2, pp. 159–60; E. Bennett, *The Post Office and its Story* (London, 1912), pp. 223–7; H. Robinson, *Britain's Post Office* (Oxford, 1953), pp. 190–1; M. J. Daunton, *Royal Mail* (London, 1985), pp. 159–60.

3 *Union Postale*, vol. 2, no. 1 (January 1877), p. 16.

4 *Times*, 15 August 1891. On the contemporary association of the UPU with civilization see Menon, *The Universal Postal Union*, p. 3.

5 Belgium, France and most of what was to become Germany had introduced a Penny Post by 1849, and other countries were planning to follow. *Union Postale*, vol. 1, no. 9 (June 1876), p. 132; vol. 2, no. 12 (December 1877), p. 246.

6 *Union Postale*, vol. 1, no. 1 (October 1875), p. 15.

7 B. R. Mitchell, *European Historical Statistics 1750–1975* (2nd edn, London, 1981), pp. 678–99.

8 *Union Postale*, vol. 1, no. 10 (July 1876), p. 163; Union Postale Universelle, *Statistique générale du service postal, année 1890* (Berne, 1892); Union Postale Universelle, *Statistique générale du service postal, année 1913* (Berne, 1915); Union Postale Universelle, *Statistique générale du service postal, année 1928* (Berne, 1930); Union Postale Universelle, *Statistique générale du service postal, année 1938* (Berne, 1940). The tables for 1938 omit the USSR: figure inferred as equivalent proportion in 1928.

9 L. G. Sandberg, 'The Case of the Impoverished Sophisticate: Human Capital and Swedish Economic Growth before World War 1', *Journal of Economic History*, XXXIX, 1 (March 1979), p. 226; E. Johansson, 'The History of Literacy in Sweden', in H. J. Graff (ed.), *Literacy and Social Development in the West* (Cambridge, 1981), pp. 165–74.

10 See the use made of these by B. Eklof in *Russian Peasant Schools: Officialdom, Village Culture and Popular Pedagogy, 1861–1914* (Berkeley, 1986).

11 W. J. F. Davies, *Teaching Reading in Early England* (London, 1973), pp. 89–90.

12 F. Furet and J. Ozouf, *Reading and Writing: Literacy in France from Calvin to Jules Ferry* (Cambridge, 1982), pp. 4–9.

13 Union Postale Universelle, *Statistique générale du service postal, année 1913* (Berne, 1915), p. 4.

14 R. D. Anderson, *Education in France 1848–1870* (Oxford, 1975), pp. 136–40.

15 I. G. Tóth, *Mivelhogy magad írást nem tudsz . . . Az írás térhódítása a müvelödésben a Kora újkori Magyarországon* (Budapest, 1996), pp. 126, 145. On the very low levels amongst the peasantry, see pp. 65, 69.

16 R. A. Houston, *Literacy in Early Modern Europe: Culture and Education 1500–1800* (London, 1988), pp. 130–54.

17 Figures 1.2 and 1.3 are derived from C. M. Cipolla, *Literacy and Development in the West* (Harmondsworth, 1969), pp. 14, 85, 89, 115, 119, 122–7; H. J. Graff, *The Legacies of Literacy* (Bloomington, 1987), p. 285; J. S. Allen, *In the Public Eye: A History of Reading in Modern France, 1800–1940* (Princeton, 1991), p. 59; P. Flora, *State, Economy, and Society in Western Europe 1815–1975*, vol. 1: *The Growth of Mass Democracies and Welfare States* (London, 1983), pp. 72–85; O. Boonstra, 'Education and Upward Social Mobility in the Netherlands, 1800–1900', unpublished paper, 1998, pp. 3–4; M. V. Ribas and X. M. Julià, *La Evolucion del Analfabetismo en España de 1887 a 1981* (Madrid, 1992), p. 166; M. Vilanova and X. Moreno, *Atlas de la Evolucion del Analfabetismo en España de 1887 a 1981* (Madrid, 1992), p. 166; J. Ruwet and Y. Wellemans, *L'Analphabétisme en Belgique (XVIIème–XIXème siècles)* (Louvain, 1978), p. 15; Registrar General of England and Wales, *Annual Reports*; R. Schofield, 'Dimensions of Illiteracy in

England 1750–1850', in Graff, *Literacy and Social Development in the West*, pp. 205, 207. The returns are all from marriage registers except Belgium, census population ten and over; Austria, recruits to 1880, census ten and over 1890–1910; Prussia, recruits; Spain, census total population to 1877, census ten and over from 1887; Prussia (male), recruits. Belgium: census (whole population); England and Wales: marriage registers; France: marriage registers; Prussia/Germany: marriage registers from 1880; Italy: marriage registers; Netherlands: marriage registers; Ireland: marriage registers; Spain: census population, ten and over; Russia: recruits from 1874, census (whole population) 1897, 1913.

18 Tóth, *Mivelhogy magad írást nem tudsz*, p. 246.

19 C.-E. Nunez, 'Literacy and Economic Growth in Spain, 1860–1977', in G. Tortella (ed.), *Education and Economic Development since the Industrial Revolution* (Valencia, 1990), p. 128.

20 M. Ballara, *Women and Literacy* (London, 1992), pp. 2–6.

21 T. U. Raun, 'The Development of Estonian Literacy in the 18th and 19th Centuries', *Journal of Baltic Studies*, 10 (1979), pp. 120–1.

22 W. B. Stephens, *Education in Britain, 1750–1914* (London, 1998), pp. 35–8; D. Vincent, *Literacy and Popular Culture: England 1750–1914* (Cambridge, 1989), pp. 24–6.

23 B. Reay, 'The Content and Meaning of Popular Literacy: Some New Evidence from Nineteenth-Century Rural England', *Past and Present*, 131 (May 1991), pp. 113–14.

24 For the use of this notion by the Italian town-dwellers of their rural neighbours see D. Marchenisi, *Il bisogno di scrivere. Usi della scrittura nell'Italia moderna* (Bari, 1992), p. 63.

25 M. Spufford, 'Literacy, Trade and Religion in the Commercial Centres of Europe', in K. Davids and J. Lucassen, *A Miracle Mirrored: The Dutch Republic in European Perspective* (Cambridge, 1995), p. 265.

26 R. Darnton, 'First Steps toward a History of Reading', *Australian Journal of French Studies*, 23, 1 (1986), p. 11.

27 Stephens, *Education in Britain, 1750–1914*, pp. 27–8.

28 See for instance the match between towns and their hinterlands in late eighteenth-century Belgium explored in Ruwet and Wellemans, *L'Analphabétisme en Belgique*, pp. 30–1.

29 J. Brooks, *When Russia Learned to Read: Literacy and Popular Literature, 1861–1917* (Princeton, 1985), p. 4.

30 Raun, 'The Development of Estonian Literacy', p. 121.

31 E. N. Anderson, 'The Prussian Volksschule in the Nineteenth Century', in G. A. Ritter (ed.), *Entstehung und Wandel der modernen Gesellschaft* (Berlin, 1970), pp. 269–70.

32 Furet and Ozouf, *Reading and Writing*, pp. 27–30.

33 W. B. Stephens, *Education, Literacy and Society, 1830–1870: The Geography of Diversity in Provincial England* (Manchester, 1987), pp. 16–17.

34 Cipolla, *Literacy and Development*, p. 19. Figures for entire population, six years and above.

35 Cipolla, *Literacy and Development*, pp. 16–17. Figures for entire population, over ten years of age.

36 Tóth, *Mivelhogy magad írást nem tudsz*, pp. 230–1.

37 P. Kenez, 'Liquidating Illiteracy in Revolutionary Russia', *Russian History*, 9, 2–3 (1982), pp. 176–7.

38 E. Johansson, 'Literacy Campaigns in Sweden', *Interchange*, 19, 3/4 (Fall/Winter 1988), pp. 148–9; N. de Gabriel, 'Literacy, Age, Period and Cohort in Spain (1900–1950)', *Paedagogica Historica*, 34, 1 (1988), pp. 30–41.

39 R. Bell, *Fate and Honour, Family and Village: Demographic and Cultural Change in Rural Italy since 1800* (Chicago, 1979), p. 160; M. J. Hefferman, 'Literacy and the Life-Cycle in Nineteenth-Century Provincial France: Some Evidence from the *Département* of Ille et Vilaine', *History of Education*, 21, 2 (June 1992), p. 151.

40 Vincent, *Literacy and Popular Culture*, pp. 26–7.

41 Ruwet, and Wellemans, *L'Analphabétisme en Belgique*, p. 48. 'Teenagers' here are those aged fifteen to twenty.

42 Furet and Ozouf, *Reading and Writing*, p. 47; Hefferman, 'Literacy and the Life-Cycle'.

43 For a rare discussion of this issue see, G. Kirkham, 'Literacy in North-West Ulster, 1680–1860', in M. Daly and D. Dickson, *The Origins of Popular Literacy in Ireland: Language Change and Educational Development 1700–1920* (Dublin, 1990), p. 79. See also, H. J. Graff, *The Labyrinths of Literacy: Reflections on Literacy Past and Present* (rev. edn, Pittsburgh, 1995), p. 49.

44 Ruwet and Wellemans, *L'Analphabétisme en Belgique (XVIIIème–XIXème siècles)*, pp. 106–8; Vincent, *Literacy and Popular Culture*, pp. 22–4.

45 Stephens, *Education in Britain, 1750–1914*, p. 26; Vincent, *Literacy and Popular Culture*, pp. 31–2.

46 Ruwet and Wellemans, *L'Analphabétisme en Belgique*, p. 106.

47 Reay, 'The Content and Meaning of Popular Literacy', pp. 105.

48 Reay, 'The Content and Meaning of Popular Literacy', pp. 118–19.

49 Marchenisi, *Il bisogno di scrivere*, p. 39.

50 Bell, *Fate and Honour*, p. 160.

51 S. Scribner and M. Cole, *The Psychology of Literacy* (Cambridge, Mass., 1981), pp. 236, 258.

52 Brooks, *When Russia Learned to Read. Literacy and Popular Literature, 1861–1917*, p. xiv.

53 I. Markussen, 'The Development of Writing Ability in the Nordic Countries of the Eighteenth and Nineteenth Centuries', *Journal of Scandinavian History*, 15, 1 (1990), pp. 40–2.

54 R. Engelsing, *Analphabetentum und Lektüre* (Stuttgart, 1973), p. 120.

55 G. Brooks, D. Foxman and T. Gorman, 'Standards in Literacy and Numeracy: 1948–1994', *National Commission on Education, Briefing* (June 1995).

56 Furet and Ozouf, *Reading and Writing*, pp. 14–17. See also the comparison between marriage register and census scores in Ruwet and Wellemans, *L'Analphabétisme en Belgique*, pp. 90–2.

57 Reay, 'The Content and Meaning of Popular Literacy', p. 113; Stephens, *Education in Britain, 1750–1914*, pp. 26–7.

58 R. Pattison, *On Literacy: The Politics of the Word from Homer to the Age of Rock* (New York, 1982), p. 140.

59 P.-J. Hélias, *The Horse of Pride* (New Haven, 1978), p. 55.

60 After 1928, national figures were still collected, but the UPU ceased publishing them on a per capita basis.

61 For sources of postal rates, see note to figure 1.1.

62 In 1876, the returns are for letters and postcards – the only mail items then in the system. By 1890 a range of other services had been added, such as printed papers, samples and postal orders.

63 The literacy levels are for males and females combined. For sources, see notes to figures 1.2 and 1.3. For sources of postal rates, see note to figure 1.1.

64 The association between modernization and literacy is critically assessed in, D. Lindmark, 'Introduction', in D. Lindmark (ed.), *Alphabeta Varia: Orality, Reading and Writing in the History of Literacy* (Umeå, 1998), p. 46.

65 E. Todd, *The Causes of Progress: Culture, Authority and Change* (Oxford, 1987), p. 131.

66 R. Chartier, 'Texts, Printing, Readings', in L. Hunt (ed.), *The New Cultural History* (Berkeley, 1989), p. 121.

67 D. Roche, *The People of Paris* (Leamington Spa, 1987), p. 199.

68 This is the central argument of H. J. Graff, *The Literacy Myth* (London, 1979), and is emphasized in his later works. See for instance, *The Legacies of Literacy*, p. 264; *The Labyrinths of Literacy*, pp. 6–18.

69 D. Barton, *Literacy: An Introduction to the Ecology of Written Language* (Oxford, 1994), pp. 4–6.

70 Vincent, *Literacy and Popular Culture*, p. 18.

71 B. Street, *Literacy in Theory and Practice* (Cambridge, 1984), p. 8.

72 On the emergence of the notion of functional literacy, see D. P. Resnick and L. B. Resnick, 'The Nature of Literacy: An Historical Exploration', *Harvard Educational Review*, 47, no. 3 (August 1977), p. 383.

73 My translation. P. Besson, *Un pâtre du Cantal* (Paris, 1914), pp. 20–1.

74 T. Cooper, *The Life of Thomas Cooper, Written by Himself* (London, 1872), pp. 57–8.

75 T. A. Jackson, *Solo Trumpet* (London, 1953), pp. 19–20.

76 K. Levine, 'Functional Literacy: Fond Illusions and False Economies', *Harvard Educational Review*, 52 (3) (August 1982), pp. 250–1; I. Kirsch and J. T. Guthrie, 'The Concept and Measurement of Functional Literacy', *Reading Research Quarterly*, 13, 4 (1977–8), p. 488.

77 Current Unesco definition of functional literacy, cited in Ballara, *Women and Literacy* p. 14.

78 M. Meek, 'Literacy: Redescribing Reading', in K. Kimberley, M. Meek and J. Miller, *New Readings: Contributions to an Understanding of Literacy* (London, 1992), pp. 226–32.

79 R. Chartier, *The Order of Books* (Cambridge, 1994), p. xi; Levine, 'Functional Literacy', p. 263.

80 Furet and Ozouf, *Reading and Writing*, p. 148.

81 For a clear statement of this approach, see, T. W. Laqueur, 'Towards a Cultural Ecology of Literacy in England', in D. P. Resnick, *Literacy in Historical Perspective* (Washington, 1983), p. 55.

Chapter 2 Learning Literacy

1 A. Errington, *Coals on Rails*, ed. P. E. H. Hair (Liverpool, 1988), p. 26.
2 Errington, *Coals on Rails*, pp. 31–2.
3 F. Furet, and J. Ozouf, *Reading and Writing: Literacy in France from Calvin to Jules Ferry* (Cambridge, 1982), p. 27.
4 H. van der Laan, 'Influences on Education and Instruction in the Netherlands, especially 1750 to 1815', in J. A. Leith (ed.), *Facets of Education in the Eighteenth Century*, Studies on Voltaire and the Eighteenth Century, 167 (Oxford, 1977), p. 295.
5 H. C. Barnard, *Education and the French Revolution* (Cambridge, 1969), pp. 166, 174.
6 T. Nipperdey, 'Mass Education and Modernization: The Case of Germany 1780–1850', *Transactions of the Royal Historical Society*, 5th ser., 27 (1977), p. 159.
7 J. V. H. Melton, *Absolutism and the Eighteenth-Century Origins of Compulsory Schooling in Prussia and Austria* (Cambridge, 1988); K. A. Schleunes, *Schooling and Society: The Politics of Education in Prussia and Bavaria 1750–1900* (Oxford, 1989), p. 37; M. Lamberti, *State, Society, and the Elementary School in Imperial Germany* (New York, 1989); R. F. Tomasson, 'The Literacy of Icelanders', *Scandinavian Studies*, 57 (1975); G. L. Seidler, 'The Reform of the Polish School System in the Era of the Enlightenment', in Leith, *Facets of Education in the Eighteenth Century*; J. F. Carrato, 'The Enlightenment in Portugal and the Educational Reforms of the Marquis of Pombal', in Leith, *Facets of Education in the Eighteenth Century*; L. Boucher, *Tradition and Change in Swedish Education* (Oxford, 1982), pp. 8–20; T. U. Raun, 'The Development of Estonian Literacy in the 18th and 19th Centuries', *Journal of Baltic Studies*, 10 (1979), p. 119.
8 R. S. Turner, 'Of Social Control and Cultural Experience: Education in the Eighteenth Century', *Central European History*, 21, 3 (September 1988), p. 303.
9 D. Vincent, 'Reading Made Strange: Context and Method in Becoming Literate in Eighteenth and Nineteenth-Century England', in I. Grosvenor, M. Lawn and K. Rousmaniere (eds), *Silences and Images: The Social History of the Classroom* (1999).
10 W. J. F. Davies, *Teaching reading in Early England* (London, 1973), p. 151. On the antiquity of most devices for teaching literacy see, I. Michael, *The Teaching of English* (Cambridge, 1987), passim.
11 See Darton and Harvey, *Children's Books in England* (London, 1805), p. 127.
12 Boucher, *Tradition and Change in Swedish Education*, pp. 7–8.
13 F. Watson, *The Encyclopaedia and Dictionary of Education* (London, 1921), IV, pp. 1571–5.

14 E. Johansson, 'Alphabeta Varia: Some Roots of Literacy in Various Countries', in D. Lindmark, *Alphabeta Varia* (Umeå, 1998), p. 128.

15 G. J. Marker, 'Primers and Literacy in Muscovy: A Taxonomic Investigation', *The Russian Review*, 48 (January 1989), pp. 1–5.

16 R. M. Wiles, 'The Relish for Reading in Provincial England Two Centuries Ago', in P. Korshin (ed.), *The Widening Circle: Essays on the Circulation of Literature in Eighteenth-Century Europe* (Philadelphia, 1976), p. 111.

17 I. G. Tóth, 'Hungarian Culture in the Early Modern Age', in L. Kósa (ed.), *A Cultural History of Hungary: From the Beginnings to the Eighteenth Century* (Budapest, 1999), pp. 218, 222–3. On the wide distribution of religious literature in Sweden, see below, p. 91.

18 Especially T. Dyche's *Guide to the English Tongue* (1710); J. R. R. Adams, *The Printed Word and the Common Man: Popular Culture in Ulster 1700–1900* (Belfast, 1987), pp. 17, 19, 111.

19 D. P. Resnick, 'Historical Perspectives on Literacy and Schooling', *Daedalus*, 119, 2 (Spring 1990), p. 18.

20 L. S. Strumingher, *What Were Little Girls and Boys Made of? Primary Education in Rural France 1830–1880* (Albany, 1983), p. 14.

21 J. Jones, 'Some Account of the Writer Written by Himself', in J. Jones, *Attempts in Verse* (London, 1831), pp. 171–2.

22 B. Eklof, *Russian Peasant Schools: Officialdom, Village Culture and Popular Pedagogy, 1861–1914* (Berkeley, 1986), p. 84.

23 H. Chisick, 'School Attendance, Literacy, and Acculturation: *Petites Écoles* and Popular Education in Eighteenth-Century France', *Europa*, 3 (1979), p. 189.

24 D. Roche, *The People of Paris* (Leamington Spa, 1987), p. 207.

25 Melton, *Absolutism and the Eighteenth-Century Origins of Compulsory Schooling in Prussia and Austria*, p. 11; Schleunes, *Schooling and Society*, p. 12. The term literally means 'corner school'.

26 Schleunes, *Schooling and Society*, p. 36.

27 Adams, *The Printed Word and the Common Man*, pp. 12–15.

28 P. J. Dowling, *The Hedge Schools of Ireland* (London, 1935), pp. 47–8.

29 J. E. Gordon, *Six Letters on Irish Education* (1832), pp. 3–4, cited in Dowling, *Hedge Schools of Ireland*, p. 43.

30 For a recent example of an uncritical acceptance of these accounts see E. Hopkins, *Childhood Transformed: Working-Class Children in Nineteenth-Century England* (Manchester, 1994), pp. 131–2. On the way in which such teaching was 'effectively decertified', see M. J. Maynes, *Schooling in Western Europe* (Albany, 1985), p. 63.

31 The Anordning for Almueskolevesenet på landet i Danmark. W. Dixon, *Education in Denmark* (Copenhagen, 1958), pp. 43–8.

32 H. Mann, *Report of an Educational Tour in Germany and Parts of Great Britain and Ireland* (London, 1846), p. 32.

33 D. Vincent, *Literacy and Popular Culture* (Cambridge, 1989), p. 69.

34 My translation. A. Sylvère, *Toinou, le cri d'un enfant auvergnat* (Paris, 1980), p. 52.

35 The figures in this paragraph are taken from P. Flora, *State, Economy, and Society in Western Europe 1815–1975*, vol. 1: *The Growth of Mass Democracies and Welfare States* (London, 1983), pp. 355–449; B. R. Mitchell, *Abstract of British Historical Statistics* (Cambridge, 1971), pp. 396–8.

36 See gross public expenditure of Belgium, Denmark, Finland, France, Germany, Norway, Sweden and the United Kingdom.

37 E. Johansson, ' "To Know the Words": The Key to Oral and Reading Tradition in the Church. A Basic Theme in Christian Literacy Teaching', in Lindmark, *Alphabeta Varia*, p. 150; J. V. H. Melton, 'From Image to Word: Cultural Reform and the Rise of Literate Culture in Eighteenth-Century Austria', *Journal of Modern History*, 58 (March, 1986), p. 112.

38 On the prevailing view in the second quarter of the nineteenth century that Prussia represented the future for European education and literacy, see, Mann, *Report of an Educational Tour in Germany and Parts of Great Britain and Ireland*, p. 5.

39 R. Block, *Der Alphabetisierungsverlauf im Preussen* (Frankfurt am Main, 1985), ch. 4.2; R. Gawthrop and G. Strauss, 'Protestantism and Literacy in Early Modern Germany', *Past and Present*, 104 (1984), pp. 43–53.

40 Schleunes, *Schooling and Society*, p. 25.

41 M. Lamberti, *State, Society, and the Elementary School in Imperial Germany* (New York, 1989), p. 13.

42 V. Cousin, *Report on the State of Public Instruction in Prussia*, ed. E. W. Knight (New York, 1930), pp. 125–9.

43 R. Gibson, *A Social History of French Catholicism 1789–1914* (London, 1989), p. 93; R. Gildea, *Education in Provincial France, 1800–1914: A Study of Three Departments* (Oxford, 1983), pp. 216–17; R. D. Anderson, *Education in France 1848–1870* (Oxford, 1975), p. 17.

44 Strumingher, *What Were Little Girls and Boys Made of?*, pp. 42–6.

45 N. J. Smelser, *Social Paralysis and Social Change* (Berkeley, 1991), pp. 141–2.

46 M. Barbagli, *Education for Unemployment: Politics, Labour Markets and the School System. Italy 1859–1973* (New York, 1982), p. 56.

47 H. J. Graff, *The Legacies of Literacy* (Bloomington, 1987), p. 307.

48 Eklof, *Russian Peasant Schools*, pp. 29, 64, 155; J. Brooks, *When Russia Learned to Read* (Princeton, 1985), pp. 37–48.

49 Maynes, *Schooling in Western Europe*, p. 69.

50 J. K. Hoensch, *A History of Modern Hungary 1867–1986* (London, 1988), p. 92.

51 S. Fitzpatrick, *Education and Social Mobility in the Soviet Union 1921–1934* (Cambridge, 1979), pp. 173–5.

52 Block, *Der Alphabetisierungsverlauf im Preussen*, p. 201, table 5.17.

53 N. Atkinson, *Irish education: A History of Educational Institutions* (Dublin, 1969), p. 74; Dowling, *Hedge Schools of Ireland*, p. 22.

54 G. Ricuperati and M. Roggero, 'Educational Policies in Eighteenth-Century Italy', in Leith, *Facets of Education in the Eighteenth Century*, p. 257.

55 R. Gibson, *Social History of French Catholicism* (London, 1989), pp. 108–22.

56 Dixon, *Education in Denmark*, p. 48.
57 Cousin, *State of Public Instruction in Prussia*, p. 130.
58 A. T. Quartararo, *Women Teachers and Popular Education in Nineteenth Century France* (Newark, 1995), p. 20.
59 G. R. Galbraith, *Reading Lives: Reconstructing Childhood, Books and Schools in Britain, 1870–1920* (New York, 1997), p. 94.
60 Johansson, 'Literacy Campaigns in Sweden', p. 160.
61 C. Heywood, *Childhood in Nineteenth-Century France* (Cambridge, 1988), p. 72.
62 Schleunes, *Schooling and Society*, p. 153.
63 I. Hunter, *Rethinking the School. Subjectivity, Bureaucracy, Criticism* (St Leonards, Australia, 1994), p. xxi.
64 Watson, *The Encyclopaedia and Dictionary of Education*, I, p. 448; S. Gemie, *Women and Schooling in France, 1815–1914: Gender Authority and Identity in the Female Schooling Sector* (Keele, 1995), p. 50.
65 M. Depaepe and F. Simon, 'Is there any Place for the History of "Education" in the "History of Education"? A Plea for the History of Everyday Educational Reality in – and outside Schools', *Paedagogica Historica*, XXXI, 1 (1995), p. 11.
66 Lindmark, 'Introduction', in *Alphabeta Varia*, p. 49.
67 I. Markussen, 'The Development of Writing Ability in the Nordic Countries', Journal of Scandinavian History, 15, 1 (1990), pp. 39–40; Anderson, *Education in France*, pp. 32–3; Eklof, *Russian Peasant Schools*, p. 53; F. Watson, *The Encyclopaedia and Dictionary of Education* (London, 1921), I, p. 447.
68 See for instance the practice in late eighteenth-century Belgian church schools. J. Ruwet and Y. Wellemans, *L'Analphabétisme en Belgique* (Louvain, 1978), p. 33.
69 I. G. Tóth, *Mivelhogy magad írást nem tudsz . . . Az írás térhódítása a müvelödésben a Kora újkori Magyarországon* (Budapest, 1996), pp. 14–15, 33.
70 Mann, *Report of an Educational Tour*, p. 93.
71 Lancaster formed a school in which he developed the method in 1798. Bell, claimed to have invented the method in Madras in 1796 and proselytized it in England during the first decade of the new century.
72 K. Barkin, 'Social Control and the Volksschule in Vormärz Prussia', *Central European History*, 16 (1983), pp. 41–3.
73 Mann, *Report of an Educational Tour*, p. 58. Also, V. Cousin, *On the State of Education in Holland as regards Schools for the Working Classes and for the Poor*, trans. L. Horner (London, 1838), p. 35; Maynes, *Schooling in Western Europe*, pp. 77–8.
74 E. B. Huey, *The Psychology and Pedagogy of Reading* (1908; Cambridge, Mass., 1968), pp. 241–2. The earliest teaching aids were in turn based on Greek models.
75 From 2nd edn, 1710.
76 First published in London in 1740, and in North America in 1747. See Vincent, 'Reading Made Strange: Context and Method in becoming literate in eighteenth and nineteenth-century England', pp. 180–4.

77 Michael, *The Teaching of English*, pp. 56, 91, 117.
78 M. Matthews, *Teaching to Read, Historically Considered* (Chicago, 1966), pp. 19–74.
79 G. J. Marker, 'Primers and Literacy in Muscovy: A Taxonomic Investigation', *The Russian Review*, 48 (January 1989), pp. 1–12.
80 *Manual of the System of Teaching Reading, Writing, Arithmetick, and Needlework in the Elementary-Schools of the British and Foreign Schools Society* (London, 1816). For a later version, see, *Manual for the System of Primary Instruction, Pursued in the Model Schools of the B.F.S.S.* (London, 1831).
81 The richest insight into what might be possible in a mid-eighteenth middle-class home is supplied by the collection of materials assembled by Jane Johnson. For an introduction to her collection, see, V. Watson, 'Jane Johnson: A Very Pretty Story to Tell Children', in M. Hilton, M. Styles and V. Watson (eds), *Opening the Nursery Door: Reading, Writing and Childhood, 1600–1900* (London, 1997), pp. 31–46.
82 Maynes, *Schooling in Western Europe*, p. 62.
83 Dixon, *Education in Denmark*, p. 39. This was the founding institution of Danish teacher training, although there had been an earlier venture in Copenhagen in 1791.
84 Galbraith, *Reading Lives*, p. 17.
85 A. J. La Vopa, *Prussian Schoolteachers: Profession and Office, 1763–1848* (Chapel Hill, 1980), p. 92; A. Green, *Education and State Formation: The Rise of Education Systems in England, France and the USA* (Basingstoke, 1990), p. 23; Maynes, *Schooling in Western Europe*, p. 76.
86 M. J. Maynes, 'Schooling and Hegemony', *Journal of Interdisciplinary History*, 13, 3 (Winter 1983), p. 519.
87 Maynes, *Schooling in Western Europe*, p. 62.
88 Gildea, *Education in Provincial France*, p. 227; La Vopa, *Prussian Schoolteachers*, p. 30.
89 W. B. Stephens, *Education in Britain, 1750–1914* (London, 1998), p. 78.
90 Maynes, *Schooling in Western Europe*, pp. 61–2.
91 This remained a central issue in inter-war Russia, as the Bolsheviks mounted their mass literacy campaigns. Fitzpatrick, *Education and Social Mobility in the Soviet Union 1921–1934*, p. 171.
92 Barbagli, *Education for Unemployment*, p. 59.
93 Johansson, 'Literacy Campaigns in Sweden', p. 136. Also, E. Johansson, 'Popular Literacy in Scandinavia about 1600–1900', *Historical Social Research*, 34 (1985), p. 123.
94 Cited in Brooks, *When Russia Learned to Read*, p. 37.
95 Cited in Vincent, *Literacy and Popular Culture*, p. 87.
96 Cited in Heywood, *Childhood in Nineteenth-Century France*, p. 72.
97 F. A. Kittler, *Discourse Networks 1800/1900*, trans. M. Metteer (Stanford, 1990), pp. 28–53.
98 J. Laurie, *First Steps to Reading* (London, 1862), Preface. See also the contemporary publication, W. J. Unwin, *Infant School Reader* (London, 1861).
99 Mathews, *Teaching to Read Historically Considered*, pp. 49–50, 75–101; Brooks, *When Russia Learned to Read*, p. 50; Huey, *The Psychology and Ped-*

agogy of Reading, p. 259. Mann discusses the need to move away from exclusive reliance on the alphabet in *Report of an Educational Tour*, pp. 103–5.

100 Galbraith, *Reading Lives*, p. 127.

101 J. Gill, *Introductory Text-Book to School Management* (2nd edn, London, 1857).

102 M. Jackson, *Literacy* (London, 1993), p. 50.

103 R. Thabault, *Education and Change in a Village Community: Mazières-en-Gâtine, 1848–1914* (London, 1971), p. 121.

104 F. Paulsen, *German Education Past and Present* (London, 1908), pp. 246–61.

105 Quartararo, *Women Teachers and Popular Education in Nineteenth Century France*, p. 116. Under the Casati law in Italy, public elementary school teachers in Italy required a certificate of morality signed by the mayor. Barbagli, *Education for Unemployment*, pp. 54–5.

106 For a particularly clear account of this curriculum see Heywood, *Childhood in Nineteenth-Century France*, pp. 61, 73–4.

107 P.-J. Hélias, *The Horse of Pride: Life in a Breton Village* (New Haven, 1978), pp. 207–8.

108 Flora, *State, Economy, and Society in Western Europe 1815–1975*, vol. 1, pp. 553–633.

109 Mann, *Report of an Educational Tour*, p. 185. Also, V. Cousin, *Report on the State of Public Instruction in Prussia*, ed. E. W. Knight (New York, 1930), p. 131.

110 J. M. McNair, *Education for a Changing Spain* (Manchester, 1984), pp. 24–6.

111 Brooks, *When Russia Went to School*, pp. xv, 43–4.

112 Hoensch, *A History of Modern Hungary*, p. 46.

113 A point stressed by K. Barkin, 'Social Control and the Volksschule in Vormärz Prussia', *Central European History*, 16 (1983), p. 32.

114 B. Reay, 'The Content and Meaning of Popular Literacy', *Past and Present*, 131 (May 1991), p. 98.

115 Literacy rates as in figure 1.2. Attendance rates from Flora, *State, Economy, and Society in Western Europe 1815–1975*, vol. 1, pp. 553–633.

116 Data from UPU returns (see figure 1.2) and Flora, *State, Economy, and Society in Western Europe 1815–1975*, vol. 1, pp. 556–633 (Belgian attendance figures are 1895).

117 See, for instance, Block's account of Prussia, where the consolidation of public elementary education did not take place until literacy levels were already over 90 per cent. Block, *Der Alphabetisierungsverlauf im Preussen*, ch. 4.2.

118 Eklof, *Russian Peasant Schools*, p. 392.

119 See the survey of France, Germany and England in L. Clark, 'The Socialization of Girls in the Primary Schools of the Third Republic', *Journal of Social History*, 15, 4 (Summer 1982), p. 685.

120 See for instance the experience of female pupils in French elementary education. L. Clark, *Schooling the Daughters of Marianne: Textbooks and the Socialisation of Girls in Modern French Primary Schools* (Albany, 1984), pp. 5, 10–14.

121 The fullest and most nuanced account of this process is to be found in A. Davin, *Growing up Poor: Home, School and Street in London 1870–1914* (London, 1996), pp. 116–73. Also, J. Purvis, *Hard Lessons: The Lives and Education of Working-Class Women in Nineteenth-Century England* (Cambridge, 1989), pp. 80–93.

122 See for instance the growing emphasis on domestic training in French elementary schools, which accompanied the increasing equality of basic literacy instruction in the Third Republic. Quartararo, *Women Teachers and Popular Education in Nineteenth Century France*, p. 99; Clark, *Schooling the Daughters of Marianne*, pp. 9, 16, 57–8, 61. On Britain see Galbraith, *Reading Lives*, p. 97.

123 Davin, *Growing up Poor*, pp. 87, 101; Purvis, *Hard Lessons*, p. 78.

124 A survey of French schoolgirls in 1899 found that these were the least favourite lessons. Clark, 'The Socialization of Girls in the Primary Schools of the Third Republic', p. 687.

Chapter 3   Economic Development

1 F. Furet and J. Ozouf, *Reading and Writing* (Cambridge, 1982), p. 312; G. Ricuperati and R. Roggero, 'Educational Policies in Eighteenth-Century Italy', in J. A. Leith, *Facets of Education in the Eighteenth Century* (Oxford, 1977), p. 259.

2 C. M. Cipolla, *Literacy and Development in the West* (Harmondsworth, 1969), p. 87. The most recent statement of the general association is D. S. Landes, *The Wealth and Poverty of Nations: Why Some are So Rich and Some So Poor* (London, 1998), p. 250.

3 Discussed in L. Petterson, 'Reading and Writing Skills and the Agrarian Revolution: Scanian Peasants during the Age of Enclosure', *Scandinavian Economic History Review*, XLIV, 3 (1996), p. 44; L. G. Sandberg, 'Ignorance, Poverty and Economic Backwardness in the Early Stages of European Industrialization: Variations on Alexander Gerschenkron's Grand Scheme', *Journal of European Economic History*, II, 3 (Winter 1982), pp. 675–8, 681. Further support to the argument that illiteracy retards growth is given in G. Tortella, 'Patterns of Economic Retardation and Recovery in South-Western Europe in the Nineteenth and Twentieth Centuries', *Economic History Review* (1994), pp. 1–21.

4 C. A. Anderson, 'Literacy and Schooling on the Development Threshold: Some Historical Cases', in C. A. Anderson and M. J. Bowman (eds), *Education and Economic Development* (London, 1966), p. 347. Also, M. J. Bowman and C. A. Anderson, 'Concerning the Role of Education in Development', in C. Geertz (ed.), *Old Societies and New States* (New York, 1963), p. 252.

5 R. A. Houston, *Literacy in Early Modern Europe* (London, 1988), p. 131. Also, R. Chartier, 'The Practical Impact of Writing', in R. Chartier, (ed.), *A History of Private Life*, vol. 3: *Passions of the Renaissance* (Cambridge, Mass.,

1989), p. 116; M. Spufford, 'Literacy, Trade and Religion in the Commercial Centres of Europe', in K. Davids and J. Lucassen, *A Miracle Mirrored* (Cambridge, 1995), p. 231.

6 D. F. Mitch, 'The Role of Human Capital in the First Industrial Revolution', in J. Mokyr (ed.), *The British Industrial Revolution* (Boulder, Colo., 1993), p. 291.

7 D. Vincent, *Literacy and Popular Culture* (Cambridge, 1989), pp. 96–7. See also R. Schofield, 'Dimensions of Illiteracy in England 1750–1850', in H. J. Graff (ed.), *Literacy and Social Development in the West* (Cambridge, 1981), p. 211.

8 C.-E. Nunez, 'Literacy and Economic Growth in Spain, 1860–1977', in G. Tortella (ed.), *Education and Economic Development since the Industrial Revolution* (Valencia, 1990), p. 128.

9 See, for instance, the summaries of Belgian, Dutch and Swedish returns in H. J. Graff, *Legacies of Literacy*, (Bloomington, 1987), pp. 304, 307, 310.

10 On France, see, C. Heywood, *Childhood in Nineteenth-Century France* (Cambridge, 1988), p. 69. On Russia, see, A. Kahan, 'Determinants of the Incidence of Literacy in Rural Nineteenth-Century Russia', in C. A. Anderson and M. J. Bowman (eds), *Education and Economic Development* (London, 1966), p. 302; B. Eklof, *Russian Peasant Schools* (Berkeley, 1986), p. 356; on the English countryside, B. Reay, 'The Content and Meaning of Popular Literacy: Some New Evidence from Nineteenth-Century Rural England', *Past and Present*, 131 (May 1991), pp. 93–6.

11 The possibilities are summarized in Cipolla, *Literacy and Development in the West*, pp. 87–8. See also W. R. Lee, *Population Growth, Economic Development and Social Change in Bavaria* (New York, 1977), p. 338. For a useful critique see, Levine, 'Functional Literacy: Fond Illusions and False Economies', *Harvard Educational Review*, 52 (3) (August 1982), pp. 257–9.

12 For an early attack on the possibilities of the 'global approach' to the relationship between literacy and economic growth, see M. Blaug, 'Literacy and Economic Development', *School Review*, 74 (Winter 1966), p. 407. He made the point at greater length in *An Introduction to the Economics of Education* (London, 1970), pp. 63–6, 83, 100. For later surveys of the problem see, K. H. Jarausch, 'The Old "New History of Education": A German Reconsideration', *History of Education Quarterly*, 26, 2 (Summer 1986), p. 235; H. J. Graff, *The Labyrinths of Literacy* (rev. edn, Pittsburgh, 1995), esp. pp. 19, 51, 273; Nunez, 'Literacy and Economic Growth in Spain, 1860–1977', p. 125.

13 For a discussion of the concept of luxury in overstretched family budgets, see, D. Vincent, *Poor Citizens: The State and the Poor in Twentieth Century Britain* (London, 1991), pp. 9–10.

14 D. Levine, 'Education and Family Life in Early Industrial England', *Journal of Family History*, 4, 4 (Winter 1979), pp. 373–9; Vincent, *Literacy and Popular Culture*, p. 26.

15 R. Lowery, *Robert Lowery, Radical and Chartist*, ed. B. Harrison and P. Hollis (London, 1979), p. 45. 'Lenny' was William Lennie's *Principles of English Grammar*.

16 E. Le Roy Ladurie, 'The Conscripts of 1868' and 'Rural Civilisation', in *The Territory of the Historian* (Hassocks, 1979), p. 56.

17 M. A. Marrus, 'Folklore as an Ethnographic Source: A "Mise au Point"', in J. Beauroy, M. Bertrand and E. T. Gargan (eds), *The Wolf and the Lamb: Popular Culture in France from the Old Regime to the Twentieth Century* (Saratoga, Calif., 1977), p. 122.

18 J. M. McNair, *Education for a Changing Spain* (Manchester, 1984), p. 25.

19 S. Tanguiane, *Literacy and Illiteracy in the World: Situation: Trends and Prospects* (Paris, 1990), p. 39.

20 R. F. Tomasson, 'The Literacy of Icelanders', *Scandinavian Studies*, 57 (1975), p. 70.

21 M. Sanderson, 'Social Change and Elementary Education in Industrial Lancashire 1780–1840', *Northern History*, 3 (1968), pp. 131–54; 'Literacy and Social Mobility in the Industrial Revolution in England', *Past and Present*, 56 (1972), pp. 82–9. Also W. B. Stephens, *Education, Literacy and Society, 1830–1870* (Manchester, 1987), pp. 3–4, 6, 58; S. Nicholas, 'Literacy and the Industrial Revolution', in Tortella, *Education and Economic Development since the Industrial Revolution*, pp. 51–8; S. J. Nicholas and J. M. Nicholas, 'Male Literacy, "Deskilling" and the Industrial Revolution', *Journal of Interdisciplinary History*, 23 (Summer 1992), pp. 3–16.

22 A point made by two early responses to Sanderson: E. G. West, 'Literacy and the Industrial Revolution', *Economic History Review*, 2nd ser., XXXI (1978), pp. 371–2, 382; T. W. Laqueur, 'The Cultural Origins of Popular Literacy in England, 1500–1800', *Oxford Review of Education*, 11, 3 (1974), pp. 96–107. Nicholas [see note 21 above] avoids this problem by using transportation data, although there remain problems of how far it is safe to generalize from these.

23 Nunez, 'Literacy and Economic Growth in Spain, 1860–1977', p. 129.

24 Stephens, *Education in Britain, 1750–1914*, p. 33.

25 On Belgium, see Graff, *Legacies of Literacy*, p. 306; on France, see Furet and Ozouf, *Reading and Writing*, pp. 203–18.

26 R. Block, *Der Alphabetisierungsverlauf im Preussen des 19. Jarhunderts* (Frankfurt am Main, 1995), pp. 181–93, tables 5.10 and 5.11.

27 Vincent, *Literacy and Popular Culture*, pp. 97–100; J. Grayson, 'Literacy, Schooling and Industrialisation: Worcestershire. 1760–1850', in W. B. Stephens (ed.), *Studies in the History of Literacy: England and North America* (Leeds, 1983), pp. 54–67; Stephens, *Education in Britain, 1750–1914*, p. 57.

28 See the debate between, R. D. Anderson, 'Education and the State in Nineteenth-Century Scotland', *Economic History Review*, 36 (1983), p. 525, and D. M. Mason, 'School Attendance in Nineteenth-Century Scotland', *Economic History Review*, 38 (1985), pp. 278–81.

29 Block, *Der Alphabetisierungsverlauf im Preussen*, p. 197, table 5.14.

30 R. D. Anderson, *Education in France 1848–1870* (Oxford, 1975), pp. 69–70; J. Brooks, *When Russia Learned to Read* (Princeton, 1985), pp. 13, 15; C. Tilly, 'Did the Cake of Custom Break?', in J. Merriman (ed.), *Class Consciousness and Class Experience in Nineteenth-Century Europe* (New York, 1979), p. 37;

Graff, *Legacies of Literacy*, p. 311; Mitch, 'The Role of Human Capital in the First Industrial Revolution', p. 300; S. Nicholas, 'Literacy and the Industrial Revolution', p. 55; Nicholas and Nicholas, 'Male literacy, "Deskilling" and the Industrial Revolution', p. 3; de Gabriel, 'Literacy, Age, Period and Cohort in Spain (1900–1950)', p. 47.

31 Le Roy Ladurie, 'The Conscripts of 1868', p. 45; Graff, *Legacies of Literacy*, p. 311; Mitch, 'The Role of Human Capital in the First Industrial Revolution', p. 300.

32 W. H. Sewell, *Structure and Mobility: The Men and Women of Marseille, 1820–1870* (Cambridge, 1985), pp. 169–71, 196.

33 Vincent, *Literacy and Popular Culture*, pp. 98–100.

34 Furet and Ozouf, *Reading and Writing*, p. 40.

35 S. A. Harrop, 'Literacy and Educational Attitudes as Factors in the Industrialisation of North-East Cheshire, 1760–1830', in Stephens, *Studies in the History of Literacy*, pp. 37–53.

36 Stephens, *Education, Literacy and Society, 1830–1870*, pp. 37–53.

37 See for instance Rainer Block's assessment of the significance of the economic power of industrialized regions of Prussia for the advancement of literacy. Block, *Der Alphabetisierungsverlauf im Preussen*, pp. 147–8.

38 Mitch, *The Rise of Popular Literacy*, appendix A, pp. 213–14.

39 Vincent, *Literacy and Popular Culture*, p. 97.

40 I. Berend, 'Economy and Education: The Hungarian Case', in Tortella, *Education and Economic Development since the Industrial Revolution*, p. 178.

41 B. Brierley, *Home Memories, and Recollections of a Life* (Manchester and London, [1886]), pp. 30–1. The brother was born in 1828.

42 Reay, 'The Content and Meaning of Popular Literacy', pp. 104–5.

43 R. Darnton, 'First Steps toward a History of Reading', *Australian Journal of French Studies*, 23, 1 (1986), p. 11. Also, D. Roche, *The People of Paris* (Leamington Spa, 1987), p. 200.

44 Mitch, *The Rise of Popular Literacy in Victorian England*, pp. 14–18, 200–1. Also, Mitch, 'The Role of Human Capital in the First Industrial Revolution', p. 291.

45 J.-L. Ménétra, *Journal of My Life*, trans. Arthur Goldhammer (New York, 1986), p. 98.

46 Ménétra, *Journal of My Life*, p. 98.

47 See Eklof, *Russian Peasant Schools*, p. 444.

48 I. G. Tóth, *Mivelhogy magad írást nem tudsz* (Budapest, 1996), pp. 90–2; Brooks, *When Russia Learned to Read*, pp. 5–10; Weber, *Peasants into Frenchmen*, p. 473.

49 D. Marchenisi, *Il bisogno di scrivere* (Bari, 1992), p. 64.

50 Heywood, *Childhood in Nineteenth-Century France*, pp. 288–9.

51 R. Engelsing, *Analphabetentum und Lektüre* (Stuttgart, 1973), p. 105.

52 D. F. Mitch, *The Rise of Popular Literacy in Victorian England* (Philadelphia, 1992), pp. 22–3, calculates that at the end of the third quarter of the nineteenth century, the premium might amount to 13 per cent of the wage of an unskilled labourer.

53 D. Mitch, 'Inequalities which Every One may Remove': Occupational Recruitment, Endogamy, and the Homogeneity of Social Origins in Victorian England', in A. Miles and D. Vincent (eds), *Building European Society* (Manchester, 1993), pp. 140–61; Mitch, *The Rise of Popular Literacy in Victorian England*, p. 69.

54 Mitch, *The Rise of Popular Literacy in Victorian England*, p. 200.

55 A. J. La Vopa, *Prussian Schoolteachers: Profession and Office 1763–1848* (Chapel Hill, 1980), p. 40.

56 K. A. Schleunes, 'Enlightenment, Reform, Reaction: The Schooling Revolution in Prussia', *Central European History* 12, 4 (December 1979), p. 332.

57 M. Lamberti, *State, Society, and the Elementary School in Imperial Germany* (New York, 1989), p. 21.

58 K. A. Schleunes, *Schooling and Society* (Oxford, 1989), p. 230; Crew found in his study in Bochum that the numbers making the key move to the *Gymnasium* were rising very slowly at the end of the century, reaching 10.5 per cent by 1906. D. Crew, 'Definitions of Modernity: Social Mobility in a German Town 1880–1901', *Journal of Social History*, 7, 1 (Fall 1973), pp. 63–6.

59 Eklof, *Russian Peasant Schools*, pp. 25, 47, 439, 453–7.

60 J. R. Gillis, *The Development of European Society 1770–1870*, (Boston, 1977), p. 221; Anderson, *Education in France 1848–1870*, pp. 14–15; Heywood, *Childhood in Nineteenth-Century France*, p. 91.

61 R. Pethybridge, *The Social Prelude to Stalinism* (London, 1974), pp. 137–40.

62 R. Grew and P. J. Harrigan, with J. Whitney, 'The Availability of Schooling in Nineteenth-Century France' *Journal of Interdisciplinary History*, 14, 1 (Summer 1983), p. 61; Anderson, *Education in France 1848–1870*, pp. 140–57. For the achievement of this certificate, and its limited value to the possessor, see, P. Besson, *Un pâtre du Cantal* (Paris, 1914), p. 26.

63 J. Guinchard (ed.), *Sweden: Historical and Statistical Handbook* (2nd edn, Stockholm, 1914), vol. 1, p. 351.

64 See below, p. 82.

65 F. K. Ringer, *Education and Society in Modern Europe* (Bloomington, 1979), p. 117.

66 L. Boucher, *Tradition and Change in Swedish Education* (Oxford, 1982), pp. 8–20; W. Dixon, *Education in Denmark* (Copenhagen, 1958), pp. 94–105.

67 Ringer, *Education and Society in Modern Europe*, p. 181.

68 J. Floud, 'The Educational Experience of the Adult Population of England and Wales as at July 1949', in D. V. Glass (ed.), *Social Mobility in Britain* (London, 1954), pp. 117–18; D. Vincent, 'Mobility, bureaucracy and careers in twentieth-century Britain', in Miles and Vincent, *Building European Society*, pp. 222–3.

69 M. Sanderson, *Educational Opportunity and Social Change in England* (London, 1987), p. 26.

70 M. Barbagli, *Education for Unemployment: Politics, Labour Markets, and the School System. Italy, 1859–1973* (New York, 1982), p. 127.

71 Crew, 'Definitions of Modernity: Social Mobility in a German Town', p. 54; N. J. Smelser, *Social Paralysis and Social Change* (Berkeley, 1991), p. 273.

72 For a vigorous assertion of the optimistic position, which takes in secondary as well as primary education, see, P. J. Harrigan, 'Social Mobility and Schooling in History: Recent Methods and Conclusions', *Historical Reflections*, 10 (Spring 1983), pp. 128–40.

73 Mitch, *The Rise of Popular Literacy*, pp. 23–32; Vincent, *Literacy and Popular Culture*, pp. 129–32.

74 Sewell, *Structure and Mobility: The Men and Women of Marseille, 1820–1870*, pp. 251–3.

75 A. Miles, 'How Open was Nineteenth-Century British Society? Social Mobility and Equality of Opportunity, 1839–1914', in Miles and Vincent, *Building European Society*, p. 34.

76 G. Crossick, 'The Emergence of the Lower Middle Class in Britain: A Discussion', in G. Crossick (ed.), *The Lower Middle Class in Britain* (London, 1977), p. 19.

77 Union Postale Universelle, *Statistique générale du service postal, année 1890* (Berne, 1892), p. 4; Union Postale Universelle, *Statistique générale du service postal, année 1913* (Berne, 1915), p. 4 (1913 figures exclude Belgium).

78 T. Myllyntaus, 'Education in the Making of Modern Finland', in Tortella, *Education and Economic Development since the Industrial Revolution*, pp. 161–2.

79 Tortella, 'Patterns of Economic Retardation and Recovery in South-Western Europe in the Nineteenth and Twentieth Centuries', p. 14. Also, above, pp. 63–4.

80 Nunez, 'Literacy and Economic Growth in Spain, 1860–1977', p. 131.

81 B. N. Mironov, 'The Effect of Education on Economic Growth: The Russian Variant, Nineteenth–Twentieth Centuries', in Tortella, *Education and Economic Development since the Industrial Revolution*, p. 117. Similar calculations are made for Canada in G. W. Bertram, *The Contribution of Education to Economic Growth* (Ottawa, 1968), pp. 61–2.

82 N. F. R. Crafts, 'Exogenous or Endogenous Growth? The Industrial Revolution Reconsidered', *Journal of Economic History*, 55, 4 (December 1995), p. 765.

83 Stephens, *Education in Britain, 1750–1914*, p. 56.

84 Blaug, 'Literacy and Economic Development', p. 400. See Bowman and Anderson, 'Concerning the Role of Education in Development', pp. 252–3, 261.

85 Furet and Ozouf, *Reading and Writing*, p. 27.

86 L. G. Sandberg, 'The Case of the Impoverished Sophisticate: Human Capital and Swedish Economic Growth before World War 1', *Journal of Economic History*, XXXIX, 1 (March 1979), pp. 227–31.

87 Pettersson, 'Reading and Writing Skills and the Agrarian Revolution: Scanian Peasants during the Age of Enclosure', p. 210.

88 K. H. O'Rourke and J. G. Williamson, 'Education, Globalization and Catch-up: Scandinavia in the Swedish Mirror', *Scandinavian Economic Review*, 3 (1996), p. 302; also pp. 296–301.

89 O'Rourke and Williamson, 'Education, Globalization and Catch-up: Scandinavia in the Swedish Mirror', p. 302.

90 A. Nilsson and L. Pettersson, 'Literacy and Economic Growth: The Swedish 19th Century Experience', unpublished paper, November 1996, p. 12; Pettersson, 'Reading and Writing Skills and the Agrarian Revolution', pp. 214–20.
91 A. Nilsson and L. Pettersson, 'Some Hypotheses regarding Education and Economic Growth in Sweden during the First Half of the Nineteenth Century', in Tortella, *Education and Economic Development since the Industrial Revolution*, p. 214; Nilsson and Pettersson, 'Literacy and Economic Growth: The Swedish 19th Century Experience', pp. 5–6.
92 G. A. Male, *Education in France* (Washington, 1963), p. 15.
93 D. C. McClelland, 'Does Education Accelerate Economic Growth?', *Economic Development and Cultural Change*, 14 (April 1966), p. 259; Mironov, 'The Effect of Education on Economic Growth', pp. 113, 117; Tortella, 'Patterns of Economic Retardation and Recovery in South-Western Europe', p. 16.
94 For literacy figures, see figures 1.2 and 1.3 above. For gross domestic product (per capita, in 1990 Geary-Khamis dollars), see A. Maddison, *Monitoring the World Economy 1820–1992* (Paris, 1995), pp. 194, 196, 200.
95 Barbagli, *Education for Unemployment*, p. 74.
96 M. Dintenfass, *The Decline of Industrial Britain 1870–1980* (London, 1992), p. 37.
97 P. Lundgren, 'Educational Expansion and Economic Growth in Nineteenth-Century Germany: A Quantitative Study', in L. Stone (ed.), *Schooling and Society* (Baltimore, 1976).
98 P. L. Robertson, 'Technical Education in the Marine Engineering Industries 1863–1914', *Economic History Review*, 2nd ser., XVII (1974), pp. 234–5.
99 Crafts, 'Exogenous or Endogenous Growth? p. 768; Nicholas, 'Literacy and the Industrial Revolution', p. 59.
100 G. Tortella and L. Sandberg, 'Education and Economic Development since the Industrial Revolution: A Summary Report', in Tortella, *Education and Economic Development since the Industrial Revolution*, p. 10.
101 Nunez, 'Literacy and Economic Growth in Spain, 1860–1977', in Tortella, *Education and Economic Development since the Industrial Revolution*, p. 124; Tortella, 'Patterns of Economic Retardation and Recovery in South-Western Europe', pp. 12–13.
102 Myllyntaus, 'Education in the Making of Modern Finland', pp. 165–6. Research on the contemporary world economy also suggests that it is secondary education, rather than primary education or literacy, which is significantly correlated with economic growth. See R. J. Barro and X. Sala-i-Martin, *Economic Growth* (New York, 1995), pp. 431–6.
103 Gross domestic product is per capita, in 1990 Geary-Khamis dollars, divided by 100. Maddison, *Monitoring the World Economy 1820–1992*, pp. 194, 196, 198, 200. For postal data, see figure 1.2 above. See below, ch. 4, p. 101 for statistical correlations.
104 Sweden and Norway, for instance, have roughly similar ratios of GDP to postal rates, but completely different proportions of pig-iron production to

the post. For pig-iron production see B. R. Mitchell, *European Historical Statistics 1750–1975* (2nd edn, London, 1981), pp. 414–15.
105 Figures based on a comparison for postal rates and GDP in 1876 and 1913. The smallest gap was Great Britain, the largest of the countries for which data are available, was Portugal. Sources, see note 103 above.
106 Barbagli, *Education for Unemployment*, pp. 74–6.

Chapter 4 Reading and Writing

1 B. Shaw, *The Family Records of Benjamin Shaw Mechanic of Dent, Dolphinholme and Preston, 1772–1841*, ed. A. G. Crosby (Stroud, 1991), pp. 27–8. Shaw was a mill mechanic. He was compelled to marry his sweetheart the following year when she became pregnant.
2 H. Miller, *My Schools and Schoolmasters; or, The Story of my Education* (1854, 13th edn, London, 1869), p. 287.
3 D. Alston, 'The Fallen Meteor: Hugh Miller and Local Tradition', and D. Vincent, 'Miller's Improvement: A Classic Tale of Self-advancement?', in M. Shortland (ed.), *Hugh Miller and the Controversies of Victorian Science* (Oxford, 1996), pp. 206–39.
4 P. Burke, *Popular Culture in Early Modern Europe* (London, 1978), pp. 3–22.
5 On the ambiguities of Scott's work as a collector see, D. Vincent, 'The Decline of the Oral Tradition in Popular Culture', in R. D. Storch (ed.), *Popular Culture and Custom in Nineteenth-Century England* (London, 1982), pp. 20–47.
6 C. A. Macartney, *The Habsburg Empire 1790–1918* (London, 1969), p. 223.
7 See, for instance, R. M. Dorson, *The British Folklorists* (London, 1968); N. Z. Davis, 'The Historian and Popular Culture', in J. Beauroy, M. Bertrand and E. T. Gargan (eds), *The Wolf and the Lamb: Popular Culture in France from the Old Regime to the Twentieth Century* (Saratoga, Calif., 1977).
8 E. Weber, *Peasants into Frenchmen* (London, 1977), p. 471; R. D. Anderson, *Education in France* (Oxford, 1975), p. 148.
9 M. A. Marrus, 'Folklore as an Ethnographic Source: A "Mise au Point"', in Beauroy, Bertrand and Gargan, *The Wolf and the Lamb* pp. 110–22; J. Boyarin, 'Introduction', in J. Boyarin (ed.), *The Ethnography of Reading* (Berkeley and Los Angeles, 1993), pp. 1–8.
10 E. Johansson, 'Literacy Campaigns in Sweden' *Interchange*, 19, 3/4 (Fall/Winter 1988), p. 94.
11 R. F. Tomasson, 'The Literacy of Icelanders', *Scandinavian Studies*, 57 (1975), p. 69.
12 D. Vincent, 'Reading in the Working Class Home', in J. K. Walton and J. Walvin (eds), *Leisure in Britain, 1780–1939* (Manchester, 1983), pp. 210–11.
13 R. Chartier, 'The *Bibliothèque bleue* and Popular Reading', in *The Cultural Uses of Print in Early Modern France* (Princeton, 1987), pp. 240–64; S. T. Nalle, 'Literacy and Culture in Early Modern Castile', *Past and Present*, 125

(November 1989), p. 82; J. Brooks, 'Studies of the Reader in the 1920s', *Russian History*, 9, 2–3 (1982), p. 87.

14 M. Spufford *Small Books and Pleasant Histories* (London, 1981), p. 101.

15 A. L. Lloyd, *Folk Song in England* (London, 1975), p. 20; R. S. Thompson, 'The Development of the Broadside Ballad Trade and its Influence upon the Transmission of English Folksongs', Ph.D. thesis, Cambridge University, 1974, p. 215.

16 D. O Hogáin, 'Folklore and Literature: 1700–1850', in M. Daly and D. Dickson, *The Origins of Popular Literacy in Ireland: Language Change and Educational Development 1700–1920* (Dublin, 1990), p. 2.

17 Cited in, O Hogáin, 'Folklore and Literature: 1700–1850', p. 4.

18 I. G. Tóth, *Mivelhogy magad írást nem tudsz* (Budapest, 1996), pp. 320–1.

19 J. S. Allen, *In the Public Eye: A History of Reading in Modern France, 1800–1940* (Princeton, 1991), p. 5; J. Brooks, *When Russia Learned to Read* (Princeton, 1985), p. 27; R. Chartier, 'Texts, Printing, Readings', in L. Hunt (ed.), *The New Cultural History* (Berkeley, 1989), p. 153.

20 R. Darnton, 'First Steps toward a History of Reading', *Australian Journal of French Studies*, 23, 1 (1986), p. 14; C. Heywood, *Childhood in Nineteenth-Century France* (Cambridge, 1988), pp. 75–80.

21 Tomasson, 'The Literacy of Icelanders', pp. 71–2.

22 On the street-sellers, see, C. Mayhew, *London Labour and the London Poor* (London, 1861), vol. I, pp. 234, 297; D. Roche, *The People of Paris* (Leamington Spa, 1987), p. 221.

23 J. R. R. Adams, *The Printed Word and the Common Man* (Belfast, 1987), pp. 34, 121.

24 C. Knight, *London* (London, 1875–7), vol. I, p. 144. Also A. J. Lee, *The Origins of the Popular Press in England 1855–1914* (London, 1976), p. 35.

25 H. Vizetelly, *Berlin under the New Empire* (London, 1879), vol. I, p. 26.

26 I. Markussen, 'The Development of Writing Ability in the Nordic Countries of the Eighteenth and Nineteenth Centuries', *Journal of Scandinavian History*, 15, 1 (1990), p. 50; Roche, *The People of Paris*, p. 220.

27 W. Farish, *The Autobiography of William Farish: The Struggles of a Hand-Loom Weaver* (privately printed, 1889), pp. 11–12.

28 T. Judt, 'The Impact of the Schools, Provence 1871–1914', in H. J. Graff (ed.), *Literacy and Social Development in the West* (Cambridge, 1981), p. 267. See also, E. Berenson, *Populist Religion and Left-Wing Politics in France, 1830–1852* (Princeton, 1984), pp. 169–75.

29 R. Chartier, *The Order of Books* (Cambridge, 1994), p. 19.

30 See for instance the impact of the Russian streets in Brooks, *When Russia Learned to Read*, p. 12. On English posters and advertisements see the early contemporary study, [J. D. Burn], *The Language of the Walls* (Manchester, 1855), p. 3.

31 J. Gutteridge, *Lights and Shadows in the Life of an Artisan* (Coventry, 1893), republished in *Master and Artisan in Victorian England*, ed. and intro. V. E. Chancellor (London, 1969), p. 85.

32 Adams, *The Printed Word and the Common Man*, pp. 43–8.

33 D. Vincent, 'Reading Made Strange', in I. Grosvenor et al. (eds), *Silences and Images* (New York, 1999), pp. 181–97.

34 D. Hall, 'Introduction', and R. Chartier, 'Culture as Appropriation: Popular Cultural Uses in Early Modern France', in S. L. Kaplan (ed.), *Understanding Popular Culture: Europe from the Middle Ages to the Nineteenth Century* (Berlin, 1984), pp. 9, 230; J. Devlin, *The Superstitious Mind: French Peasants and the Supernatural in the Nineteenth Century* (New Haven, 1987), p. 218.

35 Anderson, *Education in France*, p. 170.

36 E. Weber, 'Religion and Superstition in Nineteenth-Century France', *Historical Journal*, 31 (June 1988), p. 399.

37 Memoir of J. T. Petzet, a pupil between 1806 and 1812, cited in K. A. Schleunes, *Schooling and Society* (Oxford, 1989), p. 84.

38 B. Holbek, 'What the Illiterate Think of Writing', in K. Schousboe, and M. Trolle Larsen (eds), *Literacy and Society* (Copenhagen, 1989), p. 192.

39 B. Eklof, *Russian Peasant Schools* (Berkeley, 1986), p. 274; Devlin, *The Superstitious Mind*, pp. 37–8.

40 See, for instance the study of nineteenth-century rural England in M. Pickering, 'The Four Angels of the Earth: Popular Cosmology in a Victorian Village', *Southern Folklore Quarterly*, 45 (1981), pp. 7–12.

41 J. Lawson, *Letters to the Young on Progress in Pudsey during the Last Sixty Years* (Stanningley, 1887), pp. 68–9.

42 C. Garrett, 'Witches and Cunning Folk in the Old Régime', in Beauroy, Bertrand and Gargan, *The Wolf and the Lamb: Popular Culture in France from the Old Regime to the Twentieth Century*, pp. 59–62; Weber, *Peasants into Frenchmen*, p. 25; Devlin, *The Superstitious Mind*, p. 45.

43 D. Vincent, *Literacy and Popular Culture* (Cambridge, 1989), pp. 175–6.

44 Lawson, *Letters to the Young*, p. 71.

45 Amongst the editions were, *Napoleon's Book of Fate* (London and Otley, n.d.), and *Napoleon Bonaparte's Book of Fate* (Glasgow, n.d.). For an account of their popularity, see J. Harland, and T. T. Wilkinson, *Lancashire Folk-Lore* (London, 1882), p. 121.

46 Toth, *Mivelhogy magad írást nem tudsz*, p. 321.

47 See above, pp. 68–70.

48 A. Somerville, *The Autobiography of a Working Man* (1848; London, 1951), p. 45. Anson's book was first published in 1748.

49 Somerville, *The Autobiography of a Working Man*, p. 47.

50 R. Chartier, 'Introduction: An Ordinary Kind of Writing', in R. Chartier, A. Boureau, and C. Dauphin, *Correspondence: Models of Letter-Writing from the Middle Ages to the Nineteenth Century* (Cambridge, 1997).

51 F. Staff, *'The Valentine' and its Origins* (London, 1969), pp. 25–38; W. H. Cremer, *St. Valentine's Day and Valentines* (London, 1971), pp. 10–13.

52 This phrase appeared at the head of all revisions of the original treaty. See, for instance, Universal Postal Union, *Convention of Paris, as modified by the Additional Act of Lisbon* (London, 1885), p. 1; *Convention of Vienna* (London, 1891), p. 1; *Convention of Washington* (London, 1898), p. 1.

53 *Union Postale*, vol. 1, no. 1 (October, 1875), p. 15.

54 The role of postal co-operation in the development of international co-operation is explored in E. Luard, *International Agencies: The Emerging Framework of Interdependence* (London, 1977), pp. 11–26.

55 Railway data from B. R. Mitchell, *European Historical Statistics* (Cambridge, 1971), pp. 629–40. For postal data see figure 1.2 above.

56 See figures 1.1, 1.2, 1.3, 1.5, 2.2, 3.1, 4.1 above.

57 Union Postale Universelle, *Statistique générale du service postal, année 1890* (Berne, 1892), p. 6.

58 Anderson, *Education in France*, p. 169.

59 R. Thabault, *Education and Change in a Village Community* (London, 1971), pp. 133–5.

60 E. Shorter, 'The "Veillée" and the Great Transformation', in Beauroy, Bertrand and Gargan, *The Wolf and the Lamb: Popular Culture in France from the Old Regime to the Twentieth Century*, p. 137; G. R. Galbraith, *Reading Lives* (New York, 1997), p. 25.

61 G. J. Marker, 'Russia and the "Printing Revolution": Notes and Observations', *Slavic Review*, 41, 2 (Summer 1982), pp. 277–81.

62 Adams, *The Printed Word and the Common Man*, p. 132.

63 P. Saenger, *Space Between Words: The Origins of Silent Reading* (Stanford, 1997), pp. 256–76 and *passim*.

64 R. Chartier, 'The Practical Impact of Writing' in Chartier, *A History of Private Life*, vol. 3: *Passions of the Renaissance* (Cambridge, Mass., 1989), p. 140.

65 Chartier, *The Order of Books*, p. 8.

66 L. James, *Fiction for the Working Man* (Harmondsworth, 1974), p. 44. Vincent, *Literacy and Popular Culture*, p. 213.

67 Anderson, *Education in France 1848–1870*, p. 147; Weber, *Peasants into Frenchmen*, p. 454; R. Gildea, *Education in Provincial France* (Oxford, 1983), p. 248;

68 Allen, *In the Public Eye*, p. 66.

69 Allen, *In the Public Eye*, p. 5.

70 Chartier, *The Order of Books*, p. 17; Darnton, 'First Steps toward a History of Reading', p. 12.

71 Brooks, 'Studies of the Reader in the 1920s', p. 88.

72 A. F. Westin, *Privacy and Freedom* (New York, 1967), p. 7; J. Michael, 'Privacy', in P. Wallington (ed.), *Civil Liberties 1984* (Oxford, 1984), pp. 134–5; A. R. Miller, *The Assault on Privacy* (Ann Arbor, 1971), p. 25.

73 Chartier, 'Introduction: An Ordinary Kind of Writing', in, Chartier, Boureau, and Dauphin, *Correspondence*, pp. 13–15; D. Vincent, *The Culture of Secrecy: Britain 1832–1998* (Oxford, 1998), p. 19.

74 J.-L. Ménétra, *Journal of My Life* (New York, 1986), p. 172.

75 Adams, *The Printed Word and the Common Man*, pp. 47–8.

76 D. Landes, *Revolution in Time* (Cambridge, Mass., 1983), p. 287.

77 H. Robinson, *Britain's Post Office* (Oxford, 1953), pp. 102–17.

78 D. Marchenisi, *Il bisogno di scrivere* (Bari, 1982), pp. 82–3.

79 L. S. Strumingher, *What Were Little Girls and Boys Made of?* (Albany, 1983), p. 136.

80 W. J. Ong, *Orality and Literacy* (London, 1982), p. 97; Burke, *Popular Culture in Early Modern Europe*, p. 179.

81 I. G. Tóth, ' "Chimes and Ticks": The Concept of Time in the Minds of Peasants and the Lower Gentry Class in Hungary in the 17th and 18th Centuries', Central European University, *History Department Yearbook* (1994–5), pp. 15–37; Tóth, *Mivelhogy magad írást nem tudsz*, pp. 83–4.

82 J. V. H. Melton, *Absolutism and the Eighteenth-Century Origins of Compulsory Schooling in Prussia and Austria* (Cambridge, 1988), pp. 105, 110, 140; F. Furet and J. Ozouf, *Reading and Writing* (Cambridge, 1982), p. 137.

83 See, for instance, J. Ruwet and Y. Wellemans, *L'Analphabétisme en Belgique* (Louvain, 1978), p. 73; G. J. Marker, 'Russia and the "Printing Revolution" ', *Slavic Review*, 41, 2 (Summer 1982), p. 281; L. James, *Print and the People 1819–1851* (Harmondsworth, 1978), pp. 49–59; B. Capp, *Astrology and the Popular Press: English Almanacks 1500–1800* (London, 1979), pp. 238–69.

84 R. Engelsing, *Analphabetentum und Lektüre* (Stuttgart, 1973), pp. 118–19.

85 Weber, *Peasants into Frenchmen*, pp. 461–4; Vincent, *Literacy and Popular Culture*, pp. 192–3; I. Markussen, 'The Development of Writing Ability in the Nordic Countries of the Eighteenth and Nineteenth Centuries', *Journal of Scandinavian History*, 15, 1 (1990), p. 50.

86 Pickering, 'The Four Angels of the Earth: Popular Cosmology in a Victorian Village', pp. 12–14.

87 Adams, *The Printed Word and the Common Man*, p. 87.

88 R. M. Friedman, *Appropriating the Weather* (Ithaca, 1989), p. 3.

89 M. Perkins, *Visions of the Future: Almanacs, Time, and Cultural Change 1775–1870* (Oxford, 1996), pp. 197–230.

90 Friedman, *Appropriating the Weather*. p. 4.

91 P. Besson, *Un pâtre du Cantal* (Paris, 1914), pp. 18–20.

92 Marrus, 'Folklore as an Ethnographic Source: A "Mise au Point" ', p. 118.

93 Pickering, 'The Four Angels of the Earth: Popular Cosmology in a Victorian Village', p. 7.

94 E. Durkheim, *Suicide* (London, 1952), pp. 164–9.

95 R. Gildea, 'Education in Nineteenth-Century Brittany: Ille-et-Vilaine, 1800–1914', *Oxford Review of Education*, 2, 3 (1976), p. 228; Thabault, *Education and Change in a Village Community*, p. 44.

96 Brooks, *When Russia Learned to Read*, p. 31.

97 A. J. La Vopa, *Prussian Schoolteachers* (Chapel Hill, 1980), p. 14.

98 Eklof, *Russian Peasant Schools*, p. 23.

99 N. M. Frieden, 'Child Care: Medical Reform in a Traditionalist Culture', in D. L. Ransel (ed.), *The Family in Imperial Russia* (Urbana, 1976), pp. 239–51.

100 A. Martynova, 'Life of the Pre-Revolutionary Village as Reflected in Popular Lullabies', in D. L. Ransel (ed.), *The Family in Imperial Russia* (Urbana, 1976), pp. 179–82.

101 Weber, 'Religion and Superstition in Nineteenth-Century France', pp. 410–15.

102 C. Tilly, 'Population and Pedagogy in France', *History of Education Quarterly*, 13 (Summer 1973), pp. 122–4.

103 Vincent, *Literacy and Popular Culture*, pp. 168, 170.
104 Strumingher, *What Were Little Girls and Boys Made of?*, p. 9.
105 R. Gibson, *A Social History of French Catholicism 1789–1914* (London, 1989), pp. 134–57; Devlin, *The Superstitious Mind*, pp. 1–6.
106 Anderson, *Education in France 1848–1870*, p. 146.
107 Vincent, *Literacy and Popular Culture*, pp. 174–5.
108 Allen, *In the Public Eye*, p. 48. On the extent of this market and its decline in the second half of the nineteenth century, see S. Eliot, *Some Patterns and Trends in British Publishing, 1800–1919* (London, 1994), section C.
109 J. Sperber, *Popular Catholicism in Nineteenth-Century Germany* (Princeton, 1984), p. 58.
110 C. Ford, 'Religion and Popular Culture in Modern Europe', *Journal of Modern History*, 65 (March 1993), p. 166; Devlin, *The Superstitious Mind*, pp. 68–71.
111 Darnton, 'First Steps toward a History of Reading', p. 8.
112 Raun, 'The Development of Estonian Literacy in the 18th and 19th Centuries', *Journal of Baltic Studies*, 10 (1979), p. 120.
113 B. Reay, 'The Content and Meaning of Popular Literacy', *Past and Present*, 131 (May 1991), pp. 116–17.
114 For a particularly full account of the entrepreneurial zeal of the publishing arm of churches see, L. Howsam, *Cheap Bibles: Nineteenth-Century Publishing and the British and Foreign Bible Society* (Cambridge, 1991), pp. 75–120.
115 Brooks, *When Russia Learned to Read*, p. 31.
116 Tóth, *Mivelhogy magad írást nem tudsz*, p. 320.
117 Gibson, *A Social History of French Catholicism*, p. 235.
118 Weber, *Peasants into Frenchmen*, p. 228; Vincent, *Literacy and Popular Culture*, pp. 50–1.
119 Judt, 'The Impact of the Schools, Provence 1871–1914', p. 264.
120 Eklof, *Russian Peasant Schools*, p. 227.
121 B. N. Mironov, 'The Effect of Education on Economic Growth: The Russian Variant, Nineteenth–Twentieth Centuries', in G. Tortella (ed.), *Education and Economic Development since the Industrial Revolution* (Valencia, 1990), p. 120.
122 Shorter, 'The "Veillée" and the Great Transformation', p. 137.
123 J. Clare, 'Sketches in the Life of John Clare', in E. Robinson (ed.), *John Clare's Autobiographical Writings* (Oxford, 1983), p. 5.
124 J. Clare, 'Autobiographical Fragments', in Robinson, *John Clare's Autobiographical Writings*, p. 48. Most of these titles are identified in note 21 to the Robinson edition. The works comprised chapbooks, textbooks, herbals, astrology, histories, theological and devotional works from the seventeenth and eighteenth centuries.
125 Galbraith, *Reading Lives*, p. 33.
126 See for instance the developments in the urban market in Russia around the end of the nineteenth century. L. McReynolds, *The News under Russia's Old Regime: The Development of a Mass-Circulation Press* (Princeton, 1991), p. 26.

127 Darnton, 'First Steps toward a History of Reading', p. 9. Also, P. P. Clark, 'The Beginnings of Mass Culture in France', *Social Research*, 45 (1978), pp. 281–90.
128 Engelsing, *Analphabetentum und Lektüre*, p. 110.
129 Brooks, *When Russia Learned to Read*, p. xv.
130 Vincent, *Literacy and Popular Culture*, pp. 37–8.
131 G. A. Codding, *The Universal Postal Union* (New York, 1964), pp. 39–40.

Chapter 5   The Boundaries of Literacy

1 A. Green, *Education and State Formation* (Basingstoke, 1990), p. 309.
2 T. Nipperdey, 'Mass Education and Modernization: The Case of Germany 1780–1850', *Transactions of the Royal Historical Society*, 5th ser., 27 (1977), pp. 155, 161–2; A. J. La Vopa, *Prussian Schoolteachers* (Chapel Hill, 1980), p. 37.
3 G. L. Seidler, 'The Reform of the Polish School System in the Era of the Enlightenment', in J. A. Leith (ed.), *Facets of Education in the Eighteenth Century* (Oxford, 1977), p. 337.
4 J. Ruwet and Y. Wellemans, *L'Analphabétisme en Belgique* (Louvain, 1978), pp. 83–6.
5 J. Guinchard (ed.), *Sweden: Historical and Statistical Handbook*, 2 vols (2nd edn, Stockholm, 1914), p. 378.
6 R. Birn, 'Deconstructing Popular Culture: The *Bibliothèque Bleue* and its Historians', *Australian Journal of French Studies*, 23, 1 (1986), p. 32.
7 F. Furet and J. Ozouf, *Reading and Writing* (Cambridge, 1982), p. 97.
8 J. S. Allen, *In the Public Eye* (Princeton, 1991), pp. 9, 32, 52, 86, 94; I. Collins, *The Government and the Newspaper Press in France, 1814–1881* (London, 1959).
9 R. Gildea, *Education in Provincial France* (Oxford, 1983), p. 247.
10 The Act was one of the Six Acts passed against radical political protest in 1819. W. H. Wickwar, *The Struggle for the Freedom of the Press* (London, 1927), pp. 138–40.
11 Cited in D. Vincent, *Literacy and Popular Culture* (Cambridge, 1989), p. 233.
12 On the eighteenth-century tradition of free expression, and the contrast between French and British controls during the revolutionary crisis, see, H. Barker, *Newspapers, Politics and English Society, 1700–1850* (London, 1999), ch. 3.
13 J. Watson, 'Reminiscences of James Watson', in D. Vincent (ed.), *Testaments of Radicalism* (London, 1977), p. 109.
14 Watson, 'Reminiscences of James Watson', p. 110.
15 P. Hollis, *The Pauper Press* (Oxford, 1970), pp. 27–9.
16 Watson, 'Reminiscences of James Watson', p. 112. The stamp was in fact fourpence halfpenny until 1836.
17 The arguments were cogently summarized in H. Brougham, 'Taxes on Knowledge', *Edinburgh Review*, LXII (October 1835), pp. 130–1.

18 J. Curran, 'The Press as an Agency of Social Control: An Historical Perspective', in G. Boyce, J. Curran and P. Wingate (eds), *Newspaper History from the Seventeenth Century to the Present Day* (London, 1978), p. 63.
19 Cited in Vincent, *Literacy and Popular Culture*, p. 235.
20 Hollis, *Pauper Press*, p. 38. On the long-established tradition of reading newspapers aloud, see L. Brown, *Victorian News and Newspapers* (Oxford, 1985), p. 27.
21 H. F. Schulte, *The Spanish Press 1470–1966: Print, Power, and Politics* (Chicago, 1968), pp. 116–219.
22 L. McReynolds, *The News under Russia's Old Regime: The Development of a Mass-Circulation Press* (Princeton, 1991), pp. 22–4.
23 J. Brooks, *When Russia Learned to Read* (Princeton, 1985), pp. 64, 66, 105, 110, 299.
24 D. Vincent, *The Culture of Secrecy* (Oxford, 1998), pp. 1–99, 18–19, 21–2, 29–30, 116–20. On the French tradition, which was both more active and more open, see, E. Vaillé, *Le Cabinet noir* (Paris, 1950).
25 Union Postale Universelle, *Statistique générale du service postal, année 1913* (Berne, 1915).
26 Cited in L. E. Holmes, *The Kremlin and the Schoolhouse* (Bloomington, 1991), p. 4.
27 Brooks, *When Russia Learned to Read*, p. xx.
28 H. J. Graff, *The Labyrinths of Literacy* (rev. edn, Pittsburgh, 1995), pp. 277–9.
29 S. Fitzpatrick, *Education and Social Mobility in the Soviet Union* (Cambridge, 1979), p. 169.
30 Holmes, *The Kremlin and the Schoolhouse*, pp. 23–37.
31 R. Pethybridge, 'Spontaneity and Illiteracy in 1917', in R. C. Elwood (ed.), *Reconsiderations on the Russian Revolution* (Cambridge, Mass., 1976), pp. 84–8.
32 Cited in E. N. Anderson, 'The Prussian Volksschule in the Nineteenth Century', in G. A. Ritter (ed.), *Entstehung und Wandel der modernen Gesellschaft* (Berlin, 1970), p. 272. Also, K. Barkin, 'Social Control and the Volksschule in Vormärz Prussia', *Central European History*, 16 (1983), pp. 36–7.
33 S. J. Seregny, *Russian Teachers and Peasant Revolution* (Bloomington, 1989), p. 2.
34 N. J. Smelser, *Social Paralysis and Social Change* (Berkeley, 1991), pp. 323–9.
35 M. J. Maynes, *Schooling in Western Europe* (Albany, 1985), pp. 70–1.
36 M. J. Burrows, 'Education and the Third Republic', *Historical Journal*, 28, 1 (March 1985), p. 257.
37 A. K. Pugh, 'Factors Affecting the Growth of Literacy', in G. Brooks, A. K. Pugh and N. Hall, *Further Studies in the History of Reading* (Widnes, 1993), p. 3.
38 A. Burns, *The Power of the Written Word: The Role of Literacy in the History of Western Civilisation* (New York, 1989), p. 287; Nipperdey, 'Mass Education and Modernization', pp. 160–1.
39 R. Pattison, *On Literacy* (New York, 1982), p. 152.

40 T. Judt, 'The Impact of the Schools, Provence 1871–1914', in H. J. Graff (ed.), *Literacy and Social Development in the West* (Cambridge, 1981), p. 262.

41 J. S. Coleman, 'Introduction: Education and Political Development', in J. S. Coleman (ed.), *Education and Political Development* (Princeton, 1965), p. 19.

42 Cited in R. D. Anderson, *Education in France* (Oxford, 1975), p. 137.

43 Furet and Ozouf, *Reading and Writing*, p. 125.

44 See for instance the eager exploitation by democratic socialist movements in France in the 1840s and 1850s of the railways, the reformed postal service and the growing network of commercial travellers. E. Berenson, *Populist Religion and Left-Wing Politics in France, 1830–1852* (Princeton, 1984), pp. 127, 132, 135–7.

45 Cited in Vincent, *Literacy and Popular Culture*, p. 139.

46 For detailed case studies see, S. Shipley, 'The Libraries of the Alliance Cabinet Makers' Association in 1879', *History Workshop*, 1 (Spring 1976); H.-J. Steinberg, 'Workers' Libraries in Germany before 1914', *History Workshop*, 1 (Spring 1976). Also, R. E. Johnson, *Peasant and Proletarian: The Working Class of Moscow in the Late Nineteenth Century* (New Brunswick, NJ, 1979), p. 102.

47 R. Block, *Der Alphabetisierungsverlauf im Preussen* (Frankfurt am Main, 1995), pp. 136, 213–14, tables 5.26, 5.27. 5.28; R. Engelsing, *Analphabetentum und Lektüre* (Stuttgart, 1973), pp. 106–8.

48 Vincent, *Literacy and Popular Culture*, pp. 254–8.

49 D. Geary, 'Working-Class Culture in Imperial Germany', in R. Fletcher (ed.), *Bernstein to Brandt* (London, 1987), pp. 11–16.

50 M. Vilanova, 'Anarchism, Political Participation and Illiteracy in Barcelona between 1934 and 1936', *American Historical Review*, 97, 1 (February 1992), p. 105.

51 J. Steinberg, 'The Historian and the *Questione della Lingua*', in P. Burke and R. Porter (eds), *The Social History of Language* (Cambridge, 1987), p. 204.

52 La Vopa, *Prussian Schoolteachers*, p. 64; F. A. Kittler, *Discourse Networks 1800/1900* (Stanford, 1990), pp. 35–8.

53 D. P. Resnick, 'Historical Perspectives on Literacy and Schooling', *Daedalus*, 119, 2 (Spring 1990), pp. 22–4.

54 P. Higonnet, 'The Politics of Linguistic Terrorism and Grammatical Hegemony during the French Revolution', *Social History*, 5, 1 (January 1980), pp. 41–51.

55 H. C. Barnard, *Education and the French Revolution* (Cambridge, 1969), pp. 72–3; Furet and Ozouf, *Reading and Writing*, p. 93.

56 L. Pettersson, 'Reading and Writing Skills and the Agrarian Revolution, *Scandinavian Economic History Review*, XLIV, 3 (1996), p. 208.

57 E. Johansson, 'Popular Literacy in Scandinavia about 1600–1900', *Historical Social Research*, 34 (1985), p. 61; I. Markussen, 'The Development of Writing Ability in the Nordic Countries of the Eighteenth and Nineteenth Centuries', *Journal of Scandinavian History*, 15, 1 (1990).

58 K. A. Schleunes, *Schooling and Society* (Oxford, 1989), p. 100.

59 J. K. Hoensch, *A History of Modern Hungary 1867–1986* (London, 1988), p. 11.
60 C. A. Macartney, *The Habsburg Empire 1790–1918* (London, 1969), pp. 223–4, 723–6.
61 I. G. Tóth, *Mivelhogy magad írást nem tudsz* (Budapest, 1996), p. 232. After the upheavals of the immediate post-war period, the policy was largely renewed in 1923. Macartney, *The Habsburg Empire 1790–1918*, p. 69.
62 M. Clark, *Modern Italy 1871–1995* (London, 1996), pp. 34–5; Resnick, 'Historical Perspectives on Literacy and Schooling', p. 24.
63 On the Rome government's ambitions see, M. Barbagli, *Education for Unemployment* (New York, 1982), pp. 52–5.
64 F. Watson, *Encyclopaedia and Dictionary of Education* (London, 1921), II, p. 904; R. Bell, *Fate and Honour, Family and Village: Demographic and Cultural Change in Rural Italy since 1800* (Chicago, 1979), p. 158. On the eve of the Second World War, enrolment in schools in the north was 82 per cent of the six–fourteen age group, and 60 per cent in the south. Barbagli, *Education for Unemployment*, p. 156.
65 D. Marchenisi, *Il bisogno di scrivere* (Bari, 1992), pp. 150–1.
66 H. Innes, *The Rhetorical Class Book, or the Principles and Practice of Elocution* (London, 1834), p. 12, cited in Vincent, *Literacy and Popular Culture*, p. 80. Also, J. Lawson, *Letters to the Young* (Stamningley, 1887), p. 85.
67 Gildea, *Education in Provincial France*, p. 222.
68 Allen, *In the Public Eye*, p. 69.
69 Furet and Ozouf, *Reading and Writing*, p. 282.
70 E. Weber, 'Who Sang the Marseillaise?', in J. Beauroy, M. Bertrand and E. T. Gargan, *The Wolf and the Lamb* (Saratoga, Calif., 1977), pp. 164–6.
71 L. S. Strumingher, *What Were Little Girls and Boys Made of?* (Albany, 1983), p. 35.
72 Anderson, *Education in France 1848–1870*, pp. 168–9; G. R. Galbraith, *Reading Lives* (New York, 1997), pp. 121–2.
73 Macartney, *The Habsburg Empire 1790–1918*, p. 726.
74 Judt, 'The Impact of the Schools, Provence 1871–1914', pp. 264–5; Allen, *In the Public Eye*, p. 69; Block, *Der Alphabetisierungsverlauf im Preussen*, pp. 151–2, ch. 4.2.
75 Furet and Ozouf, *Reading and Writing*, p. 297; Clark, *Modern Italy 1871–1995*, p. 35.
76 T. Myllyntaus, 'Education in the Making of Modern Finland', in G. Tortella (ed.), *Education and Economic Development since the Industrial Revolution* (Valencia, 1990), pp. 156–7.
77 G. Williams, 'Language, Literacy and Nationalism in Wales', *History*, 56 (February 1971), p. 11.
78 Schleunes, *Schooling and Society*, p. 100.
79 Block, *Der Alphabetisierungsverlauf im Preussen*, pp. 202–5, table 5.18.
80 M. Lamberti, *State, Society, and the Elementary School in Imperial Germany* (New York, 1989), pp. 109, 124, 140. See also the support of the Catholic Church in Spain for teaching the catechism in Castilian. M. Andrés and J. F. A. Braster, 'The Rebirth of the "Spanish Race": The State, Nationalism

and Education in Spain, 1875–1931', *European History Quarterly*, 29, 1 (1999), pp. 87–8.

81 P.-J. Hélias, *The Horse of Pride* (New Haven, 1978), p. 151.

82 Bell, *Fate and Honour*, pp. 159–60; Clark, *Modern Italy 1871–1995*, p. 169.

83 Steinberg, 'The Historian and the *Questione della Lingua*', p. 198.

84 A. R. Zolberg, 'The Making of Flemings and Walloons: Belgium: 1830–1914', *Journal of Interdisciplinary History*, 5, 2 (Autumn 1974), p. 194.

85 E. Weber, *Peasants into Frenchmen* (London, 1977), pp. 495–6.

86 C. Tilly, 'Did the Cake of Custom Break?', in J. Merriman (ed.), *Class Consciousness and Class Experience in Nineteenth-Century Europe* (New York, 1979).

87 R. Chartier, *The Order of Books* (Cambridge, 1994), pp. 7–16.

88 For a useful taxonomy of categories of culture, see, N. Z. Davis, 'The Historian and Popular Culture', in Beauroy, Bertrand and Gargan, *The Wolf and the Lamb*, pp. 9–12. On the limited value of the category of popular culture, see J. Rose, 'Rereading the English Common Reader: A Preface to a History of Audiences', *Journal of the History of Ideas*, 53 (1992), p. 58.

89 For this definition of mass culture see, B. Waites, T. Bennett and G. Martin (eds), *Popular Culture: Past and Present* (London, 1982), p. 15.

90 D. Hall, 'Introduction', in S. L. Kaplan, (ed.), *Understanding Popular Culture: Europe from the Middle Ages to the Nineteenth Century* (Berlin, 1984), pp. 5–14; P. Anderson, *The Printed Image and the Transformation of Popular Culture 1790–1860* (Oxford, 1991), p. 7.

91 D. Roche, 'Jacques-Louis Ménétra: An Eighteenth-Century Way of Life', in J.-L. Ménétra, *Journal of My Life* (New York, 1986), p. 257.

92 Vincent, *Literacy and Popular Culture*, pp. 212–13.

93 R. Chartier, 'Culture as Appropriation: Popular Cultural Uses in Early Modern France', in Kaplan, *Understanding Popular Culture: Europe from the Middle Ages to the Nineteenth Century*, pp. 229–35.

94 D. Roche, *The People of Paris* (Leamington Spa, 1987), p. 215.

95 B. Brierley, *Ab-O'Th'Yate's Dictionary; or, Walmsley Fowt Skoomester* (Manchester, 1881), p. 128.

96 M. Shiach, *Discourse on Popular Culture* (Cambridge, 1989), p. 72.

97 R. Chartier, 'Culture as Appropriation: Popular Cultural Uses in Early Modern France', p. 235; R. W. Scribner, 'Is a History of Popular Culture Possible?', *History of European Ideas*, 10, 2 (1989), p. 181.

98 Scribner, 'Is a History of Popular Culture Possible?', p. 181.

99 See, for instance, G. L. Craik, *The Pursuit of Knowledge under Difficulties* (London, 1830–1), vol. 1, p. 418.

100 Shiach, *Discourse on Popular Culture*, p. 97.

101 R. Biernacki, *The Fabrication of Labour: Germany and Britain, 1640–1914* (Berkeley, 1997), pp. 34–5. Emphasis in original.

102 R. Darnton, 'First Steps toward a History of Reading', *Australian Journal of French Studies*, 23, 1 (1986), p. 9.

Bibliography

Adams, J. R. R., *The Printed Word and the Common Man: Popular Culture in Ulster 1700–1900* (Belfast, 1987).

Allen, J. S., *In the Public Eye: A History of Reading in Modern France, 1800–1940* (Princeton, 1991).

Allen, W. O. B. and McClure, E., *Two Hundred Years: The History of the Society for Promoting Christian Knowledge* (London, 1898).

Alston, D., 'The Fallen Meteor: Hugh Miller and Local Tradition', in Shortland, M. (ed.), *Hugh Miller and the Controversies of Victorian Science* (Oxford, 1996).

Alston, P. L., *Education and the State in Tsarist Russia* (Stanford, 1969).

Altick, R. D., *The English Common Reader* (Chicago, 1957).

Anderson, C. A., 'Patterns and Variability in the Distribution and Diffusion of Schooling', in Anderson, C. A. and Bowman, M. J. (eds), *Education and Economic Development* (London, 1966).

Anderson, C. A., 'Literacy and Schooling on the Development Threshold: Some Historical Cases', in Anderson, C. A. and Bowman, M. J. (eds), *Education and Economic Development* (London, 1966).

Anderson, E. N., 'The Prussian Volksschule in the Nineteenth Century', in Ritter, G. A. (ed.), *Entstehung und Wandel der modernen Gesellschaft* (Berlin, 1970).

Anderson, P., *The Printed Image and the Transformation of Popular Culture 1790–1860* (Oxford, 1991).

Anderson, R. D., *Education in France 1848–1870* (Oxford, 1975).

Anderson, R. D., 'Education and the State in Nineteenth-Century Scotland', *Economic History Review*, 36 (1983).

Anderson, R. D., *Education and the Scottish People 1750–1918* (Oxford, 1995).

Andrés, M. and Braster, J. F. A., 'The Rebirth of the "Spanish Race": The State, Nationalism and Education in Spain, 1875–1931', *European History Quarterly*, 29, 1 (1999).

Atkinson, N., *Irish Education: A History of Educational Institutions* (Dublin, 1969).

Baines, F. E., *Forty Years at the Post Office* (London, 1895).

Bajkó, M., 'The Development of Hungarian formal education in the eighteenth century', in Leith, J. A. (ed.), *Facets of Education in the Eighteenth Century*, Studies on Voltaire and the Eighteenth Century, 167 (Oxford, 1977).

Ballara, M., *Women and Literacy* (London, 1992).

Barbagli, M., *Education for Unemployment: Politics, Labour Markets, and the School System. Italy, 1859–1973* (New York, 1982).

Barker, H., *Newspapers, Politics and English Society, 1700–1850* (London, 1999).

Barkin, K., 'Social Control and the Volksschule in Vormärz Prussia', *Central European History*, 16 (1983).

Barnard, H. C., *Education and the French Revolution* (Cambridge, 1969).

Barro, R. J. and Sala-i-Martin, X., *Economic Growth* (New York, 1995).

Barton, D., *Literacy: An Introduction to the Ecology of Written Language* (Oxford, 1994).

Barton, H. A., 'Popular Education in Sweden: Theory and Practice', in Leith, J. A. (ed.), *Facets of Education in the Eighteenth Century*, Studies on Voltaire and the Eighteenth Century, 167 (Oxford, 1977).

Bell, R., *Fate and Honour, Family and Village: Demographic and Cultural Change in Rural Italy since 1800* (Chicago, 1979).

Bennett, E., *The Post Office and its Story* (London, 1912).

Berend, I., 'Economy and Education: The Hungarian Case', in Tortella, G. (ed.), *Education and Economic Development since the Industrial Revolution* (Valencia, 1990).

Berenson, E., *Populist Religion and Left-Wing Politics in France, 1830–1852* (Princeton, 1984).

Berlanstein, L. B., 'Growing up as Workers in Nineteenth-Century Paris: The Case of the Orphans of the Prince Imperial', *French Historical Studies*, 11 (Fall 1980).

Bertram, G. W., *The Contribution of Education to Economic Growth* (Ottawa, 1968).

Besson, P., *Un pâtre du Cantal* (Paris, 1914).

Biernacki, R., *The Fabrication of Labour: Germany and Britain, 1640–1914* (Berkeley, 1997).

Birn, R., 'Deconstructing Popular Culture: The *Bibliothèque Bleue* and its Historians', *Australian Journal of French Studies*, 23, 1 (1986).

Blaug, M., 'Literacy and Economic Development', *School Review*, 74 (Winter 1966).

Blaug, M., *An Introduction to the Economics of Education* (London, 1970).

Block, R., *Der Alphabetisierungsverlauf im Preussen des 19. Jarhunderts* (Frankfurt am Main, 1995).

Boonstra, O., 'Education and Upward Social Mobility in the Netherlands, 1800–1900', unpublished paper, 1998.

Boucher, L., *Tradition and Change in Swedish Education* (Oxford, 1982).

Bourdieu, P. and Passeron, J.-C., *Reproduction in Education, Society and Culture* (London, 1977).

Bowman, M. J. and Anderson, C. A., 'Concerning the Role of Education in Development', in Geertz, C. (ed.), *Old Societies and New States* (New York, 1963).

Boyarin, J. (ed.), *The Ethnography of Reading* (Berkeley and Los Angeles, 1993).

Brewer, J., 'Reconstructing the Reader: Prescriptions, Texts and Strategies in Anna Larpent's Reading', in Raven, J., Small, H. and Tadmor, N. (eds), *The Practice and Representation of Reading in England* (Cambridge, 1996).

Brierley, B., *Ab'O'Th'Yate's Dictionary; or, Walmsley Fowt Skoomester* (Manchester, 1881).

Brierley, B., *Home Memories, and Recollections of a Life* (Manchester and London, [1886]).

Brooks, G., Foxman, D. and Gorman, T., 'Standards in Literacy and Numeracy: 1948–1994', National Commission on Education, Briefing (June 1995).

Brooks, J., 'Studies of the Reader in the 1920s', *Russian History*, 9, 2–3 (1982).

Brooks, J., *When Russia Learned to Read: Literacy and Popular Literature, 1861–1917* (Princeton, 1985).

Brougham, H., 'Taxes on Knowledge', *Edinburgh Review*, LXII (October 1835).

Brown, L., *Victorian News and Newspapers* (Oxford, 1985).

Burke, P., *Popular Culture in Early Modern Europe* (London, 1978).

Burke, P., 'From Pioneers to Settlers: Recent Studies of the History of Popular Culture', *Comparative Studies in Society and History*, 25, 1 (January 1983).

[Burn, J. D.], *The Language of the Walls* (Manchester, 1855).

Burnette, J. and Mitch, D. F., 'Literacy and Skill Development in a Declining Agricultural Sector: The Case of Eighteenth- and Nineteenth-Century English Farm Workers', paper to International Economic History Conference, Madrid, 1998.

Burns, A., *The Power of the Written Word: The Role of Literacy in the History of Western Civilisation* (New York, 1989).

Burrows, M. J., 'Education and the Third Republic', *Historical Journal*, 28, 1 (March 1985).

Capp, B., *Astrology and the Popular Press: English Almanacks 1500–1800* (London, 1979).

Carrato, J. F., 'The Enlightenment in Portugal and the Educational Reforms of the Marquis of Pombal', in Leith, J. A. (ed.), *Facets of Education in the Eighteenth Century*, Studies on Voltaire and the Eighteenth Century, 167 (Oxford, 1977).

Casteleyn, M., *A History of Literacy and Libraries in Ireland: The Long Traced Pedigree* (Aldershot, 1984).

de Certeau, M., *The Practice of Everyday Life* (Berkeley, 1988).

Chartier, R., 'Culture as Appropriation: Popular Cultural Uses in Early Modern France', in Kaplan, S. L. (ed.), *Understanding Popular Culture: Europe from the Middle Ages to the Nineteenth Century* (Berlin, 1984).

180   *Bibliography*

Chartier, R., 'The *Bibliothèque Bleue* and Popular Reading', in *The Cultural Uses of Print in Early Modern France* (Princeton, 1987).

Chartier, R., 'The Practical Impact of Writing', in Chartier, R. (ed.), *A History of Private Life*, vol. 3: *Passions of the Renaissance* (Cambridge, Mass., 1989).

Chartier, R., 'Texts, Printing, Readings', in Hunt, L. (ed.), *The New Cultural History* (Berkeley, 1989).

Chartier, R., *The Order of Books* (Cambridge, 1994).

Chartier, R., Boureau, A. and Dauphin, C., *Correspondence: Models of Letter-Writing from the Middle Ages to the Nineteenth Century* (Cambridge, 1997).

Chisick, H., 'School Attendance, Literacy, and Acculturation: *Petites Écoles* and Popular Education in Eighteenth-Century France', *Europa*, 3 (1979).

Cipolla, C. M., *Literacy and Development in the West* (Harmondsworth, 1969).

Clare, J., 'Sketches in the Life of John Clare' and 'Autobiographical Fragments', in Robinson, E. (ed.), *John Clare's Autobiographical Writings* (Oxford, 1983).

Clark, L., 'The Socialization of Girls in the Primary Schools of the Third Republic', *Journal of Social History*, 15, 4 (Summer 1982).

Clark, L., *Schooling the Daughters of Marianne: Textbooks and the Socialisation of Girls in Modern French Primary Schools* (Albany, 1984).

Clark, M., *Modern Italy 1871–1995* (London, 1996).

Clark, P. P., 'The Beginnings of Mass Culture in France', *Social Research*, 45 (1978).

Clark, S., 'French Historians and Early Modern Popular Culture', *Past and Present*, 100 (1983).

Codding, G. A., *The Universal Postal Union* (New York, 1964).

Coleman, J. S., 'Introduction: Education and Political Development', in Coleman, J. S. (ed.), *Education and Political Development* (Princeton, 1965).

Collins, I., *The Government and the Newspaper Press in France, 1814–1881* (London, 1959).

Cooper, T., *The Life of Thomas Cooper, Written by Himself* (London, 1872).

Cousin, V., *On the State of Education in Holland as regards Schools for the Working Classes and for the Poor*, trans. Horner, L. (London, 1838).

Cousin, V., *Report on the State of Public Instruction in Prussia*, ed. Knight, E. W. (New York, 1930).

Covino, W. A., *Magic, Rhetoric, and Literacy: An Eccentric History of the Composing Imagination* (Albany, 1994).

Crafts, N. F. R., 'Exogenous or Endogenous Growth? The Industrial Revolution Reconsidered', *Journal of Economic History*, 55, 4 (December 1995).

Craik, G. L., *The Pursuit of Knowledge under Difficulties* (London, 1830–1).

Cremer, W. H., *St. Valentine's Day and Valentines* (London, 1971).

Crew, D., 'Definitions of Modernity: Social Mobility in a German Town 1880–1901', *Journal of Social History*, 7, 1 (Fall 1973).

Crisp, O., 'Labour and Industrialisation in Russia', in Mathias, P. and Postan, M. M. (eds), *The Cambridge Economic History of Modern Europe*, VII, 2 (Cambridge, 1978).

Cross, N., *The Common Writer: Life in Nineteenth-Century Grub Street* (Cambridge, 1985).

Crossick, G., 'The Emergence of the Lower Middle Class in Britain: A Discussion', in Crossick, G. (ed.), *The Lower Middle Class in Britain* (London, 1977).

Cullen, L. M., 'Patrons, Teachers and Literacy in Irish: 1700–1850', in Daly, M. and Dickson, D. (eds), *The Origins of Popular Literacy in Ireland: Language Change and Educational Development 1700–1920* (Dublin, 1990).

Curran, J., 'The Press as an Agency of Social Control: An Historical Perspective', in Boyce, G., Curran, J. and Wingate, P. (eds), *Newspaper History from the Seventeenth Century to the Present Day* (London, 1978).

Dahl, S., 'Travelling Pedlars in Nineteenth Century Sweden', *Scandinavian Economic History Review*, 7 (1959).

Daly, M., 'Literacy and Language Change in the Late Nineteenth and Early Twentieth Centuries', in Daly, M. and Dickson, D. (eds), *The Origins of Popular Literacy in Ireland: Language Change and Educational Development 1700–1920* (Dublin, 1990).

Danhieux, L. 'Literate or Semi-Literate?', *Local Population Studies*, 18 (Spring 1977).

Darnton, R., 'Reading, Writing, and Publishing in Eighteenth-Century France: A Case Study in the Sociology of Literature', in Gilbert, F. and Graubard, S. R. (eds), *Historical Studies Today* (New York, 1972).

Darnton, R., 'First Steps toward a History of Reading', *Australian Journal of French Studies*, 23, 1 (1986).

Darton and Harvey, *Children's Books in England* (London, 1805).

Daunton, M. J., *Royal Mail* (London, 1985).

Davies, W. J. F., *Teaching Reading in Early England* (London, 1973).

Davin, A., *Growing up Poor: Home, School and Street in London 1870–1914* (London, 1996).

Davis, N. Z., 'The Historian and Popular Culture', in Beauroy, J., Bertrand, M. and Gargan, E. T. (eds), *The Wolf and the Lamb: Popular Culture in France from the Old Regime to the Twentieth Century* (Saratoga, Calif., 1977).

Depaepe, M. and Simon, F., 'Is there any Place for the History of "Education" in the "History of Education"? A Plea for the History of Everyday Educational Reality in – and outside Schools', *Paedagogica Historica*, XXXI, 1 (1995).

Devlin, J., *The Superstitious Mind: French Peasants and the Supernatural in the Nineteenth Century* (New Haven, 1987).

Dilworth, T., *A New Guide to the English Tongue* (1793).

Dintenfass, M., *The Decline of Industrial Britain 1870–1980* (London, 1992).

Dixon, W., *Education in Denmark* (Copenhagen, 1958).

Dorson, R. M., *The British Folklorists* (London, 1968).

Dowling, P. J., *The Hedge Schools of Ireland* (London, 1935).

Dowling, P. J., *A History of Irish Education* (Cork, 1971).

Durkheim, E., *Suicide* (London, 1952).

Dyche, T., *Guide to the English Tongue* (2nd edn, London, 1710).

Eklof, B., *Russian Peasant Schools: Officialdom, Village Culture and Popular Pedagogy, 1861–1914* (Berkeley, 1986).

Eklof, B., 'Worlds in Conflict: Patriarchal Authority, Discipline and the Russian School, 1861–1914', *Slavic Review*, 50, 4 (Winter 1991).

Eklof, B., 'The Adequacy of Basic Schooling in Rural Russia: Teachers and their Craft, 1880–1914', *History of Education Quarterly*, 26, 2 (Summer 1986).

Eklof, B., 'Russian Literacy Campaigns 1861–1939', in Arnove, R. F. and Graff, H. J. (eds), *National Literacy Campaigns: Historical and Comparative Perspectives* (New York, 1987).

Eliot, S., *Some Patterns and Trends in British Publishing, 1800–1919* (London, 1994).

Engelsing, R., *Analphabetentum und Lektüre* (Stuttgart, 1973).

Engelstein, L., 'Print Culture and the Transformation of Imperial Russia: Three New Views', *Comparative Studies in Society and History*, 31 (October 1989).

Errington, A., *Coals on Rails*, ed. Hair, P. E. H. (Liverpool, 1988).

Farish, W., *The Autobiography of William Farish: The Struggles of a Hand-Loom Weaver* (privately printed, 1889).

Fitzpatrick, S., *Education and Social Mobility in the Soviet Union 1921–1934* (Cambridge, 1979).

Flora, P., *State, Economy, and Society in Western Europe 1815–1975*, vol. 1: *The Growth of Mass Democracies and Welfare States* (London, 1983).

Floud, J. 'The Educational Experience of the Adult Population of England and Wales as at July 1949', in Glass, D. V. (ed.), *Social Mobility in Britain* (London, 1954).

Ford, C., 'Religion and Popular Culture in Modern Europe', *Journal of Modern History*, 65 (March 1993).

Frieden, N. M., 'Child Care: Medical Reform in a Traditionalist Culture', in Ransel, D. L. (ed.), *The Family in Imperial Russia* (Urbana, 1976).

Frieden, N. M., *Russian Physicians in an Era of Reform and Revolution, 1856–1905* (Princeton, 1981).

Friedman, R. M., *Appropriating the Weather* (Ithaca, 1989).

Fulbrook, M., 'Education and Absolutism in Eighteenth-Century Germany', *Historical Journal*, 34, 3 (September 1991).

Fullerton, R. A., 'Creating a Mass Book Market in Germany: The Story of the "Colporteur Novel" 1870–1890', *Journal of Social History*, 10, 3 (March 1977).

Furet, F. and Ozouf, J., *Reading and Writing: Literacy in France from Calvin to Jules Ferry* (Cambridge, 1982).

de Gabriel, N., 'Literacy, Age, Period and Cohort in Spain (1900–1950), *Paedagogica Historica*, 34, 1 (1998).

Galbraith, G. R., *Reading Lives: Reconstructing Childhood, Books and Schools in Britain, 1870–1920* (New York, 1997).

Galenson, D., 'Literacy and Age in Preindustrial England: Quantitative Analysis', *Economic Development and Cultural Change*, 29, 4 (July 1981).

Gardner, P., *The Lost Elementary Schools of Victorian England* (London, 1985).

Garrett, C., 'Witches and Cunning Folk in the Old Régime', in Beauroy, J., Bertrand, M. and Gargan, E. T. (eds), *The Wolf and the Lamb: Popular Culture in France from the Old Regime to the Twentieth Century* (Saratoga, Calif., 1977).

Gawthrop, R., 'Literacy Drives in Preindustrial Germany', in Arnove, R. F. and

Graff, H. J. (eds), *National Literacy Campaigns: Historical and Comparative Perspectives* (New York, 1987).

Gawthrop, R. and Strauss, G., 'Protestantism and Literacy in Early Modern Germany', *Past and Present*, 104 (1984).

Geary, D., 'Working-Class Culture in Imperial Germany', in Fletcher, R. (ed.), *Bernstein to Brandt* (London, 1987).

Gemie, S., *Women and Schooling in France, 1815–1914: Gender Authority and Identity in the Female Schooling Sector* (Keele, 1995).

Gibson, R., *A Social History of French Catholicism 1789–1914* (London, 1989).

Gildea, R., 'Education in Nineteenth-Century Brittany: Ille-et-Vilaine, 1800–1914', *Oxford Review of Education*, 2, 3 (1976).

Gildea, R., *Education in Provincial France, 1800–1914: A Study of Three Departments* (Oxford, 1983).

Gillis, J. R., *The Development of European Society 1770–1870* (Boston, 1977).

Gilmore, W. J., *Reading Becomes a Necessity of Life, 1760–1830* (Knoxville, 1989).

Gold, C., 'Educational Reform in Denmark, 1784–1814', in Leith, J. A. (ed.), *Facets of Education in the Eighteenth Century*, Studies on Voltaire and the Eighteenth Century, 167 (Oxford, 1977).

Graff, H. J., *The Literacy Myth* (London, 1979).

Graff, H. J., *The Legacies of Literacy* (Bloomington, 1987).

Graff, H. J., *The Labyrinths of Literacy: Reflections on Literacy Past and Present* (rev. edn, Pittsburgh, 1995).

Gray, W. S., *The Teaching of Reading and Writing* (Paris and London, 1956).

Grayson, J., 'Literacy, Schooling and Industrialisation: Worcestershire. 1760–1850', in Stephens, W. B. (ed.), *Studies in the History of Literacy: England and North America* (Leeds, 1983).

Green, A., *Education and State Formation: The Rise of Education Systems in England, France and the USA* (Basingstoke, 1990).

Grew, R. and Harrigan, P. J., with Whitney, J., 'The Availability of Schooling in Nineteenth-Century France', *Journal of Interdisciplinary History*, 14, 1 (Summer 1983).

Guinchard, J. (ed.), *Sweden: Historical and Statistical Handbook*, 2 vols (2nd edn, Stockholm, 1914).

Gutteridge, J., *Lights and Shadows in the Life of an Artisan* (Coventry, 1893), republished in *Master and Artisan in Victorian England*, ed. and intro. Chancellor, V. E. (London, 1969).

Hall, D., 'Introduction', in Kaplan, S. L. (ed.), *Understanding Popular Culture: Europe from the Middle Ages to the Nineteenth Century* (Berlin, 1984).

Harland, J. and Wilkinson, T. T., *Lancashire Folk-Lore* (London, 1882).

Harrigan, P. J., 'Social Mobility and Schooling in History: Recent Methods and Conclusions', *Historical Reflections*, 10 (Spring 1983).

Harrop, S. A. 'Literacy and Educational Attitudes as Factors in the Industrialisation of North-East Cheshire, 1760–1830', in Stephens, W. B. (ed.), *Studies in the History of Literacy: England and North America* (Leeds, 1983).

Hefferman, M. J., 'Literacy and the Life-Cycle in Nineteenth-Century Provincial France: Some Evidence from the *Département* of Ille et Vilaine', *History of Education*, 21, 2 (June 1992).

Hélias, P.-J., *The Horse of Pride: Life in a Breton Village* (New Haven, 1978).

Heywood, C., *Childhood in Nineteenth-Century France* (Cambridge, 1988).

Higonnet, P., 'The Politics of Linguistic Terrorism and Grammatical Hegemony during the French Revolution', *Social History* 5, 1 (January 1980).

Hoensch, J. K., *A History of Modern Hungary 1867–1986* (London, 1988).

Holbek, B., 'What the Illiterate Think of Writing', in Schousboe, K. and Trolle Larsen, M. (eds), *Literacy and Society* (Copenhagen, 1989).

Hollis, P., *The Pauper Press* (Oxford, 1970).

Holmes, L. E., *The Kremlin and the Schoolhouse* (Bloomington, 1991).

Hopkins, E., *Childhood Transformed: Working-Class Children in Nineteenth-Century England* (Manchester, 1994).

Houston, R. A., *Literacy in Early Modern Europe: Culture and Education 1500–1800* (London, 1988).

Howsam, L., *Cheap Bibles: Nineteenth-Century Publishing and the British and Foreign Bible Society* (Cambridge, 1991).

Huey, E. B., *The Psychology and Pedagogy of Reading* (1908; Cambridge, Mass., 1968).

Hunt, L., 'Introduction: History, Culture, and Text', in Hunt, L. (ed.), *The New Cultural History* (Berkeley, 1989).

Hunter, I., *Rethinking the School: Subjectivity, Bureaucracy, Criticism* (St Leonards, Australia, 1994).

Innes, H., *The British Child's Spelling Book* (London, 1835).

Jackson, M., *Literacy* (London, 1993).

Jackson, T. A., *Solo Trumpet* (London, 1953).

James, L., *Fiction for the Working Man* (Harmondsworth, 1974).

James, L., *Print and the People 1819–1851* (Harmondsworth, 1978).

Janos, A. C., *The Politics of Backwardness in Hungary 1825–1945* (Princeton, 1982).

Jarausch, K. H., 'The Old "New History of Education": A German Reconsideration', *History of Education Quarterly*, 26, 2 (Summer 1986).

Johansson, E., 'The History of Literacy in Sweden', in Graff, H. J. (ed.), *Literacy and Social Development in the West* (Cambridge, 1981).

Johansson, E., 'Popular Literacy in Scandinavia about 1600–1900', *Historical Social Research*, 34 (1985).

Johansson, E., 'Literacy Campaigns in Sweden', *Interchange*, 19, 3/4 (Fall/Winter 1988).

Johansson, E., 'Alphabeta Varia: Some Roots of Literacy in Various Countries', in Lindmark, D. (ed.), *Alphabeta Varia: Orality, Reading and Writing in the History of Literacy* (Umeå, 1998).

Johansson, E., 'The Postliteracy Problem: Illusion or Reality in Modern Society?', in Lindmark, D. (ed.), *Alphabeta Varia: Orality, Reading and Writing in the History of Literacy* (Umeå, 1998).

Johansson, E., ' "To Know the Words": The Key to Oral and Reading Tradition in the Church. A Basic Theme in Christian Literacy Teaching', in Lindmark,

D. (ed.), *Alphabeta Varia: Orality, Reading and Writing in the History of Literacy* (Umeå, 1998).

Johnson, R. E., *Peasant and Proletarian: The Working Class of Moscow in the Late Nineteenth Century* (New Brunswick, NJ, 1979).

Jones, J., 'Some Account of the Writer Written by Himself', in Jones, J., *Attempts in Verse* (London, 1831).

Jones, W., *The Jubilee Memorial of the Religious Tract Society* (London, 1850).

Judt, T., 'The Impact of the Schools, Provence 1871–1914' in Graff, H. J. (ed.), *Literacy and Social Development in the West* (Cambridge, 1981).

Kahan, A., 'Determinants of the Incidence of Literacy in Rural Nineteenth-Century Russia', in Anderson, C. A. and Bowman, M. J. (eds), *Education and Economic Development* (London, 1966).

Kenez, P., 'Liquidating Illiteracy in Revolutionary Russia', *Russian History*, 9, 2–3 (1982).

Khleif, B. B., *Language, Ethnicity, and Education in Wales* (The Hague, 1980).

Kirkham, G., 'Literacy in North-West Ulster, 1680–1860', in Daly, M. and Dickson, D. (eds), *The Origins of Popular Literacy in Ireland: Language Change and Educational Development 1700–1920* (Dublin, 1990).

Kirsch, I. and Guthrie, J. T., 'The Concept and Measurement of Functional Literacy', *Reading Research Quarterly* 13, 4 (1977–8).

Kittler, F. A., *Discourse Networks 1800/1900*, trans. Metteer, M. (Stanford, 1990).

Klancher, J. P., *The Making of English Reading Audiences, 1790–1832* (Madison, 1987).

Knight, C., *London* (London, 1875–7).

Koenker, D., 'Urban Families, Working-Class Youth Groups, and the 1917 Revolution in Moscow', in Ransel, D. L. (ed.), *The Family in Imperial Russia* (Urbana, 1976).

Kselman, T. A., *Death and the Afterlife in Modern France* (Princeton, 1993).

van der Laan, H., 'Influences on Education and Instruction in the Netherlands, especially 1750 to 1815', in Leith, J. A. (ed.), *Facets of Education in the Eighteenth Century*, Studies on Voltaire and the Eighteenth Century, 167 (Oxford, 1977).

Lamberti, M., *State, Society, and the Elementary School in Imperial Germany* (New York, 1989).

Landes, D. S., *Revolution in Time* (Cambridge, Mass., 1983).

Landes, D. S., *The Wealth and Poverty of Nations: Why Some are So Rich and Some So Poor* (London, 1998).

Lankshear, C. with Lawler, M., *Literacy, Schooling and Revolution* (New York, 1987).

Laqueur, T. W., 'The Cultural Origins of Popular Literacy in England, 1500–1800', *Oxford Review of Education*, 11, 3 (1974).

Laqueur, T. W., 'Literacy and Social Mobility in the Industrial Revolution', *Past and Present*, 64 (1974).

Laqueur, T. W., *Religion and Respectability: Sunday Schools and Working Class Culture 1780–1850* (New Haven, 1976).

Laqueur, T. W., 'Towards a Cultural Ecology of Literacy in England', in Resnick, D. P., *Literacy in Historical Perspective* (Washington, 1983).

La Vopa, A. J., *Prussian Schoolteachers: Profession and Office, 1763–1848* (Chapel Hill, 1980).

Lawson, J., *Letters to the Young on Progress in Pudsey during the Last Sixty Years* (Stanningley, 1887).

Lee, A. J., *The Origins of the Popular Press in England 1855–1914* (London, 1976).

Lee, W. R., *Population Growth, Economic Development and Social Change in Bavaria 1750–1850* (New York, 1977).

Le Roy Ladurie, E., 'The Conscripts of 1868' and 'Rural Civilisation', in *The Territory of the Historian* (Hassocks, 1979).

Levine, D., 'Education and Family Life in Early Industrial England', *Journal of Family History*, 4, 4 (Winter 1979).

Levine, K., 'Functional Literacy: Fond Illusions and False Economies', *Harvard Educational Review*, 52 (3) (August 1982).

Lindmark, D. (ed.), *Alphabeta Varia: Orality, Reading and Writing in the History of Literacy* (Umeå, 1998).

Litak, S., 'The Parochial School Network in Poland prior to the Establishment of the Commission of National Education (First Half of the Nineteenth Century)', *Acta Poloniae Historica*, 27 (1973).

Lloyd, A. L., *Folk Song in England* (London, 1975).

Logan, J., 'Sufficient to their Needs: Literacy and Elementary Schooling in the Nineteenth Century', in Daly, M. and Dickson, D. (eds), *The Origins of Popular Literacy in Ireland: Language Change and Educational Development 1700–1920* (Dublin, 1990).

Lovett, W., *The Life and Struggles of William Lovett* (1876; London, 1967).

Lowery, R., *Robert Lowery, Radical and Chartist*, ed. Harrison, B. and Hollis, P. (London, 1979).

Luard, E., *International Agencies: The Emerging Framework of Interdependence* (London, 1977).

Lundgren, P., 'Educational Expansion and Economic Growth in Nineteenth-Century Germany: A Quantitative Study', in Stone, L. (ed.), *Schooling and Society* (Baltimore, 1976).

McAleer, J., *Popular Reading and Publishing in Britain 1914–1950* (Oxford, 1992).

Macartney, C. A., *October Fifteenth: A History of Modern Hungary, 1929–1945*, 2 vols. (Edinburgh, 1956, 1957).

Macartney, C. A., *The Habsburg Empire 1790–1918* (London, 1969).

McClelland, C. E., 'From Compulsory Schooling to Free University in Central and West European Education', *Comparative Studies in Society and History*, 32 (January 1990).

McClelland, D. C., 'Does Education Accelerate Economic Growth?', *Economic Development and Cultural Change*, 14 (April 1966).

Mace, J., 'Mothers and the Appetite for Reading: Family Literacy in Past and Present', in Polkey, P., *Women's Lives into Print* (London, 1998).

McNair, J. M., *Education for a Changing Spain* (Manchester, 1984).

McPhee, P., 'Historians, Germs and Culture-Brokers: The Circulation of Ideas in the Nineteenth-Century Countryside', *Australian Journal of French Studies*, 23, 1 (1986).

McReynolds, L., *The News under Russia's Old Regime: The Development of a Mass-Circulation Press* (Princeton, 1991).

Maddison, A., *Monitoring the World Economy 1820–1992* (Paris, 1995).

Male, G. A., *Education in France* (Washington, 1963).

Mann, H., *Report of an Educational Tour in Germany and Parts of Great Britain and Ireland* (London, 1846).

Manual for the System of Primary Instruction, Pursued in the Model Schools of the B.F.S.S. (London, 1831).

Manual of the System of Teaching Reading, Writing, Arithmetick, and Needlework in the Elementary-Schools of the British and Foreign Schools Society (London, 1816).

Marchenisi, D., *Il bisogno di scrivere. Usi della scrittura nell'Italia moderna* (Bari, 1992).

Marker, G. J., 'Russia and the "Printing Revolution": Notes and Observations', *Slavic Review*, 41, 2 (Summer 1982).

Marker, G. J., 'Primers and Literacy in Muscovy: A Taxonomic Investigation', *Russian Review*, 48 (January 1989).

Markoff, J. 'Some Effects of Literacy in Eighteenth-Century France', *Journal of Interdisciplinary History*, 17, 2 (Autumn 1986).

Markussen, I. 'The Development of Writing Ability in the Nordic Countries of the Eighteenth and Nineteenth Centuries', *Journal of Scandinavian History*, 15, 1 (1990).

Marrus, M. A., 'Folklore as an Ethnographic Source: A "Mise au Point"', in Beauroy, J., Bertrand, M. and Gargan, E. T. (eds), *The Wolf and the Lamb: Popular Culture in France from the Old Regime to the Twentieth Century* (Saratoga, Calif., 1977).

Martin, H.-J., 'The Bibliothèque Bleue: Literature for the Masses in the *Ancien Régime*', *Publishing History*, 3 (1978).

Martynova, A., 'Life of the Pre-Revolutionary Village as Reflected in Popular Lullabies', in Ransel, D. L. (ed.), *The Family in Imperial Russia* (Urbana, 1976).

Mason, D. M., 'School Attendance in Nineteenth-Century Scotland', *Economic History Review*, 38 (1985).

Matthews, M., *Teaching to Read, Historically Considered* (Chicago, 1966).

Mayhew, C., *London Labour and the London Poor* (London, 1861).

Maynes, M. J., 'The Virtues of Archaism: The Political Economy of Schooling in Europe, 1750–1850', *Comparative Studies in Society and History*, 21 (1979).

Maynes, M. J., 'Schooling and Hegemony', *Journal of Interdisciplinary History*, 13, 3 (Winter 1983).

Maynes, M. J., *Schooling in Western Europe* (Albany, 1985).

Meek, M., 'Literacy: Redescribing Reading', in Kimberley, K., Meek, M. and Miller, J., *New Readings: Contributions to an Understanding of Literacy* (London, 1992).

Melton, J. V. H., 'From Image to Word: Cultural Reform and the Rise of Literate Culture in Eighteenth-Century Austria', *Journal of Modern History*, 58 (March 1986).

Melton, J. V. H., *Absolutism and the Eighteenth-Century Origins of Compulsory Schooling in Prussia and Austria* (Cambridge, 1988).

Ménétra, J.-L., *Journal of My Life*, trans. Goldhammer, A. (New York, 1986).

Menon, M. A. K., *The Universal Postal Union* (New York, 1965).

Michael, I., *The Teaching of English* (Cambridge, 1987).

Michael, J., 'Privacy', in Wallington, P. (ed.), *Civil Liberties 1984* (Oxford, 1984).

Miles, A., 'How Open was Nineteenth-Century British Society? Social Mobility and Equality of Opportunity, 1839–1914', in Miles, A. and Vincent, D. (eds), *Building European Society* (Manchester, 1993).

Miller, A. R., *The Assault on Privacy* (Ann Arbor, 1971).

Miller, H., *My Schools and Schoolmasters; or, The Story of my Education* (1854; 13th edn, London, 1869).

Mironov, B. N., 'The Effect of Education on Economic Growth: The Russian Variant, Nineteenth–Twentieth Centuries', in Tortella, G. (ed.), *Education and Economic Development since the Industrial Revolution* (Valencia, 1990).

Mitch, D. F., 'Education and Economic Growth: Another Axiom of Indispensability? From Human Capital to Human Capabilities', in Tortella, G. (ed.), *Education and Economic Development since the Industrial Revolution* (Valencia, 1990).

Mitch, D. F., *The Rise of Popular Literacy in Victorian England: The Influence of Private Choice and Public Policy* (Philadelphia, 1992).

Mitch, D. F., 'Inequalities which Every One may Remove': Occupational Recruitment, Endogamy, and the Homogeneity of Social Origins in Victorian England', in Miles, A. and Vincent, D. (eds), *Building European Society* (Manchester, 1993).

Mitch, D. F., 'The Role of Human Capital in the First Industrial Revolution', in Mokyr, J. (ed.), *The British Industrial Revolution* (Boulder, Colo., 1993).

Mitchell, B. R., *Abstract of British Historical Statistics* (Cambridge, 1971).

Mitchell, B. R., *European Historical Statistics 1750–1975* (2nd edn, London, 1981).

Mulhall, M. G., *Balance-Sheet of the World for Ten Years 1870–1880* (London, 1881).

Mulhall, M. G., *Dictionary of Statistics* (London, 1892).

Myllyntaus, T., 'Education in the Making of Modern Finland', in Tortella, G. (ed.), *Education and Economic Development since the Industrial Revolution* (Valencia, 1990).

Nalle, S. T., 'Literacy and Culture in Early Modern Castile', *Past and Present*, 125 (November 1989).

Nicholas, S. J., 'Literacy and the Industrial Revolution', in Tortella, G. (ed.), *Education and Economic Development since the Industrial Revolution* (Valencia, 1990).

Nicholas, S. J. and Nicholas, J. M., 'Male Literacy, "Deskilling" and the Industrial Revolution', *Journal of Interdisciplinary History*, 23 (Summer 1992).

Nilsson, A. and Pettersson, L., 'Some Hypotheses regarding Education and Economic Growth in Sweden during the First Half of the Nineteenth Century', in Tortella, G. (ed.), *Education and Economic Development since the Industrial Revolution* (Valencia, 1990).

Nilsson, A. and Pettersson, L., 'Literacy and Economic Growth: The Swedish 19th Century Experience', unpublished paper, November 1996.

Nilsson, A. and Pettersson, L., 'Literacy, Land Reform, and Economic Development in 19th Century Scania', unpublished paper, 1996.

Nipperdey, T., 'Mass Education and Modernization: The Case of Germany 1780–1850', *Transactions of the Royal Historical Society*, 5th ser., 27 (1977).

Nunez, C.-E., 'Literacy and Economic Growth in Modern Spain', Ph.D., New York University, 1989.

Nunez, C.-E., 'Literacy and Economic Growth in Spain, 1860–1977', in Tortella, G. (ed.), *Education and Economic Development since the Industrial Revolution* (Valencia, 1990).

Ó Cíosáin, N., 'Printed Popular Literature in Irish 1750–1850: Presence and Absence', in Daly, M. and Dickson, D. (eds), *The Origins of Popular Literacy in Ireland: Language Change and Educational Development 1700–1920* (Dublin, 1990).

O Hogáin, D., 'Folklore and Literature: 1700–1850', in Daly, M. and Dickson, D. (eds), *The Origins of Popular Literacy in Ireland: Language Change and Educational Development 1700–1920* (Dublin, 1990).

Okenfuss, M. J., *The Discovery of Childhood in Russia: The Evidence of the Slavic Primer* (Newstonville, 1980).

Ólason, V., *The Traditional Ballads of Iceland* (Reykjavík, 1982).

Ong, W. J., *Orality and Literacy* (London, 1982).

O'Rourke, K. H. and Williamson, J. G., 'Education, Globalization and Catch-up: Scandinavia in the Swedish Mirror', *Scandinavian Economic Review*, 3 (1996).

Pattison, R., *On Literacy: The Politics of the Word from Homer to the Age of Rock* (New York, 1982).

Paulsen, F., *German Education Past and Present* (London, 1908).

Perkins, M., *Visions of the Future: Almanacs, Time, and Cultural Change 1775–1870* (Oxford, 1996).

Pethybridge, R., *The Social Prelude to Stalinism* (London, 1974).

Pethybridge, R., 'Spontaneity and Illiteracy in 1917', in Elwood, R. C. (ed.), *Reconsiderations on the Russian Revolution* (Cambridge, Mass., 1976).

Pettersson, L., 'Reading and Writing Skills and the Agrarian Revolution: Scanian Peasants during the Age of Enclosure', *Scandinavian Economic History Review*, XLIV, 3 (1996).

Pickering, M., 'The Four Angels of the Earth: Popular Cosmology in a Victorian Village', *Southern Folklore Quarterly*, 45 (1981).

Post Office Archive.

Preston, S. H. and Haines, M. R., *Fatal Years: Child Mortality in Late Nineteenth-Century America* (Princeton, 1991).

Prothero, I., *Radical Artisans in England and France, 1830–1870* (Cambridge, 1997).

Pugh, A. K., 'Factors Affecting the Growth of Literacy', in Brooks, G., Pugh, A. K. and Hall, N., *Further Studies in the History of Reading* (Widnes, 1993).

Purvis, J., *Hard Lessons: The Lives and Education of Working-Class Women in Nineteenth-Century England* (Cambridge, 1989).

Quartararo, A. T., *Women Teachers and Popular Education in Nineteenth Century France* (Newark, 1995).

Rath, R., 'Training for Citizenship in Austrian Elementary Schools during the Reign of Francis I', *Journal of Central European Affairs*, IV (July 1944).

Raun, T. U., 'The Development of Estonian Literacy in the 18th and 19th Centuries', *Journal of Baltic Studies*, 10 (1979).

Raven, J., Small, H. and Tadmor, N. (eds), *The Practice and Representation of Reading in England* (Cambridge, 1996).

Reay, B., 'The Content and Meaning of Popular Literacy: Some New Evidence from Nineteenth-Century Rural England', *Past and Present*, 131 (May 1991).

Resnick, D. P., 'Historical Perspectives on Literacy and Schooling', *Daedalus*, 119, 2 (Spring 1990).

Resnick, D. P. and Resnick, L. B., 'The Nature of Literacy: An Historical Exploration', *Harvard Educational Review*, 47, 3 (August 1977).

Ribas, M. V. and Julià, X. M., *La Evolucion del Analfabetismo en España de 1887 a 1981* (Madrid, 1992).

Ricuperati, G. and Roggero, M., 'Educational Policies in Eighteenth-Century Italy', in Leith, J. A. (ed.), *Facets of Education in the Eighteenth Century*, Studies on Voltaire and the Eighteenth Century, 167 (Oxford, 1977).

Ringer, F. K., *Education and Society in Modern Europe* (Bloomington, 1979).

Robertson, P. L., 'Technical Education in the Marine Engineering Industries 1863–1914', *Economic History Review*, 2nd ser., XVII (1974).

Robinson, H., *Britain's Post Office* (Oxford, 1953).

Roche, D., *The People of Paris* (Leamington Spa, 1987).

Rose, J., 'Rereading the English Common Reader: A Preface to a History of Audiences', *Journal of the History of Ideas*, 53 (1992).

Rose, J., 'Willingly to School: The Working-Class Response to Elementary Education in Britain 1875–1918', *Journal of British Studies* 32, 2 (April 1993).

Ruwet, J. and Wellemans, Y., *L'Analphabétisme en Belgique (XVIIIème–XIXème siècles)* (Louvain, 1978).

Saenger, P., *Space Between Words: The Origins of Silent Reading* (Stanford, 1997).

Sandberg, L. G., 'The Case of the Impoverished Sophisticate: Human Capital and Swedish Economic Growth before World War 1', *Journal of Economic History*, XXXIX, 1 (March 1979).

Sandberg, L. G., 'Ignorance, Poverty and Economic Backwardness in the Early Stages of European Industrialisation: Variations on Alexander Gerschenkron's Grand Scheme', *Journal of European Economic History*, II, 3 (Winter 1982).

Sanderson, M., 'Social Change and Elementary Education in Industrial Lancashire 1780–1840', *Northern History*, 3 (1968).

Sanderson, M., 'Literacy and Social Mobility in the Industrial Revolution in England', *Past and Present*, 56 (1972).

Sanderson, M., *Educational Opportunity and Social Change in England* (London, 1987).

Schleunes, K. A., 'Enlightenment, Reform, Reaction: The Schooling Revolution in Prussia', *Central European History* 12, 4 (December 1979).

Schleunes, K. A., *Schooling and Society: The Politics of Education in Prussia and Bavaria 1750–1900* (Oxford, 1989).

Schofield, R., 'Dimensions of Illiteracy in England 1750–1850', in Graff, H. J. (ed.), *Literacy and Social Development in the West* (Cambridge, 1981).

Schulte, H. F., *The Spanish Press 1470–1966: Print, Power, and Politics* (Chicago, 1968).

Scribner, R. W., 'Is a History of Popular Culture Possible?', *History of European Ideas* 10, 2 (1989).

Scribner, S. and Cole, M., *The Psychology of Literacy* (Cambridge, Mass., 1981).

Seccombe, W., *Weathering the Storm: Working-Class Families from the Industrial Revolution to the Fertility Decline* (London, 1993).

Seidler, G. L., 'The Reform of the Polish School System in the Era of the Enlightenment', in Leith, J. A. (ed.), *Facets of Education in the Eighteenth Century*, Studies on Voltaire and the Eighteenth Century, 167 (Oxford, 1977).

Seregny, S. J., *Russian Teachers and Peasant Revolution: The Politics of Education in 1905* (Bloomington, 1989).

Sewell, W. H., *Structure and Mobility: The Men and Women of Marseille, 1820–1870* (Cambridge, 1985).

Shaw, B., *The Family Records of Benjamin Shaw Mechanic of Dent, Dolphinholme and Preston, 1772–1841*, ed. Crosby, A. G. (Stroud, 1991).

Shiach, M., *Discourse on Popular Culture* (Cambridge, 1989).

Shipley, S., 'The Libraries of the Alliance Cabinet Makers' Association in 1879', *History Workshop*, 1 (Spring 1976).

Shorter, E., 'The "Veillée" and the Great Transformation', in Beauroy, J., Bertrand, M. and Gargan, E. T. (eds), *The Wolf and the Lamb: Popular Culture in France from the Old Regime to the Twentieth Century* (Saratoga, Calif., 1977).

Singer, B., 'The Village Schoolmaster as Outsider', in Beauroy, J., Bertrand, M. and Gargan, E. T. (eds), *The Wolf and the Lamb: Popular Culture in France from the Old Regime to the Twentieth Century* (Saratoga, Calif., 1977).

Smelser, N. J., *Social Paralysis and Social Change* (Berkeley, 1991).

Smout, T. C., 'Born Again at Cambuslang: New Evidence on Popular Religion and Literacy in Eighteenth-Century Scotland', *Past and Present*, 97 (1982).

Soltow, L. and Stevens, E., *The Rise of Literacy and the Common School in the United States* (Chicago, 1981).

Somerville, A., *The Autobiography of a Working Man* (1848; London, 1951).

Sperber, J., *Popular Catholicism in Nineteenth-Century Germany* (Princeton, 1984).

Spufford, M., *Small Books and Pleasant Histories* (London, 1981).

Spufford, M., 'Literacy, Trade and Religion in the Commercial Centres of Europe', in Davids, K. and Lucassen, J., *A Miracle Mirrored: The Dutch Republic in European Perspective* (Cambridge, 1995).

Staff, F., *'The Valentine' and its Origins* (London, 1969).

Statistique générale du service postal dans les pays de L'Union Postale Universelle.

Steinberg, H.-J., 'Workers' Libraries in Germany before 1914', *History Workshop*, 1 (Spring 1976).

Steinberg, J., 'The Historian and the *Questione della Lingua*', in Burke, P. and Porter, R. (eds), *The Social History of Language* (Cambridge, 1987).

Stephens, W. B., *Education, Literacy and Society, 1830–1870: The Geography of Diversity in Provincial England* (Manchester, 1987).

Stephens, W. B., *Education in Britain, 1750–1914* (London, 1998).

Street, B., *Literacy in Theory and Practice* (Cambridge, 1984).

Strumingher, L. S., *What Were Little Girls and Boys Made of? Primary Education in Rural France 1830–1880* (Albany, 1983).

Sutherland, G., 'Education', in Thompson, F. M. L. (ed.), *The Cambridge Social History of Britain 1750–1950*, vol. 3 (Cambridge, 1990).

Sylvère, A., *Toinou, le cri d'un enfant auvergnat* (Paris, 1980).

Tanguiane, S., *Literacy and Illiteracy in the World: Situation: Trends and Prospects* (Paris, 1990).

Thabault, R., *Education and Change in a Village Community: Mazières-en-Gâtine, 1848–1914* (London, 1971).

Thompson, E. P., 'Time, Work-Discipline, and Industrial Capitalism', *Past and Present*, 38 (1967).

Thompson, R. S., 'The Development of the Broadside Ballad Trade and its Influence upon the Transmission of English Folksongs', Ph.D. thesis, Cambridge University, 1974.

Tilly, C., 'Population and Pedagogy in France', *History of Education Quarterly*, 13 (Summer 1973).

Tilly, C., 'Did the Cake of Custom Break?', in Merriman, J. (ed.), *Class Consciousness and Class Experience in Nineteenth-Century Europe* (New York, 1979).

Todd, E., *The Causes of Progress: Culture, Authority and Change* (Oxford, 1987).

Tomasson, R. F., 'The Literacy of Icelanders', *Scandinavian Studies*, 57 (1975).

Tortella, G., 'Patterns of Economic Retardation and Recovery in South-Western Europe in the Nineteenth and Twentieth Centuries', *Economic History Review*, XLII, 1 (1994).

Tortella, G. and Sandberg, L., 'Education and Economic Development since the Industrial Revolution: A Summary Report', in Tortella, G. (ed.), *Education and Economic Development since the Industrial Revolution* (Valencia, 1990).

Tóth, I. G., 'How Many Hungarian Noblemen Could Read in the Eighteenth Century?', Central European University, *History Department Yearbook* (1993).

Tóth, I. G., 'Noble Women Learning to Write in Western Hungary between the Sixteenth and Eighteenth Centuries', Central European University, History Department Working Paper Series, 1 (1994).

Tóth, I. G., '"Chimes and Ticks": The Concept of Time in the Minds of Peasants and the Lower Gentry Class in Hungary in the 17th and 18th Centuries', Central European University, *History Department Yearbook* (1994–5).

Tóth, I. G., *Mivelhogy magad írást nem tudsz . . . Az írás térhódítása a müvelödésben a Kora újkori Magyarországon* (Budapest, 1996).

Tóth, I. G., 'Hungarian Culture in the Early Modern Age', in Kósa, L. (ed.), *A Cultural History of Hungary: From the Beginnings to the Eighteenth Century* (Budapest, 1999).

Turner, R. S., 'Of Social Control and Cultural Experience: Education in the Eighteenth Century', *Central European History*, 21, 3 (September 1988).

UNICEF, *The State of the World's Children, 1984* (Oxford, 1983).

Union Postale.

Union Postale Universelle, *Statistique générale du service postal, année 1890* (Berne, 1892).

Union Postale Universelle, *Statistique générale du service postal, année 1913* (Berne, 1915).

Universal Postal Union, *Convention of Paris, 1 June 1878* (London, 1885).

Universal Postal Union, *Convention of Vienna* (London, 1891).

Vaillé, E., *Le Cabinet noir* (Paris, 1950).

Vilanova, M. 'Anarchism, Political Participation and Illiteracy in Barcelona between 1934 and 1936', *American Historical Review*, 97, 1 (February 1992).

Vilanova, M., and Moreno, X., *Atlas de la Evolucion del Analfabetismo en España de 1887 a 1981* (Madrid, 1992).

Vincent, D., 'The Decline of the Oral Tradition in Popular Culture', in Storch, R. D. (ed.), *Popular Culture and Custom in Nineteenth-Century England* (London, 1982).

Vincent, D., 'Reading in the Working-Class Home', in Walton, J. K. and Walvin, J. (eds), *Leisure in Britain 1780–1939* (Manchester, 1983).

Vincent, D., *Literacy and Popular Culture: England 1750–1914* (Cambridge, 1989).

Vincent, D., *Poor Citizens: The State and the Poor in Twentieth Century Britain* (London, 1991).

Vincent, D., 'Mobility, Bureaucracy and Careers in Twentieth-Century Britain', in Miles, A. and Vincent, D. (eds), *Building European Society* (Manchester, 1993).

Vincent, D., 'Miller's Improvement: A Classic Tale of Self-Advancement?', in Shortland, M. (ed.), *Hugh Miller and the Controversies of Victorian Science* (Oxford, 1996).

Vincent, D., *The Culture of Secrecy: Britain 1832–1998* (Oxford, 1998).

Vincent, D., 'Reading Made Strange: Context and Method in Becoming Literate in Eighteenth and Nineteenth-Century England', in Grosvenor, I., Lawn, M. and Rousmaniere, K. (eds), *Silences and Images: The Social History of the Classroom* (New York, 1999).

Vizetelly, H., *Berlin under the New Empire* (London, 1879).

Waites, B., Bennett, T. and Martin, G. (eds), *Popular Culture: Past and Present* (London, 1982).

Watson, F., *The Encyclopaedia and Dictionary of Education*, 4 vols. (London, 1921).

Watson, J., 'Reminiscences of James Watson', in Vincent, D. (ed.), *Testaments of Radicalism* (London, 1977).

Watson, V., 'Jane Johnson: A Very Pretty Story to Tell Children', in Hilton, M., Styles, M. and Watson, V. (eds), *Opening the Nursery Door: Reading, Writing and Childhood, 1600–1900* (London, 1997).

Webb, R. K., 'Working Class Readers in Early Victorian England', *English Historical Review*, 65 (1950).

Weber, E., *Peasants into Frenchmen: The Modernisation of Rural France 1870–1914* (London, 1977).

Weber, E., 'Who Sang the Marseillaise?', in Beauroy, J., Bertrand, M. and Gargan, E. T. (eds), *The Wolf and the Lamb: Popular Culture in France from the Old Regime to the Twentieth Century* (Saratoga, Calif., 1977).

Weber, E., 'Cultures Apart', *Journal of the History of Ideas*, 40 (1979).

Weber, E., 'Religion and Superstition in Nineteenth-Century France', *Historical Journal*, 31 (June 1988).

West, E. G., 'Literacy and the Industrial Revolution', *Economic History Review*, 2nd ser., XXXI (1978).

Westin, A. F., *Privacy and Freedom* (New York, 1967).

Westwood, J. N., *A History of Russian Railways* (London, 1964).

Wickwar, W. H., *The Struggle for the Freedom of the Press* (London, 1927).

Wiles, R. M., 'The Relish for Reading in Provincial England Two Centuries Ago', in Korshin, P. (ed.), *The Widening Circle: Essays on the Circulation of Literature in Eighteenth-Century Europe* (Philadelphia, 1976).

Williams, G., 'Language, Literacy and Nationalism in Wales', *History*, 56 (February 1971).

Zolberg, A. R., 'The Making of Flemings and Walloons: Belgium: 1830–1914', *Journal of Interdisciplinary History*, 5, 2 (Autumn 1974).

Index